Frommer's®

W9-BDF-384

PORTABLE

Puerto Rico

4th Edition

by Darwin Porter & Danforth Prince

Here's what critics say about Frommer's:

"Amazingly easy to use. Very portable, very complete."

—*Booklist*

"Detailed, accurate, and easy-to-read information for all price ranges."

—*Glamour Magazine*

1807
WILEY
2007

Wiley Publishing, Inc.

Published by:

WILEY PUBLISHING, INC.

111 River St.
Hoboken, NJ 07030-5774

ISBN: 978-0-470-10052-3
Editor: Myka Carroll DelBarrio
Production Editor: Lindsay Conner
Photo Editor: Richard Fox
Cartographer: Guy Ruggiero
Anniversary Logo Design: Richard Pacifico
Production by Wiley Indianapolis Composition Services

For information on our other products and services or to obtain technical
support, please contact our Customer Care Department within the U.S. at
800/762-2974, outside the U.S. at 317/572-3993 or fax 317/572-4002.

Wiley also publishes its books in a variety of electronic formats. Some con-
tent that appears in print may not be available in electronic formats.

Manufactured in the United States of America

5   4   3   2   1

Contents

List of Maps

ABOUT THE AUTHORS

As a team of veteran travel writers, **Darwin Porter** and **Danforth Prince** have produced numerous warm-weather-destination titles for Frommer's, including the bestselling *Frommer's Caribbean,* as well as guides to Puerto Rico, Jamaica, the Virgin Islands, the Bahamas, and Bermuda. Porter, a former bureau chief of the *Miami Herald,* is also a Hollywood biographer and author of *Katharine the Great* (devoted to Katharine Hepburn) and *Howard Hughes: Hell's Angel.* Prince was formerly employed by the Paris bureau of the *New York Times* and is today president of Blood Moon Productions and other media-related firms.

AN INVITATION TO THE READER

In researching this book, we discovered many wonderful places—hotels, restaurants, shops, and more. We're sure you'll find others. Please tell us about them, so we can share the information with your fellow travelers in upcoming editions. If you were disappointed with a recommendation, we'd love to know that, too. Please write to:

Frommer's Portable Puerto Rico, 4th Edition
Wiley Publishing, Inc. • 111 River St. • Hoboken, NJ 07030-5774

AN ADDITIONAL NOTE

Please be advised that travel information is subject to change at any time—and this is especially true of prices. We therefore suggest that you write or call ahead for confirmation when making your travel plans. The authors, editors, and publisher cannot be held responsible for the experiences of readers while traveling. Your safety is important to us, however, so we encourage you to stay alert and be aware of your surroundings. Keep a close eye on cameras, purses, and wallets, all favorite targets of thieves and pickpockets.

FROMMER'S STAR RATINGS, ICONS & ABBREVIATIONS

Every hotel, restaurant, and attraction listing in this guide has been ranked for quality, value, service, amenities, and special features using a **star-rating system.** In country, state, and regional guides, we also rate towns and regions to help you narrow down your choices and budget your time accordingly. Hotels and restaurants are rated on a scale of zero (recommended) to three stars (exceptional). Attractions, shopping, nightlife, towns, and regions are rated according to the following scale: zero stars (recommended), one star (highly recommended), two stars (very highly recommended), and three stars (must-see).

In addition to the star-rating system, we also use **seven feature icons** that point you to the great deals, in-the-know advice, and unique experiences that separate travelers from tourists. Throughout the book, look for:

Finds	Special finds—those places only insiders know about
Fun Fact	Fun facts—details that make travelers more informed and their trips more fun
Kids	Best bets for kids and advice for the whole family
Moments	Special moments—those experiences that memories are made of
Overrated	Places or experiences not worth your time or money
Tips	Insider tips—great ways to save time and money
Value	Great values—where to get the best deals

The following **abbreviations** are used for credit cards:

AE	American Express	DISC	Discover	V	Visa
DC	Diners Club	MC	MasterCard		

FROMMERS.COM

Now that you have this guidebook to help you plan a great trip, visit our website at **www.frommers.com** for additional travel information on more than 3,500 destinations. We update features regularly to give you instant access to the most current trip-planning information available. At Frommers.com, you'll find scoops on the best airfares, lodging rates, and car rental bargains. You can even book your travel online through our reliable travel booking partners. Other popular features include:

- Online updates to our most popular guidebooks
- Vacation sweepstakes and contest giveaways
- Newsletter highlighting the hottest travel trends
- Online travel message boards with featured travel discussions

The Best of Puerto Rico

Whatever you want to do on a tropical vacation or business trip—play on the beach with the kids (or gamble away their college funds), enjoy a romantic honeymoon, or have a little fun after a grueling negotiating session—you'll find it in Puerto Rico.

Here are our picks for the best that Puerto Rico has to offer.

1 The Best Beaches

White sandy beaches put Puerto Rico and its offshore islands on tourist maps in the first place. Many other Caribbean destinations have only jagged coral outcroppings or black volcanic-sand beaches that get very hot in the noonday sun. The best beaches are labeled on the "Puerto Rico" map on p. 9.

- **Best for Singles (Straight & Gay):** Sandwiched between the Condado and Isla Verde beaches along San Juan's beachfront, **Ocean Park Beach** attracts more adults and less of the family trade. Only Isla Verde beach to the east matches Ocean Park for its broad beach and good swimming. The people-watching here is nothing compared to the well-stuffed bikinis (both male and female) found on South Miami Beach or Rio de Janeiro. However, for the Caribbean, Ocean Park is as good as it gets. Because many gay boardinghouses lie in Ocean Park, a lot of the beach here is frequented by gay young men, mainly from New York. However, straight people looking to meet someone while wearing swimwear will find plenty of lookers (and perhaps takers). See p. 117.
- **Best Beach for Families:** Winning without contest, **Luquillo Beach,** 30 miles (48km) east of San Juan, has better sands and clearer waters than any beach in San Juan. The vast sandy beach opens onto a crescent-shaped bay edged by a coconut grove. Coral reefs protect the crystal-clear lagoon from the often rough Atlantic waters that can buffet the northern coast, making Luquillo a good place for young children to swim.

Much photographed because of its white sands, Luquillo also has tent sites and other facilities, including picnic areas with changing rooms, lockers, and showers. See p. 146.

- **Best for Swimming:** Whereas on much of the northwest coast of Puerto Rico, rough Atlantic waters often deter bathers but attract surfers (see below), the south coast waters are calmer. On the south coast, **Playa de Ponce,** outside Ponce, Puerto Rico's second-largest city, consists of a long strip of beautiful white sand that opens onto the tranquil waters of the Caribbean. Less crowded than Condado and Luquillo, Playa de Ponce is an ideal place to swim year-round in clearer, less polluted waters than those along the more heavily populated northern coastline. See p. 157.

- **Best for Windsurfing:** Rincón's winter surf, especially at **Playa Higüero,** puts Malibu to shame. Today surfers from all over the world are attracted to Rincón, which they have dubbed "Little Malibu." From Borinquén Point south to Rincón, nearly all the beaches along the western coast are ideal for surfing from November to April. As the windsurfing capital of the Caribbean, the Rincón area was put on the map when it was the site of the 1968 world surfing championships. Some of the 16-foot (4.9m) breakers here equal those on the north shore of Oahu. See p. 172.

2 The Best Golf & Tennis

- **Westin Rio Mar Beach Golf Resort & Spa** (Rio Grande; ✆ **888/627-8556** or 787/888-6000): A 45-minute drive from San Juan on the northeast coast, the 6,145-yard (5,619m) Rio Mar Golf Course is shorter than those at both Palmas del Mar and Dorado East. One avid golfer recommended it to "those whose games and egos have been bruised by the other two courses." Wind here can seriously influence the outcome of your game. The greens fees are a lot lower than those of its two major competitors. See p. 147.

- **Ponce Hilton & Casino** (Ponce; ✆ **787/259-7676**): It's not only the most luxurious hotel along the southern coast of Puerto Rico, but is also home to the beautiful 27-hole golf course, the **Costa Caribe Golf & Country Club** (✆ **787/ 812-2650**). The landscaped holes command views of the ocean and mountains, and three nines can be played in 18-hole combinations as conceived by golf architect Bruce Besse. Not only that, but the Hilton also has the best tennis courts along the southern coast. See p. 160.

- **El Conquistador Resort & Golden Door Spa** (Las Croabas; *C* **800/468-5228** or 787/863-1000): This sprawling resort east of San Juan is one of the island's finest tennis retreats, with seven Har-Tru courts and a pro on hand to offer guidance and advice. If you don't have a partner, the hotel will find one for you. Only guests of the hotel are allowed to play here. See p. 190.
- **Palmas del Mar Country Club** (Humacao; *C* **787/285-2256**): Lying on the southeast coast on the grounds of a former coconut plantation, the Palmas del Mar resort boasts the second-leading course in Puerto Rico—a par-72, 6,803-yard (6,221m) layout designed by Gary Player. Crack golfers consider holes 11 through 15 the toughest five successive holes in the Caribbean. See p. 194.

3 The Best Natural Wonders

- **El Yunque** (*C* **787/888-1880** for information): Forty-five minutes by road east of San Juan in the Luquillo Mountains and protected by the U.S. Forest Service, El Yunque is Puerto Rico's greatest natural attraction. Some 100 billion gallons of rain fall annually on this home to four forest types, containing 240 species of tropical trees. Families can walk one of the dozens of trails that wind past waterfalls, dwarf vegetation, and miniature flowers, while the island's colorful parrots fly overhead. You can hear the sound of Puerto Rico's mascot, the *coquí,* a small frog. See p. 143.
- **Río Camuy Caves** (*C* **787/898-3100**): Some 2½ hours west of San Juan, visitors board a tram to descend into this forest-filled sinkhole at the mouth of the Clara Cave. They walk the footpaths of a 170-foot-high (52m) cave to a deeper sinkhole. Once they're inside, a 45-minute tour helps everyone, including kids, learn to differentiate stalactites from stalagmites. At the Pueblos sinkhole, a platform overlooks the Camuy River, passing through a network of cave tunnels. See p. 140.

- **Las Cabezas de San Juan Nature Reserve** (© 787/722-5882): This 316-acre (128ha) nature reserve about 45 minutes from San Juan encompasses seven different ecological systems, including forestland, mangroves, lagoons, beaches, cliffs, and offshore coral reefs. Five days a week (Wed–Sun), the park staff conducts tours in Spanish and English, the latter at 2pm only. Each tour lasts 2½ hours and is conducted with electric trolleys that traverse most of the park. Tours end with a climb to the top of the still-working 19th-century lighthouse for views over Puerto Rico's eastern coast and nearby Caribbean islands. Call to reserve space. The cost is a relative bargain at $5 for adults, $2 for seniors and children under 11. See "Las Cabezas de San Juan Nature Reserve" on p. 188.

4 The Best Family Resorts

- **Condado Plaza Hotel & Casino** (San Juan; © 800/468-8588 or 787/721-1000): This resort offers Camp Taíno, a regular program of activities and special events for children ages 5 to 12. The cost of $25 per child includes lunch. The main pool has a kids' water slide that starts in a Spanish castle turret, plus a toddler pool. For teenagers, the hotel has a video game room, tennis courts, and various organized activities. For the whole family, the resort offers two pools and opens onto a public beach. It also has the best collection of restaurants of any hotel on the Condado. See p. 66.
- **Westin Rio Mar Beach Golf Resort & Spa** (Palmer; © 888/627-8556 or 787/888-6000): Here you'll find family fun for the entire brood. Opening onto Rio Mar Beach, the resort is known for its varied restaurants, pools, golf courses, tennis courts, spa, casino, and also the best children's programs east of San Juan. Many rooms are spacious enough to house the entire gang. See p. 147.
- **El Conquistador Resort & Golden Door Spa** (Las Croabas; © 800/468-5228 or 787/863-1000): Located 31 miles (50km) east of San Juan, this resort offers Camp Coquí on Palomino Island for children 3 to 12 years of age. The hotel's free water taxi takes kids to the island for a half- or full day of watersports and nature hikes. This resort has some of the best facilities and restaurants in eastern Puerto Rico. See p. 190.

5 The Best Big Resort Hotels

- **Ritz-Carlton San Juan Hotel, Spa & Casino** (San Juan; ✆ **800/241-3333** or 787/253-1700): At last Puerto Rico has a Ritz-Carlton, and this truly deluxe, oceanfront property is one of the island's most spectacular resorts. Guests are pampered in a setting of elegance and beautifully furnished guest rooms. Hotel dining is second only to that at El San Juan, and a European-style spa features 11 treatments "for body and beauty." See p. 75.

- **Ponce Hilton & Casino** (Ponce; ✆ **787/259-7676**): This is the most elaborate resort along the southern coast, spread over an 80-acre (32ha) landscaped tract of land right on the beach, a 10-minute drive from the center of Ponce. Many guests check in and never leave the premises, as the resort has a wide array of gardens, a giant pool, a fitness center, a casino, a nightclub, and various restaurants and bars. It is preferred by many discerning visitors who want to escape the hustle and bustle of San Juan itself. See p. 160.

- **Westin Rio Mar Beach Golf Resort & Spa** (Río Grande; ✆ **800/627-8556** or 787/888-6000): This $180-million 481-acre (195ha) resort, 19 miles (31km) east of the San Juan airport, is one of the three largest hotels in Puerto Rico. Despite its size, personal service and style are hallmarks of the property. Twelve restaurants and lounges boast an array of cuisines. Along with its proximity to two golf courses, entertainment—including an extensive program of live music—is a key ingredient in the hotel's success. See p. 147.

- **El Conquistador Resort & Golden Door Spa** (Las Croabas; ✆ **800/468-5228** or 787/863-1000): The finest resort in Puerto Rico, this is a world-class destination—a sybaritic haven for golfers, honeymooners, families, and anyone else. Three intimate "villages" combine with one grand hotel, draped along 300-foot (91m) bluffs overlooking both the Atlantic and the Caribbean at Puerto Rico's northeastern tip. The 500 landscaped acres (202ha) include tennis courts, an 18-hole Arthur Hills–designed championship golf course, and a marina filled with yachts and charter boats. See p. 190.

6 The Best Attractions

- **The Historic District of Old San Juan:** There's nothing like it in the Caribbean. Partially enclosed by old walls dating from the 17th century, Old San Juan was designated a U.S. National Historic Zone in 1950. Some 400 massively restored buildings fill this district, which is chockablock with tree-shaded squares, monuments, and open-air cafes, as well as shops, restaurants, and bars. If you're interested in history, there is no better stroll in the West Indies. See "Seeing the Sights" in chapter 6.

- **Castillo de San Felipe del Morro** (Old San Juan): Located in Old San Juan and nicknamed El Morro, this fort was originally built in 1540. It guards the bay from a rocky promontory on the northwestern tip of the old city. Rich in history and legend, the site covers enough territory to accommodate a 9-hole golf course. See p. 108.

- **The Historic District of Ponce:** Second only to Old San Juan in terms of historic significance, the central district of Ponce is a blend of Ponce Creole and Art Deco building styles, dating mainly from the 1890s to the 1930s. One street, Calle Isabel, offers an array of Ponceño architectural styles, which often incorporate neoclassic details. The city underwent a massive restoration preceding the celebration of its 300th anniversary in 1996. See "Ponce" in chapter 8.

- **Museo de Arte de Ponce** (Ponce): This museum has the finest collection of European and Latin American art in the Caribbean. The building was designed by Edward Durell Stone, who also designed the Museum of Modern Art in New York City. Contemporary works by Puerto Ricans are displayed, as well as works by an array of old masters, including Renaissance and baroque pieces from Italy. See p. 154.

- **Tropical Agriculture Research Station:** These tropical gardens contain one of the largest collections of tropical species intended for practical use. These include cacao, fruit trees, spices, timbers, and ornamentals. Adjacent to the Mayagüez campus of the University of Puerto Rico, the site attracts botanists from around the world. See p. 166.

2

Planning Your Trip to Puerto Rico

This chapter discusses the where, when, and how of your trip to Puerto Rico—everything required to plan your trip and get on the road. Here we've concentrated on what you need to do *before* you go.

1 The Regions in Brief

The most important geographical and political divisions are detailed here.

SAN JUAN

The largest and best-preserved complex of Spanish colonial architecture in the Caribbean, Old San Juan (founded in 1521) is the oldest capital city under the U.S. flag. Once a linchpin of Spanish dominance in the Caribbean, it has three major fortresses, miles of solidly built stone ramparts, a charming collection of antique buildings, and a modern business center. The city's economy is the most stable and solid in all of Latin America.

San Juan is the site of the official home and office of the governor of Puerto Rico *(La Fortaleza),* the 16th-century residence of Ponce de León's family, and several of the oldest places of Christian worship in the Western Hemisphere. Its bars, restaurants, shops, and nightclubs attract an animated group of fans. In recent years, the old city has become surrounded by densely populated modern buildings, including an ultramodern airport, which makes San Juan one of the most dynamic cities in the West Indies.

THE NORTHWEST: ARECIBO, RIO CAMUY, RINCON & MORE

The region's districts include the following:

AGUADILLA Christopher Columbus landed near Aguadilla during his second voyage to the New World in 1493. Today the town has a busy airport, fine beaches, and a growing tourism-based infrastructure. It is also the center of Puerto Rico's lace-making industry, a craft imported here many centuries ago by immigrants from Spain, Holland, and Belgium.

ARECIBO　Located on the northern coastline a 2-hour drive west of San Juan, Arecibo was originally founded in 1556. Although little remains of its original architecture, the town is well-known to physicists and astronomers around the world because of the radar/radio-telescope that fills a concave depression between six of the region's hills. Equal in size to 13 football fields and operated jointly by the National Science Foundation and Cornell University, it studies the shape and formation of galaxies by deciphering radio waves from space.

RINCON　Named after the 16th-century landowner Don Gonzalo Rincón, who donated its site to the poor of his district, the tiny town of Rincón is famous throughout Puerto Rico for its world-class surfing and beautiful beaches. The lighthouse that warns ships and boats away from dangerous offshore reefs is one of the most powerful in Puerto Rico.

RIO CAMUY CAVE PARK　Located near Arecibo, this park's greatest attraction is underground, where a network of rivers and caves provides some of the most enjoyable spelunking in the world. At its heart lies one of the largest known underground rivers. Above-ground, the park covers 300 acres (121ha).

DORADO & THE NORTH COAST

Playa Dorado, directly east of San Juan at Dorado, is actually a term for a total of six white-sand beaches along the northern coast, reached by a series of winding roads. Dorado is the island's oldest resort town, the center of golf, casinos, and a major Hyatt resort (p. 140). You'll find 72 holes of golf, the greatest concentration in the Caribbean—all designed by Robert Trent Jones, Sr. The complex is quite family-friendly, with its Camp Coquí, which offers programs for children ages 3 to 12.

Another resort of increasing importance is also found along the north coast: **El Conquistador Resort & Golden Door Spa** (p. 190) at Palomino Island, a private island paradise with sandy beaches and recreational facilities. This resort lies near Las Croabas, a fishing village on the northeastern tip of Puerto Rico's north coast.

Challenging the Hyatt and El Conquistador is the **Westin Rio Mar Beach Golf Resort & Spa** (p. 147), which lies 19 miles (31km) to the east of the Luis Muñoz Marín International Airport.

Puerto Rico

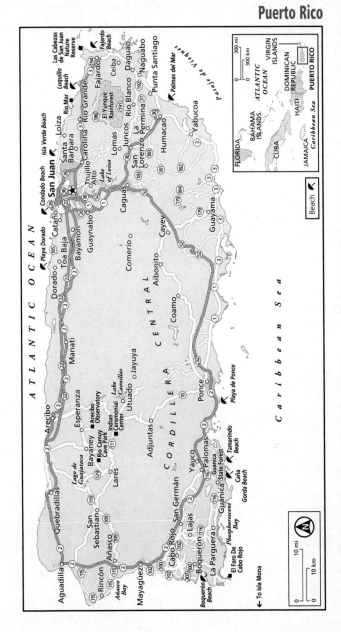

THE NORTHEAST: EL YUNQUE, A NATURE RESERVE & FAJARDO

The capital city of San Juan (see above) dominates Puerto Rico's northeast. Despite the region's congestion, there are still many remote areas, including some of the island's most important nature reserves. Among the region's most popular towns, parks, and attractions are the following:

EL YUNQUE   The rainforest in the Luquillo Mountains, 25 miles (40km) east of San Juan, El Yunque is a favorite escape from the capital. Teeming with plant and animal life, it is a sprawling tropical forest (actually a national forest) whose ecosystems are strictly protected. Some 100 billion gallons of rainwater fall here each year, allowing about 250 species of trees and flowers to flourish.

FAJARDO   Small and sleepy, this town was originally established as a supply depot for the many pirates who plied the nearby waters. Today, a host of private yachts bob at anchor in its harbor, and the many offshore cays provide visitors with secluded beaches. From Fajardo, ferryboats make choppy but frequent runs to the offshore islands of Vieques and Culebra.

LAS CABEZAS DE SAN JUAN NATURE RESERVE   About an hour's drive from San Juan, this is one of the island's newest ecological refuges. It was established in 1991 on 316 acres (128ha) of forest, mangrove swamp, offshore cays, coral reefs, and freshwater lagoons—a representative sampling of virtually every ecosystem in Puerto Rico. There is a visitor center, a 19th-century lighthouse (El Faro) that still works, and ample opportunity to forget the pressures of urban life.

THE SOUTHWEST: PONCE, MAYAGÜEZ, SAN GERMAN & MORE

One of Puerto Rico's most beautiful regions, the southwest is rich in local lore, civic pride, and natural wonders.

BOQUERON   Famous for the beauty of its beach and the abundant birds and wildlife in the nearby Boquerón Forest Reserve, this sleepy village is now ripe for large-scale tourism-related development. During the early 19th century, the island's most-feared pirate, Roberto Cofresi, terrorized the Puerto Rican coastline from a secret lair in a cave nearby.

CABO ROJO   Established in 1772, Cabo Rojo reached the peak of its prosperity during the 19th century, when immigrants from around the Mediterranean, fleeing revolutions in their own countries, arrived to establish sugar-cane plantations. Today, cattle graze peacefully on land originally devoted almost exclusively to sugar cane, and the area's many varieties of exotic birds draw bird-watchers from throughout North America. Even the offshore waters are fertile; it's estimated that nearly half of all the fish consumed in Puerto Rico are caught in waters near Cabo Rojo.

MAYAGÜEZ   The third-largest city in Puerto Rico, Mayagüez is named after the *majagua,* the Amerindian word for a tree that grows abundantly in the area. Because of an earthquake that destroyed almost everything in town in 1917, few old buildings remain. The town is known as the commercial and industrial capital of Puerto Rico's western sector. Its botanical garden is among the finest on the island.

PONCE   Puerto Rico's second-largest city, Ponce has always prided itself on its independence from the Spanish-derived laws and taxes that governed San Juan and the rest of the island. Long ago home of some of the island's shrewdest traders, merchants, and smugglers, it is enjoying a renaissance as citizens and visitors re-discover its unique cultural and architectural charms. Located on Puerto Rico's southern coast, about 90 minutes by car from the cap-ital, Ponce contains a handful of superb museums, one of the most charming main squares in the Caribbean, an ancient cathedral, dozens of authentically restored colonial-era buildings, and a num-ber of outlying mansions and the island's most opulent villas.

THE SOUTHEAST: PALMAS DEL MAR & MORE

The southeastern quadrant of Puerto Rico has some of the most heavily developed, as well as some of the least developed, sections of the island.

COAMO   Although today Coamo is a bedroom community for San Juan, originally it was the site of two different Taíno communi-ties. Founded in 1579, it now has a main square draped with bougainvillea and one of the best-known Catholic churches in Puerto Rico. Even more famous, however, are the mineral springs whose therapeutic warm waters helped President Franklin D. Roosevelt during his recovery from polio. (Some historians claim that these springs inspired the legend of the Fountain of Youth, which in turn set Ponce de León off on his vain search of Florida.)

PALMAS DEL MAR   This sprawling vacation and residential resort community is located near Humacao. A splendid golf course covers some of the grounds. Palmas del Mar is at the center of what has been called the "New American Riviera"—3 miles (4.8km) of white-sand beaches on the eastern coast of the island. Palmas del Mar is the largest resort in Puerto Rico, lying to the south of Humacao on 2,800 acres (1,133ha) of a former coconut plantation—now devoted to luxury living and the sporting life.

The Equestrian Center at Palmas is the finest riding headquarters in Puerto Rico, with trails cutting through an old plantation and jungle along the beach. The resort is ideal for families and has a supervised summer activities program for children ages 5 to 12.

2 Visitor Information

For information before you leave home, visit **www.gotopuerto rico.com** or contact one of the following **Puerto Rico Tourism Company** offices: 666 Fifth Ave., New York, NY 10013 (© **800/ 223-6530** or 212/586-6262); 3575 W. Cahuenga Blvd., Ste. 405, Los Angeles, CA 90068 (© **800/874-1230** or 323/874-5991); or 901 Ponce de Leon Blvd., Ste. 101, Coral Gables, FL 33134 (© **800/815-7391** or 305/445-9112).

In Canada, contact the company at 41–43 Colborne St., Ste. 301, Toronto, ON M5E 1E3 (© **800/667-0394** or 416/368-2680).

One of the best Caribbean websites is **Caribbean-On-Line** (www.caribbean-on-line.com), a series of virtual guidebooks full of information on hotels, restaurants, and shopping, along with sights and detailed maps of the islands. The site also includes links to online travel agents and cruise lines. Other helpful websites include **Municipality of Ponce** (www.ponceweb.org), **Tourism Association of Rincón** (www.rincon.org), and **Puerto Rico TravelMaps** (www.travelmaps.com).

A good travel agent can be a valuable source of information. Make sure your agent is a member of the American Society of Travel Agents (ASTA). If you get poor service from an ASTA agent, you can write to the **ASTA Consumer Affairs Department,** 1101 King St., Alexandria, VA 22314 (© **703/739-2782;** www.astanet.com).

3 Entry Requirements & Customs

ENTRY REQUIREMENTS

DOCUMENTS   Because Puerto Rico is a Commonwealth, **U.S. citizens** coming from mainland destinations do not need any documents to enter Puerto Rico. It is the same as crossing from Georgia into Florida. They do not need to carry proof of citizenship or produce documents. However, because of new airport security measures, it is necessary to produce a government-issued photo ID (federal, state, or local) to board a plane; this is most often a driver's license.

Be sure to carry plenty of documentation. You might need to show a government-issued photo ID (federal, state, or local) at various airport checkpoints. Be sure that your ID is up-to-date: An expired driver's license or passport, for example, might keep you from boarding a plane.

Visitors from **other countries** need a valid passport to land in Puerto Rico. For those from countries requiring a visa to enter the U.S., the same visa is necessary to enter Puerto Rico, unless these nationals are coming directly from the U.S. mainland and have already cleared U.S. Immigration and Customs there.

CUSTOMS

U.S. citizens do not need to clear Puerto Rican Customs upon arrival by plane or ship from the U.S. mainland. All non-U.S. citizens must clear Customs and are permitted to bring in items intended for their personal use, including tobacco, cameras, film, and a limited supply of liquor (usually 40 oz.).

WHAT YOU CAN TAKE HOME

U.S. CUSTOMS   On departure, U.S.-bound travelers must have their luggage inspected by the U.S. Agriculture Department because laws prohibit bringing fruits and plants to the U.S. mainland. Fruits and vegetables are not allowed, but otherwise, you can bring back as many purchased goods as you want without paying duty.

For more information, contact the **U.S. Customs & Border Protection (CBP),** 1300 Pennsylvania Ave. NW, Washington, DC 20229 (© **877/287-8867;** www.cbp.gov [click on "Travel" and then "Know Before You Go"]), and request the free pamphlet *Know Before You Go.*

CANADIAN CUSTOMS   For a clear summary of Canadian rules, write for the booklet *I Declare,* issued by the **Canada Border Services Agency** (© **800/461-9999** in Canada, or 204/983-3500; www.cbsa-asfc.gc.ca). Canada allows its citizens a C$750 exemption, and you're allowed to bring back duty-free one carton of cigarettes, one can of tobacco, 40 imperial ounces of liquor, and 50 cigars. In addition, you're allowed to mail gifts to Canada valued at less than C$60 per day, provided they're unsolicited and don't contain alcohol or tobacco (write on the package "Unsolicited gift, under $60 value"). All valuables should be declared on the Y-38 form before departure from Canada, including serial numbers of valuables already owned, such as expensive foreign cameras. *Note:* The C$750 exemption can only be used once per year and only after an absence of 7 days.

U.K. CUSTOMS   U.K. citizens returning from a non-E.U. country have a customs allowance of 200 cigarettes, 50 cigars, or 250 grams of smoking tobacco; 2 liters of still table wine; 1 liter of spirits or strong liqueurs (over 22% volume); 2 liters of fortified wine, sparkling wine, or other liqueurs; 60 cubic centimeters (ml) perfume; 250 cubic centimeters (ml) of toilet water; and £145 worth of all other goods, including gifts and souvenirs. People under 17 do not get the tobacco or alcohol allowance. For more information, contact **HM Revenue & Customs,** National Advice Service, Dorset House, Stamford St., London SE1 9PY (© **0845/010-9000** or 02920/501-261, from outside the U.K. 44/208-929-0152), or consult the website at www.hmrc.gov.uk.

AUSTRALIA CUSTOMS   The duty-free allowance in Australia is A$900, or for those under 18, A$450. Personal property mailed back from Puerto Rico should be marked "Australian goods returned" to avoid payment of duty. Upon returning to Australia, citizens can bring in 250 cigarettes or 250 grams of loose tobacco, and 2.25 liters of alcohol. If you're returning with valuable goods you already owned, such as foreign-made cameras, you should file form B263. A helpful brochure, available from Australian consulates or Customs offices, is *Know Before You Go.* For more information, contact **Australian Customs Service,** GPO Box 8, Sydney NSW 2000 (© **1300/363-263**), or see www.customs.gov.au.

NEW ZEALAND CUSTOMS   The duty-free allowance for New Zealand is NZ$700. Citizens over 17 can bring in 200 cigarettes, 50 cigars, or 250 grams of tobacco (or a mixture of all three if their combined weight doesn't exceed 250g); plus 4.5 liters of wine or beer or 1.125 milliliters of liquor. New Zealand currency does not carry import or export restrictions. Fill out a certificate of export, listing the valuables you are taking out of the country; that way, you can bring them back without paying duty. Most questions are answered in a free pamphlet available at New Zealand consulates and Customs offices: *New Zealand Customs Guide for Travellers, Notice no. 4.* For more information, contact **New Zealand Customs**

Service, The Custom House, 17–21 Whitmore St., Box 2218, Wellington (𝄞 **04/473-6099** or 0800/428-786; www.customs. govt.nz).

4 Money

CURRENCY The U.S. dollar is the coin of the realm. Keep in mind that once you leave Ponce or San Juan, you might have difficulty finding a place to exchange foreign money (unless you're staying at a large resort), so it's wise to handle your exchange needs before you head off into rural parts of Puerto Rico.

What Things Cost in Puerto Rico	US$	UK£
Taxi from airport to Condado	13.00	6.75
Average taxi fare within San Juan	6.00	3.10
Typical bus fare within San Juan	0.25–0.50	0.15–0.25
Double room at the Condado Plaza (very expensive)	369.00	191.90
Double room at El Canario by the Lagoon (moderate)	120.00	62.40
Double room at Wind Chimes Inn (inexpensive)	99.00	51.50
Lunch for one at Amadeus (moderate)	16.00	8.30
Lunch for one at Fatty's (inexpensive)	12.00	6.25
Dinner for one at Ramiro's (expensive)	54.00	28.10
Dinner for one at Ostra Cosa (moderate)	26.00	13.50
Dinner for one at La Bombonera (inexpensive)	12.00	6.25
Bottle of beer in a bar	3.00	1.55
Glass of wine in a restaurant	4.00	2.10
Roll of ASA 100 color film 36 exposures	8.50	4.40
Admission Museo de Arte	6.00	3.10
Movie ticket	6.00	3.10
Theater ticket	15.00–75.00	7.80–39.00

ATMs ATMs are linked to a network that most likely includes your bank at home. **Cirrus** (© 800/424-7787; www.mastercard. com) and **PLUS** (© 800/843-7587; www.visa.com) are the two most popular networks in the U.S.; call or check online for ATM locations at your destination. Be sure you know your four-digit PIN before you leave home, and be sure to find out your daily withdrawal limit before you depart. You can also get cash advances on your credit card at an ATM. Keep in mind that credit card companies try to protect themselves from theft by limiting the funds someone can withdraw away from home; it's therefore best to call your credit card company before you leave and let them know where you're going and how much you plan to spend. You'll get the best exchange rate if you withdraw money from an ATM, but keep in mind that many banks impose a fee every time a card is used at an ATM in a different city or bank. On top of this, the bank from which you withdraw cash may charge its own fee.

CURRENCY EXCHANGE The currency exchange facilities at any large international bank within Puerto Rico's larger cities can exchange non-U.S. currencies for dollars. You can also exchange money at the Luis Muñoz Marín International Airport. Also, you'll find foreign-exchange facilities in large hotels and at the many banks in Old San Juan or Avenida Ashford in Condado. In Ponce, look for foreign-exchange facilities at large resorts and at banks such as **Banco Popular,** Plaza Las Delicias (© 787/843-8000).

5 When to Go

CLIMATE
Puerto Rico has one of the most unvarying climates in the world. Temperatures year-round range from 75°F to 85°F (24°C–29°C). The island is wettest and hottest in August, averaging 81°F (27°C) and 7 inches of rain. San Juan and the northern coast seem to be cooler and wetter than Ponce and the southern coast. The coldest weather is in the high altitudes of the Cordillera, the site of Puerto Rico's lowest recorded temperature—39°F (4°C).

THE HURRICANE SEASON
The hurricane season, the curse of Puerto Rican weather, lasts—officially, at least—from June 1 to November 30. But there's no cause for panic. In general, satellite forecasts give adequate warnings so that precautions can be taken.

If you're heading to Puerto Rico during the hurricane season, you can call your local branch of the **National Weather Service** (listed

in your phone directory under the U.S. Department of Commerce)
for a weather forecast. You can also check the **Weather Channel**
(www.weather.com) for a 5-day forecast of your destinations.

Average Temperatures in Puerto Rico

	Jan	Feb	Mar	Apr	May	June	July	Aug	Sept	Oct	Nov	Dec
Temp. (°F)	75	75	76	78	79	81	81	81	81	81	79	77
Temp. (°C)	24	24	24	26	26	27	27	27	27	27	26	25

THE "SEASON"

In Puerto Rico, hotels charge their highest prices during the peak
winter period from mid-December to mid-April, when visitors fleeing from cold northern climates flock to the islands. Winter is the
driest season along the coasts but can be wet in mountainous areas.

If you plan to travel in the winter, make reservations 2 to 3
months in advance. At certain hotels it's almost impossible to book
accommodations for Christmas and the month of February.

SAVING MONEY IN THE OFF SEASON

Puerto Rico is a year-round destination. The island's "off season"
runs from late spring to late fall, when temperatures in the mid-80s
(about 30°C) prevail throughout most of the region. Trade winds
ensure comfortable days and nights, even in accommodations without air-conditioning. Although the noonday sun may raise the temperature to around 90°F (32°C), cool breezes usually make the
morning, late afternoon, and evening more comfortable here than
in many parts of the U.S. mainland.

Dollar for dollar, you'll spend less money by renting a summer
house or fully equipped unit in Puerto Rico than you would on
Cape Cod, Fire Island, Laguna Beach, or the coast of Maine.

The off season in Puerto Rico—roughly from mid-April to mid-
December (rate schedules vary from hotel to hotel)—amounts to a
summer sale. In most cases, hotel rates are slashed from 20% to a
startling 60%. It's a bonanza for cost-conscious travelers, especially
families who like to go on vacations together. In the chapters ahead,
we'll spell out in dollars the specific amounts that hotels charge
during the off season.

HOLIDAYS

Puerto Rico has many public holidays when stores, offices,
and schools are closed: New Year's Day, January 6 (Three Kings
Day), Washington's Birthday, Good Friday, Memorial Day, July 4,
Labor Day, Thanksgiving, Veterans Day, and Christmas, plus such
local holidays as Constitution Day (July 25) and Discovery Day

(Nov 19). Remember, U.S. federal holidays are holidays in Puerto Rico, too.

PUERTO RICO CALENDAR OF EVENTS

January

Three Kings Day, island-wide. On this traditional gift-giving day in Puerto Rico, there are festivals with lively music, dancing, parades, puppet shows, caroling troubadours, and traditional feasts. January 6.

February

Carnaval Ponceño, Ponce. The island's Carnaval celebrations feature float parades, dancing, and street parties. One of the most vibrant festivities is held in Ponce, known for its masqueraders wearing brightly painted horned masks. Live music includes the folk rhythms of the *plena,* which originated in Africa. Festivities include the crowning of a carnival queen and the closing "burial of the sardine." For more information, call ℂ **787/284-4141.** Mid-February.

Casals Festival, Performing Arts Center in San Juan. *Sanjuaneros* and visitors alike eagerly look forward to the annual Casals Festival, the Caribbean's most celebrated cultural event. The bill at San Juan's Performing Arts Center includes a glittering array of international guest conductors, orchestras, and soloists. They come to honor the memory of Pablo Casals, the renowned cellist who was born in Spain to a Puerto Rican mother.

Ticket prices for the Casals Festival range from $20 to $100. A 50% discount is offered to students, people over 60, and persons with disabilities. Tickets are available through the **Performing Arts Center** in San Juan (ℂ **787/792-5000** or 787/620-4444). Information is also available from the **Puerto Rico Tourism Company,** 666 Fifth Ave., New York, NY 10103 (ℂ **800/223-6530** or 212/586-6262), or online at www.festcasalspr.gobierno. pr. The festivities take place late February to early March.

March

Emancipation Day, island-wide. Commemoration of the emancipation of Puerto Rico's slaves in 1873, held at various venues. March 22.

April

Good Friday and Easter, island-wide. Celebrated with colorful ceremonies and processions. Varies from year to year (March 2008 and April 2009).

June

San Juan Bautista Day, island-wide. Puerto Rico's capital and other cities celebrate the island's patron saint with weeklong festivities. At midnight, Sanjuaneros and others walk backward into the sea (or nearest body of water) three times to renew good luck for the coming year. June 24.

Aibonito Flower Festival, at Road 721 next to the City Hall Coliseum, in the central mountain town of Aibonito. This annual flower-competition festival features acres of lilies, anthuriums, carnations, roses, gardenias, and begonias. For more information, call © **787/735-4070.** Last week in June and first week in July.

July

Loíza Carnival, Loíza. This annual folk and religious ceremony honors Loíza's patron saint, James (Santiago) the Apostle. Colorful processions take place, with costumes, masks, and *bomba* dancers (the *bomba* has a lively Afro-Caribbean dance rhythm). This jubilant celebration reflects the African and Spanish heritage of the region. For more information, call © **787/886-6071.** Late July through early August.

October

La Raza Day (Columbus Day), island-wide. This day commemorates Columbus's landing in the New World. October 12.

National Plantain Festival, Corozal. This annual festivity involves crafts, paintings, agricultural products, exhibition, and sale of plantain dishes; *nueva trova* music and folk ballet are performed. For more information, call © **787/859-3060.** Mid-October.

November

Festival of Puerto Rican Music, San Juan. Annual classical and folk music festival. One of its highlights is a *cuatro*-playing contest. (A *cuatro* is a guitarlike instrument with 10 strings.) For more information, call © **787/724-1844.** First week in November.

Puerto Rico Discovery Day, island-wide. This day commemorates the "discovery" by Columbus in 1493 of the already-inhabited island of Puerto Rico. Columbus is thought to have come ashore at the northwestern municipality of Aguadilla, although the exact location is unknown. November 19.

December

Old San Juan's White Christmas Festival, Old San Juan. Special musical and artistic presentations take place in stores, with window displays. December 1 through January 12.

Bacardi Artisans' Fair, San Juan. The best and largest artisans' fair on the island features more than 100 artisans who turn out to exhibit and sell their wares. The fair includes shows for adults and children, a Puerto Rican troubadour contest, rides, and typical food and drink—all sold by nonprofit organizations. It is held on the grounds of the world's largest rum-manufacturing plant in Cataño, an industrial suburb set on a peninsula jutting into San Juan Bay. For more information, call ☎ **787/788-1500.** First two Sundays in December.

YEAR-ROUND FESTIVALS

In addition to the individual events described above, Puerto Rico has two yearlong series of special events: the **Patron Saint Festivals** *(fiestas patronales)* in honor of the patron saint of each municipality, and the **Festival La Casita,** in which prominent Puerto Rican musicians, dance troupes, orchestras, and puppeteers perform every Saturday at Puerto Rico Tourism's "La Casita" Tourism Information Center, Plaza Darsenas, across from Pier 1, Old San Juan.

For more information about all these events, contact the **Puerto Rico Tourism Company,** 666 Fifth Ave., New York, NY 10103 (☎ **800/223-6530** or 212/586-6262).

6 The Active Vacation Planner

For more information on outdoor pursuits, see chapter 6.

BOATING & SAILING

The waters off Puerto Rico provide excellent boating in all seasons. Winds average 10 to 15 knots virtually year-round. Marinas provide facilities and services on par with any others in the Caribbean, and many have powerboats or sailboats for rent (crewed or bareboat charter).

Major marinas include the **San Juan Bay Marina,** Fernández Juncos Avenue (☎ 787/721-8062; www.sjbaymarina.com); **Marina Puerto Chico,** at Puerto Chico (☎ 787/863-0834; www. puerto-chico.com); and **Marina de Salinas** (☎ 787/752-8484; www.marinadesalinas.com) in Salinas. The Caribbean's largest and most modern marina, **Puerto del Rey,** RD 3 Km 51.4 (☎ 787/ 860-1000; www.puertodelrey.com), is located on the island's east coast, in Fajardo.

One of the sailing regattas in Puerto Rico is the Copa Velasco Regatta for ocean racing, at Palmas del Mar in Humacao.

For the typical visitor interested in watersports—not the serious yachter—our favorite place for fun in the surf is the aptly named **San Juan Water Fun,** Isla Verde Beach in back of the El San Juan Hotel and Casino, Avenida Isla Verde in Isla Verde, San Juan (© 787/643-4510). Here you can rent everything from a one-seater kayak for $20 per hour to a banana boat that holds 4 to 10 passengers and costs $15 per person for a 20-minute ride.

If you're staying in eastern Puerto Rico, the best place for watersports rentals is **Iguana Water Sports,** Westin Rio Mar Beach Resort, 6000 Rio Mar Blvd., Río Grande (© 787/888-6000), which has the island's best selection of small boats. Waverunners cost $100 per hour, and two-seat kayaks go for $35 per hour.

For other boating needs, we head to **Maragata Yacht Charter** (© 787/637-1802; www.maragatacharters.com), which offers a wide variety of options, including 8-hour trips to Culebra, costing $175 per person, or 3- to 4-hour snorkeling trips to Monkey Island at $65 per person. Departures are from Palmas del Mar outside Humacao. Fishing trips come in a wide range of options, depending on your needs.

CAMPING

Puerto Rico abounds in sandy beaches and forested hillsides that are suitable for erecting a tent. It is best and safest to camp only in the sites maintained by the government-sponsored **Compañías de Parques Nacionales.** Some of these are simple places where you erect your own tent, although they are outfitted with electricity and running water; some are simple cabins, sometimes with fireplaces. Showers are communal. To stay at a campsite costs between $15 and $25 per night per tent. For more information and an application to rent one of the units or reserve a site, call © 787/622-5200 or, if you speak Spanish, visit **www.parquesnacionalespr.com**.

Many sites offer very basic cabins for rent. Each cabin is equipped with a full bathroom, a stove, a refrigerator, two beds, and a table and chairs. However, most of your cooking will probably be tastier if you do it outside at one of the on-site barbecues. In nearly all cases, you must provide your own sheets and towels.

You might want to camp along or near a lovely beach. On the western coast of Puerto Rico, the best camping site is **Tres Hermanos Beach,** which opens onto Anasco Bay, lying between Rincón to the north and Mayagüez to the south.

Heading west from San Juan en route to Isabella, there are two excellent beach camps: **Cerro Gordo,** east of the city of Arecibo, and **Punta Maracayo,** to the west of Arecibo, both reached along Route 22. The Atlantic waters here can be turbulent, even in summer.

If you'd like to camp in the east of Puerto Rico, the finest site is the beach at **Seven Seas** to the south of Fajardo.

Arroyo on the southern coast to the east of the town of Guayama is yet another site on mainland Puerto Rico that has both cabins and regular campsites, although this location is a bit bare-boned.

Both Culebra and Vieques offer camping by the beach. The best for camping on Culebra is **Flamenco Beach,** on the north shore. On Vieques, the best beach camping is at **Sun Bay,** on the island's south coast.

For information about camping on or near a beach, call (C) **787/ 721-2800.**

Puerto Rico also allows camping in various state forests, provided that permits are obtained. Except for cabins at Monte Guilarte State Forest, which cost $20 per night, camping sites are available at $5 per person. For further information about permits, call the **Forest Service Office** at San Juan Bay Marina ((C) **787/724-3724**).

There are seven major on-island camping sites in various state forests: **Cambalache State Forest,** near Barceloneta; **Carite State Forest,** near Patillas; **Guajataca State Forest,** near Quebradillas; **Monte Guilarte State Forest,** near Adjuntas; **Susua State Forest,** near Yauco; **Río Abajo State Forest,** near Arecibo; and our favorite, **Toro Negro Forest Reserve,** near Villaba, where you can camp in the shadow of Puerto Rico's highest peaks.

In addition, the **Caribbean National Forest/El Yunque** allows primitive camping within the rainforest. For more information, call (C) **787/888-1880.**

It's also possible to camp at either of two wildlife refuges, **Isla de Mona Wildlife Refuge** ((C) **787/724-3640**), lying some 50 miles (80km) off the rough seas of Mona Passage, and **Lago Lucchetti Wildlife Refuge** ((C) **787/856-4887**), between Yauco and Ponce.

The **Parks and Recreation Association of Puerto Rico** ((C) **787/ 721-2800**) can provide you with a map and detailed instructions about how to reach all these sites.

DEEP-SEA FISHING

The offshore fishing here is top-notch! Allison tuna, white and blue marlin, sailfish, wahoo, dolphin fish, mackerel, and tarpon are some of the fish that can be caught in Puerto Rican waters, where some 30 world records have been broken.

Charter arrangements can be made through most major hotels and resorts. In San Juan, **Benítez Fishing Charters** sets the standard by which to judge other captains (p. 118). In Palmas del Mar, which has some of the best year-round fishing in the Caribbean, you'll find **Capt. Bill Burleson** (see "Palmas del Mar," in chapter 10).

GOLF

Home to 14 golf courses, including eight championship links, Puerto Rico is justifiably known as the "Scotland of the Caribbean." In fact, the 72 holes at the Hyatt resort at Dorado offer the greatest concentration of golf in the Caribbean.

The courses at the **Dorado Beach Golf Club** are among the 25 best courses created by Robert Trent Jones, Sr. Jack Nicklaus rates the challenging 13th hole at the Hyatt Dorado as one of the top 10 in the world. See p. 141 for more details.

On the southeast coast, crack golfers consider holes 11 through 15 at the **Golf Club at Palmas del Mar** to be the toughest five successive holes in the Caribbean. At **El Conquistador Resort & Golden Door Spa,** the spectacular $250-million resort at Las Croabas east of San Juan, the course's 200-foot (61m) changes in elevation provide panoramic vistas. With the exception of the El Conquistador Resort and Country Club, these courses are open to the public. See chapter 10 for more details on the major golf clubs east of San Juan.

HIKING

The mountainous interior of Puerto Rico provides ample opportunities for hill climbing and nature treks. These are especially appealing because panoramas open at the least-expected moments, often revealing spectacular views of the distant sea.

The most popular, most beautiful, and most spectacular trekking spot is **El Yunque,** the sprawling "jungle" maintained by the U.S. Forest Service and the only rainforest on U.S. soil.

El Yunque is part of the **Caribbean National Forest,** which lies a 45-minute drive east of San Juan. More than 250 species of trees and some 200 types of ferns have been identified here. Some 60 species of birds inhabit El Yunque, including the increasingly rare Puerto Rican parrot. Such rare birds as the elfin woods warbler, the green mango hummingbird, and the Puerto Rican lizard-cuckoo live here.

Park rangers have clearly marked the trails that are ideal for walking. See "El Yunque" in chapter 7 for more details.

A lesser forest, but one that is still intriguing to visit, is the **Maricao State Forest,** near the coffee town of Maricao. This forest is in western Puerto Rico, east of the town of Mayagüez. For more details, see p. 167.

Ponce is the best center for exploring some of the greatest forest reserves in the Caribbean Basin, notably **Toro Negro Forest Reserve** with its **Lake Guineo** (the lake at the highest elevation on the island); the **Guánica State Forest,** ideal for hiking and bird-watching; and the **Carite Forest Reserve,** a 6,000-acre (2,428ha) park known for its dwarf forest. For more details, see p. 156.

Equally suitable for hiking are the protected lands (especially the **Río Camuy Cave Park**) whose topography is characterized as "karst"—that is, limestone riddled with caves, underground rivers, and natural crevasses and fissures. Although these regions pose additional risks and technical problems for trekkers, some people prefer the opportunities they provide for exploring the territory both above and below its surface. See p. 140 for details about the Río Camuy Caves.

For more information about any of the national forest reserves of Puerto Rico, call the **Department of Sports & Recreation** at *©* 787/721-2800.

Aventuras Tierra Adentro (*©* 787/766-0470; www.aventuras pr.com) offers the best island adventure tours, focusing on hiking through virgin forests, rock climbing, or cliff jumping. Several different adventures are offered, costing $160 per person, which includes transportation from San Juan. Most of the jaunts take place on weekends.

SCUBA DIVING

The continental shelf, which surrounds Puerto Rico on three sides, is responsible for an abundance of coral reefs, caves, sea walls, and trenches for scuba diving and snorkeling.

Open-water reefs off the southeastern coast near **Humacao** are visited by migrating whales and manatees. Many caves are located near Isabela on the west coast. The **Great Trench,** off the island's south coast, is ideal for experienced open-water divers. Caves and the sea wall at **La Parguera** are also favorites. **Vieques** and **Culebra islands** have coral formations. **Mona Island** offers unspoiled reefs at depths averaging 80 feet (24m); seals are one of the attractions.

Uninhabited islands, such as **Icacos,** off the northeastern coast near Fajardo, are also popular with both snorkelers and divers.

These sites are now within reach because many of Puerto Rico's dive operators and resorts offer packages that include daily or twice-daily dives, scuba equipment, instruction, and excursions to Puerto Rico's popular attractions.

In San Juan, **Caribe Aquatic Adventures** offers an array of sailing, scuba, and snorkeling trips, as well as boat charters and fishing (p. 119).

Elsewhere on the island, several other companies offer scuba and snorkeling instruction. We provide details in each chapter.

SNORKELING

Because of its overpopulation, the waters around San Juan aren't the most ideal for snorkeling. In fact, the entire north shore of Puerto Rico fronts the Atlantic, where the waters are often turbulent. Windsurfers—not snorkelers—gravitate to the waves and surf in the northwest.

The most ideal conditions for snorkeling in Puerto Rico are along the shores of the remote islands of Vieques and Culebra. But the best snorkeling on the main island is found near the town of **Fajardo,** to the east of San Juan and along the tranquil eastern coast (p. 194).

The calm, glasslike quality of the clear Caribbean along the south shore is also ideal for snorkeling. The most developed tourist mecca here is the city of Ponce. Few rivers empty their muddy waters into the sea along the south coast, resulting in gin-clear waters offshore. You can snorkel off the coast without having to go on a boat trip. One good place is at **Playa La Parguera,** where you can rent snorkeling equipment from kiosks along the beach. This beach lies east of the town of Guánica, to the east of Ponce. Here tropical fish add to the brightness of the water, which is generally turquoise. The addition of mangrove cays in the area also makes La Parguera more alluring for snorkelers. Another good spot for snorkelers is **Caja de Muertos** off the coast of Ponce. Here a lagoon coral reef boasts a large number of fish species (p. 158).

SURFING

Puerto Rico's northwest beaches attract surfers from around the world. Called the "Hawaii of the East," Puerto Rico has hosted a number of international competitions. October through February are the best surfing months, but the sport is enjoyed in Puerto Rico from August through April. The most popular areas are from Isabela around Punta Borinquén to Rincón—at beaches such as Wilderness, Surfers, Crashboat, Los Turbos in Vega Baja, Pine Grove in Isla Verde, and La Pared in Luquillo. Surfboards are available at many watersports shops.

International competitions held in Puerto Rico have included the 1968 and 1988 World Amateur Surfing Championships, the annual Caribbean Cup Surfing Championship, and the 1989 and 1990 Budweiser Puerto Rico Surfing Challenge events.

TENNIS

Puerto Rico has approximately 100 major tennis courts. Many are at hotels and resorts; others are in public parks throughout the island. Several *paradores* also have courts. A number of courts are lighted for nighttime play.

In San Juan, the **Caribe Hilton** and the **Condado Plaza Hotel & Casino** have tennis courts. Also in the area are the **public courts** at the San Juan Central Municipal Park. See chapter 6.

WINDSURFING

The best windsurfing is found at Punta Las Marías in the Greater San Juan metropolitan area. Other spots on the island for windsurfing include Santa Isabel, Guánica, and La Parguera in the south; Jobos and Shacks in the northwest; and the island of Culebra off the eastern coast. The best advice and equipment rental is available at **Velauno,** Calle Loíza 2430, Punta Las Marías in San Juan (© **866/ PR-VELA-1** or 787/982-0543; www.velauno.com).

7 Health & Safety

STAYING HEALTHY

Puerto Rico poses no major health risks for most travelers. If you have a chronic condition, however, you should check with your doctor before visiting the islands. For conditions such as epilepsy, diabetes, or heart problems, wear a **MedicAlert Identification Tag** (© **888/633-4298;** www.medicalert.org), which will immediately alert doctors to your condition and give them access to your records through MedicAlert's 24-hour hot line.

Finding a good doctor in Puerto Rico is easy, and most speak English. See "Fast Facts: Puerto Rico," later in this chapter, for hospital locations.

If you worry about getting sick away from home, consider purchasing **medical travel insurance**, and carry your ID card in your purse or wallet. In most cases, your existing health plan will provide the coverage you need.

Pack **prescription medications** in your carry-on luggage and carry prescription medications in their original containers. Also bring along copies of your prescriptions in case you lose your medication or run out. Carry the generic name of prescription medicines, in case a local pharmacist is unfamiliar with the brand name. And don't forget **sunglasses** and an extra pair of **contact lenses** or **prescription glasses.**

Contact the **International Association for Medical Assistance to Travellers (IAMAT; ✆ 716/754-4883,** or in Canada 416/652-0137; www.iamat.org) for tips on travel and health concerns in Puerto Rico and lists of local, English-speaking doctors. If you get sick, consider asking your hotel concierge to recommend a local doctor—even his or her own. You can also try the emergency room at a local hospital; many have walk-in clinics for emergency cases that are not life-threatening. You might not get immediate attention, but you won't pay the high price of an emergency-room visit (usually a minimum of $300 just for signing your name). The United States **Centers for Disease Control and Prevention (✆ 800/394-1945;** www.cdc.gov) provides up-to-date information on necessary vaccines and health hazards by region or country.

It's best to stick to **bottled mineral water** here. Although tap water is said to be safe to drink, many visitors experience diarrhea, even if they follow the usual precautions. The illness usually passes quickly without medication if you eat simply prepared food and drink only mineral water until you recover. If symptoms persist, consult a doctor.

The **sun** can be brutal, especially if you haven't been exposed to it in some time. Experts advise that you limit your time on the beach the first day. If you do overexpose yourself, stay out of the sun until you recover. If your exposure is followed by fever or chills, a headache, or a feeling of nausea or dizziness, see a doctor.

Sandflies (or "no-see-ums") are one of the biggest insect menaces in Puerto Rico. They appear mainly in the early evening, and even if you can't see these tiny bugs, you sure can "feel-um," as any native Puerto Rican will attest. Screens can't keep them out, so you'll need to use your favorite insect repellent.

Although mosquitoes are a nuisance, they do not carry malaria in Puerto Rico. However, after a long absence, the potentially deadly **dengue fever** has returned to Puerto Rico. The disease is transmitted by the Aede mosquito, and its symptoms include fever, headaches, pain in the muscles and joints, skin blisters, and hemor-rhaging. Most of its victims lack any defense against it.

Hookworm and other **intestinal parasites** are relatively com-mon in the Caribbean, though you are less likely to be affected in Puerto Rico than on other islands. Hookworm can be contracted by just walking barefoot on an infected beach; do not walk barefoot or contact the soil with bare hands in areas where hookworm is com-mon. *Schistosomiasis* (also called *bilharzia*), caused by a parasitic fluke, can be contracted by submerging your feet in rivers and lakes infested with a certain species of snail.

Puerto Rico has been especially hard hit by **AIDS.** Exercise *at least* the same caution in choosing your sexual partners, and in practicing safe sex, as you would at home.

STAYING SAFE

The U.S. State Department issues no special travel advisories for the Commonwealth of Puerto Rico, the way it might for, say, the more troubled island of Jamaica. However, there are problems in Puerto Rico, especially muggings along San Juan's Condado and Isla Verde beaches. Auto theft and break-ins are other major problems. Do not leave valuables in cars, even when the doors are locked.

Take precautions about leaving valuables on the beach, and exer-cise extreme care if you're searching for a remote beach where there's no one in sight. The only person lurking nearby might be someone not interested in surf and sand, but a robber waiting to make off with your possessions.

Avoid wandering around the darkened and relatively deserted alleys and small streets of San Juan's Old Town at night, especially a section called El Callejón, near the intersection of calles San Sebastián and Tanca. Be especially careful along the narrow alley that connects this intersection with Calle Norzagaray. The district attracts more drug dealers than any other spot in Puerto Rico. A number of muggings also occur in Old Town's Cementerio de San Juan.

8 Specialized Travel Resources
TRAVELERS WITH DISABILITIES

The Americans with Disabilities Act is enforced as strictly in Puerto Rico as it is on the U.S. mainland—in fact, a telling example of the act's enforcement can be found in Ponce, where the sightseeing trol-leys are equipped with ramps and extra balustrades to accommodate travelers with disabilities. Unfortunately, hotels rarely give much publicity to the facilities they offer persons with disabilities, so it's always wise to contact the hotel directly, in advance, if you need special facilities. Tourist offices usually have little data about such matters.

The U.S. National Park Service offers a **Golden Access Passport** that gives free lifetime entrance to U.S. national parks, including those in Puerto Rico, for persons who are visually impaired or permanently disabled, regardless of age. You can pick up a Golden Access Passport at any NPS entrance-fee area by showing proof of medically determined disability and eligibility for receiving benefits under federal law. Besides free entry, the Golden Access Passport also offers a 50% discount on federal-use fees charged for such facilities as camping, swimming, parking, boat launching, and tours. For more information, go to www.nps.gov/fees_passes.htm or call ✆ **888/GO-PARKS.**

SATH (Society for Accessible Travel and Hospitality; ✆ **212/ 447-7284;** www.sath.org) offers a wealth of travel resources for all types of disabilities and informed recommendations on destinations, access guides, travel agents, tour operators, vehicle rentals, and companion services. **The American Foundation for the Blind** (**AFB;** ✆ **800/232-5463** or 212/502-7600; www.afb.org) provides information on traveling with Seeing Eye dogs.

GAY & LESBIAN TRAVELERS

Puerto Rico is the most gay-friendly destination in the Caribbean, with lots of accommodations, restaurants, clubs, and bars that actively cater to a gay clientele. A free monthly newsletter, *Puerto Rico Breeze,* lists items of interest to the island's gay community. It's distributed at the Atlantic Beach Hotel (p. 68) and many of the gay-friendly clubs mentioned in this book.

The **International Gay and Lesbian Travel Association** (**IGLTA;** ✆ **800/448-8550** or 954/776-2626; www.iglta.org) links travelers up with gay-friendly hoteliers, tour operators, and airline and cruise-line representatives. It offers monthly newsletters, marketing mailings, and a membership directory that's updated once a year.

Gay.com Travel (✆ **800/929-2268** or 415/644-8044; www.gay. com/travel or www.outandabout.com) is an excellent online successor to the popular **Out&About** print magazine. It provides regularly updated information about gay-owned, gay-oriented, and gay-friendly lodging, dining, sightseeing, nightlife, and shopping establishments in every important destination worldwide.

SENIOR TRAVEL

Mention the fact that you're a senior when you first make your travel reservations. All major airlines and many Puerto Rican hotels offer discounts for seniors.

Though much of the island's sporting and nightlife activity is geared toward youthful travelers, Puerto Rico also has much to offer the senior. The best source of information for seniors is the Puerto Rico Tourism Company (see "Visitor Information," earlier in this chapter), or, if you're staying in a large resort hotel, talk to the activities director or the concierge.

Members of **AARP** (formerly known as the American Association of Retired Persons), 601 E St. NW, Washington, DC 20049 (© **888/687-2277;** www.aarp.org), get discounts on hotels, airfares, and car rentals. AARP offers members a wide range of benefits, including *AARP The Magazine* and a monthly newsletter. Anyone over 50 can join.

The **U.S. National Park Service** offers a **Golden Age Passport** that gives seniors 62 or older lifetime entrance to U.S. national parks for a one-time processing fee of $10. The pass must be purchased in person at any NPS facility that charges an entrance fee. Besides free entry, a Golden Age Passport also offers a 50% discount on federal-use fees charged for such facilities as camping, swimming, parking, boat launching, and tours. For more information, visit www.nps.gov/fees_passes.htm or call © **888/GO-PARKS.**

FAMILY TRAVEL

Puerto Rico is a terrific family destination. The smallest toddlers can spend blissful hours on sandy beaches and in the shallow seawater or pools specifically constructed for them. There's no end to the fascinating pursuits available for older children, ranging from boat rides to shell collecting to horseback riding and hiking. Perhaps your children are old enough to learn to snorkel and explore the wonderland of underwater Puerto Rico. Skills such as swimming and windsurfing are taught here, and there are a variety of activities unique to the islands. Most resort hotels will advise you on what there is in the way of fun for the young, and many have play directors and supervised activities for various age groups.

Recommended family travel Internet sites include **Family Travel Forum** (www.familytravelforum.com), a comprehensive site that offers customized trip planning; **Family Travel Network** (www. familytravelnetwork.com), an award-winning site that offers travel features, deals, and tips; and **Family Travel Files** (www.thefamily travelfiles.com), which offers an online magazine and a directory of off-the-beaten-path tours and tour operators for families.

9 Getting There: Flying to Puerto Rico

Puerto Rico is by far the most accessible of the Caribbean islands, with frequent airline service. It's also the major airline hub of the Caribbean Basin.

THE AIRLINES

With San Juan as its hub for the entire Caribbean, **American Airlines** (© 800/433-7300; www.aa.com) offers nonstop daily flights to San Juan from Baltimore, Boston, Chicago, Dallas–Fort Worth, Hartford, Los Angeles, Miami, Newark, New York, Orlando, Detroit, Philadelphia, Seattle, Tampa, Fort Lauderdale, and Washington (Dulles), plus flights to San Juan from both Montreal and Toronto with changes in Chicago or Miami. There are also at least two daily flights from Los Angeles to San Juan that touch down in Dallas or Miami.

American, because of its wholly owned subsidiary **American Eagle,** is also the undisputed leader among the short-haul local commuter flights of the Caribbean. It usually flies propeller planes carrying between 34 and 64 passengers. Collectively, American Eagle and American Airlines offer service to 37 destinations on 31 islands of the Caribbean and the Bahamas, more than any other carrier.

Delta (© 800/221-1212; www.delta.com) has daily nonstop flights from Atlanta and JFK. Flights into Atlanta from around the world are frequent, with excellent connections from points throughout Delta's network in the South and Southwest. There is also one daily nonstop flight from Cincinnati.

United Airlines (© 800/241-6522; www.united.com) offers daily nonstop flights from Chicago to San Juan. United also offers flights to San Juan, some of them nonstop, from both Memphis and Minneapolis, with a schedule that varies according to the season and the day of the week. **Northwest/KLM** (© 800/225-2525; www.nwa.com) has one daily nonstop flight to San Juan from Detroit, as well as at least one connecting flight (and sometimes more) to San Juan from Detroit.

America West/US Airways (© 800/428-4322; www.usairways. com) has daily direct flights between Charlotte, North Carolina, and San Juan. The airline also offers three daily nonstop flights to

---

Tips **Before You Pack**

With the ever-changing security measures, we recommend that you check the Transportration Security Administration's website at **www.tsa.gov** as near to your departure date as possible to see the latest carry-on and baggage restrictions.

San Juan from Philadelphia, and one daily nonstop Saturday and Sunday flight to San Juan from Pittsburgh.

Continental Airlines (© **800/525-0280;** www.continental. com) flies nonstop daily from Newark, Houston, and Cleveland. The airline also flies five times a week direct to the northwestern airport outside Aguadilla, should you wish to begin your tour of Puerto Rico in the west. In winter, service is increased to daily flights. **JetBlue** (© **800/538-2583;** www.jetblue.com) flies four times a day from New York's JFK airport to San Juan and daily to Aguadilla and Ponce. **Spirit Airlines** (© **787/772-7117;** www. spiritair.com) offers two daily nonstop flights from Orlando and Boston to San Juan.

Canadians can fly **Air Canada** (© **888/247-2262;** www.air canada.com) from either Montreal or Toronto to San Juan. British travelers can take a **British Airways** (© **0870/859-9850** in the U.K., or 800/247-9297 in the U.S.; www.britishairways.com) weekly flight direct from London to San Juan on Sunday. **Lufthansa** (© **01/805-83-84-26** in Germany, or 800/399-5838 in the U.S.; www.lufthansa.com) passengers can fly on Saturday (one weekly flight) from Frankfurt to San Juan via Condor (a subsidiary operating the flight). And **Iberia** (© **902/400-500** in Spain, or 800/772-4642 in the U.S.; www.iberia.com) has two weekly flights from Madrid to San Juan, leaving on Thursday and Saturday.

FLYING FOR LESS: TIPS FOR GETTING THE BEST AIRFARE

- Passengers who can book their ticket either **long in advance or at the last minute,** or who **fly midweek** or **at less-trafficked hours**, may pay a fraction of the full fare. If your schedule is flexible, say so, and ask if you can secure a cheaper fare by changing your flight plans.
- Search **the Internet** for cheap fares.

- Keep an eye on local newspapers for **promotional specials** or **fare wars,** when airlines lower prices on their most popular routes.
- **Consolidators,** also known as bucket shops, are great sources for international tickets. Start by looking in Sunday newspaper travel sections; U.S. travelers should focus on the *New York Times, Los Angeles Times,* and *The Miami Herald.* U.K. travelers should search in *The Independent, The Guardian,* or *The Observer. Beware:* Bucket shop tickets are usually nonrefundable or rigged with stiff cancellation penalties, often as high as 50% to 75% of the ticket price, and some put you on charter airlines, which may leave at inconvenient times and experience delays. Several reliable consolidators are worldwide and available online. **STA Travel** has been the world's leading consolidator for students since purchasing Council Travel, but their fares are competitive for travelers of all ages. **ELTExpress (Flights.com)** (© 201/541-3826; www.eltexpress.com) has excellent fares worldwide. **AirTicketsDirect** (© 888/858-8884; www.airticketsdirect.com) is based in Montreal and leverages the Canadian dollar for low fares; they also book trips to places that U.S. travel agents won't touch, such as Cuba.
- Join **frequent-flier clubs.** Frequent-flier membership doesn't cost a cent, but it does entitle you to better seats, faster response to phone inquiries, and prompter service if your luggage is stolen or your flight is canceled or delayed, or if you want to change your seat. With more than 70 mileage awards programs on the market, consumers have never had more options. To play the frequent-flier game to your best advantage, consult Randy Petersen's **Inside Flyer** (www.insideflyer. com). Petersen and friends review all the programs in detail and post regular updates on changes in policies and trends.

10 Packages for the Independent Traveler

Before you start your search for the lowest airfare, you might want to consider booking your flight as part of a travel package such as an escorted tour or a package tour. What you lose in adventure, you'll gain in time and money saved when you book accommodations, and maybe even food and entertainment, along with your flight.

One good source of package deals is the airlines themselves. Most major airlines offer air/land packages, including **American Airlines**

Vacations (℗ 800/321-2121; www.aavacations.com), **Delta Vacations** (℗ 800/654-6559; www.deltavacations.com), **US Airways Vacations** (℗ 800/455-0123; www.usairwaysvacations.com), **Continental Airlines Vacations** (℗ 800/301-3800; www.covacations. com), and **United Vacations** (℗ 888/854-3899; www.united vacations.com).

Vacation Together (℗ 877/444-4547; www.vacationtogether. com) allows you to search for and book packages offered by a number of tour operators and airlines. The **United States Tour Operators Association**'s website (www.ustoa.com) has a search engine that allows you to look for operators that offer packages to a specific destination. Travel packages are also listed in the travel section of your local Sunday newspaper. **Liberty Travel** (℗ 888/271-1584; www.libertytravel.com), one of the biggest packagers in the Northeast, often runs full-page ads in Sunday papers. Or check ads in the national travel magazines such as *Budget Travel, Travel + Leisure, National Geographic Traveler,* and *Condé Nast Traveler.*

To save time comparing the price and value of all the package tours out there, consider calling **TourScan** (℗ 800/962-2080 or 203/655-8091; www.tourscan.com). Every season the company gathers and computerizes the contents of about 200 brochures containing 10,000 different vacations in the Caribbean, the Bahamas, and Bermuda. TourScan selects the best value at each hotel and condo. Two catalogs are printed each year. Each lists a broad-based choice of hotels on most of the islands of the Caribbean, in all price ranges.

Another option for general independent packages is **Just-A-Vacation** (℗ 800/683-6313 or 301/559-0510; www.justavacation. com), which specializes in all-inclusive upscale resorts in Puerto Rico.

11 Escorted General Interest Tours

An escorted tour is a structured group tour with a group leader. The price usually includes everything from airfare to hotel, meals, tours, admission costs, and local transportation.

Puerto Rico Tours, Condo Inter-Suite, Suite 5M, on Isla Verde in San Juan (℗ 787/791-5479; www.puertorico-tours.com), offers specially conducted private sightseeing tours of Puerto Rico, including trips to the rainforest, Luquillo Beach, the caves of Camuy, and other attractions, such as a restored Taíno Indian village.

Backstage Partners (© 787/748-0099; www.backstagepartners. com) offers customized tours that take in a wide range of island attractions, including eco-tours, deep-sea fishing, scuba diving and snorkeling, safaris, and golf packages.

Other leading escorted tour operators include **Atlantic San Juan Tours** (© 787/644-9841; www.puertoricoexcursions.com), which helps you take in all the major sights of the island from Ponce to El Yunque; and **Sunshine Tours** (© 866/785-3636; www.puerto-rico-sunshinetours.com), which covers much the same ground as the others.

12 Special-Interest Tours

If you'd like to explore Puerto Rico as part of a horseback-riding tour package, consult **PRwest Vacation Services** (© 888/779-3788 or 787/823-0806; www.prwest.com). A dozen well-trained Paso Fino horses are available to accommodate both the advanced and novice rider. In northwest Puerto Rico, you can explore cavernous cliffs and tropical forests—all on horseback. Tours are customized.

Several other tour operators cater to special tastes, including **Castillo Tours & Travel Service,** 2413 Laurel St., Punta Las Marías, Santurce (© 787/791-6195; www.castillotours.com), which is known for some of the best deep-sea fishing tours.

Hillbilly Tours, Route 181 Km 13.4, San Juan (© 787/760-5618), specializes in nature-based and countryside tours in the rainforest.

AdvenTours, El Yunque (© 787/889-0251; www.adventours pr.com), features customized private tours that include such activities as bird-watching, hiking, camping, visits to coffee plantations, and kayaking.

Eco Xcursion Aquática, Route 191 Km 1.7, Río Grande, Fajardo (© 787/888-2887), offers some of the best rainforest hikes and mountain-bike tours for both individuals and groups.

13 Getting Around
BY PLANE
American Eagle (© 800/433-7300; www.aa.com) flies from Luis Muñoz Marín International Airport to Mayagüez, which can be your gateway to western Puerto Rico.

Puerto Rico is the major transportation hub of the Caribbean, with the best connections for getting anywhere in the islands. In addition to American Eagle (see above), **Cape Air** (© **800/352-0714;** www.flycapeair.com) links the two major islands in the U.S. Virgins, both St. Croix and St. Thomas, as well as Tortola in the BVI, with San Juan, Ponce, Vieques, and Mayagüez.

Seaborne Airlines (© **888/359-8687;** www.seaborneonline.com) offers daily links between St. Croix and St. Thomas with San Juan. The one-way cost from the U.S. Virgin Islands to Puerto Rico is $100 per person. The planes are small and frequent, carrying 15 to 19 passengers. Often there are more than 50 flights a day.

LIAT (© **888/844-LIAT;** www.liatairline.com) provides an air link to the Lesser Antilles islands.

BY CAR

There is good news and bad news about driving in Puerto Rico. First, the good news: Puerto Rico offers some of the most scenic drives in all the Caribbean. Driving around and discovering its little hidden beaches, coastal towns, mountain villages, vast forests, and national parks is reason enough to visit the island. In fact, if you want to explore the island in any depth, driving a private car is about the only way, as public transportation is woefully inadequate.

Of course, if you want to stay only in San Juan, having a car is not necessary. You can get around San Juan on foot or by bus, taxi, and, in some cases, hotel minivan.

Now the bad news: Renting a car and driving in Puerto Rico, depending on the routes you take, can lead to a number of frustrating experiences, as our readers relate to us year after year. These readers point out that local drivers are often dangerous, as evidenced by the number of fenders with bashed-in sides. The older coastal highways provide the most scenic routes but are often congested. Some of the roads, especially in the mountainous interior, are just too narrow for automobiles. If you do rent a car, proceed with caution along these poorly paved and maintained roads, which most often follow circuitous routes. Cliffslides or landslides are not uncommon.

Some local agencies may tempt you with special reduced prices. But if you're planning to tour the island by car, you won't find any local branches that will help you if you experience trouble. And some of the agencies widely advertising low-cost deals won't take credit cards and want cash in advance. Also, watch out for "hidden" extra costs, which sometimes proliferate among the smaller and not very well-known firms, and for difficulties connected with resolving insurance claims.

If you do rent a vehicle, it's best to stick with the old reliables: **Avis** (© **800/331-1212** or 787/253-5926; www.avis.com), **Budget** (© **800/472-3325** or 787/791-0600; www.budget.com), or **Hertz** (© **800/654-3001** or 787/566-4400; www.hertz.com). Each of these companies offers minivan transport to its office and car depot. Be alert to the minimum-age requirements for car rentals in Puerto Rico. Both Avis and Hertz require that renters be 25 or older; at Budget, renters must be 21 or older, but those between the ages of 21 and 24 pay a $10 to $25 daily surcharge to the agreed-upon rental fee.

Added security comes from an antitheft double-locking mechanism that has been installed in most of the rental cars available in Puerto Rico. Car theft is common in Puerto Rico, so extra precautions are always needed.

Distances are often posted in kilometers rather than miles (1km = .62 mile), but speed limits are displayed in miles per hour.

GASOLINE   There is usually an abundant supply of gasoline in Puerto Rico, especially on the outskirts of San Juan, where you'll see all the familiar signs, such as Mobil. Gasoline stations are also plentiful along the main arteries traversing the island. However, if you're going to remote areas of the island, especially on Sunday, it's advisable to start out with a full tank. *Note:* In Puerto Rico, gasoline is sold by the liter, not by the gallon. The cost of gasoline is often somewhat cheaper than in the United States. Since gasoline prices are in a worldwide flux, it's anybody's guess what actual costs will be when you arrive on island—check locally.

DRIVING RULES   Driving rules can be a source of some confusion. Speed limits are often not posted on the island, but when they are, they're given in miles per hour. For example, the limit on the San Juan–Ponce *autopista* (expressway) is 70 mph. Speed limits elsewhere, notably in heavily populated residential areas, are much lower. Because you're not likely to know what the actual speed limit is in some of these areas, it's best to confine your speed to no more than 30 mph. The highway department places *lomas* (speed bumps) at strategic points to deter speeders. Sometimes these are called "sleeping policemen."

Like U.S. and Canadian motorists, Puerto Ricans drive on the right side of the road.

See also the "Highway Signs" box on the inside front cover of this guide.

ROAD MAPS One of the best and most detailed road maps of Puerto Rico is published by **International Travel Maps** and distributed in the United States by Rand McNally. It's available in some bookstores and is a good investment at $9.95. The tourist offices in Puerto Rico have a free map available.

BREAKDOWNS & ASSISTANCE All the major towns and cities have garages that will come to your assistance and tow your vehicle for repairs if necessary. There's no national emergency number to call in the event of a mechanical breakdown. If you have a rental car, call the rental company first. Usually, someone there will bring motor assistance to you. If your car requires extensive repairs because of a mechanical failure, a new one will be sent to replace it.

BY PUBLIC TRANSPORTATION

Cars and minibuses known as *públicos* provide low-cost transportation around the island. Their license plates have the letters "P" or "PD" following the numbers. They serve all the main towns of Puerto Rico; passengers are let off and picked up along the way, both at designated stops and when someone flags them down. Rates are set by the Public Service Commission. *Públicos* usually operate during daylight hours, departing from the main plaza (central square) of a town.

Information about *público* routes between San Juan and Mayagüez is available at **Líneas Sultana,** Calle Esteban González 898, Urbanización Santa Rita, Río Piedras (© **787/765-9377**). Information about *público* routes between San Juan and Ponce is available from **Choferes Unidos de Ponce,** Terminal de Carros Públicos, Calle Vive in Ponce (© **787/764-0540**).

Fares vary according to whether the *público* will make a detour to pick up or drop off a passenger at a specific locale. (If you want to deviate from the predetermined routes, you'll pay more than if you wait for a *público* beside the main highway.) Fares from San Juan to Mayagüez range from $12 to $15; from San Juan to Ponce, from $10 to $12. Be warned that although prices of *públicos* are low, the routes are slow, with frequent stops, often erratic routing, and lots of inconvenience.

14 Tips on Accommodations
HOTELS & RESORTS

There is no rigid classification of Puerto Rican hotels. The word "deluxe" is often used—or misused—when "first class" might be a more appropriate term. Self-described first-class hotels often aren't that nice. We've presented fairly detailed descriptions of the hotels in this book, so you'll get an idea of what to expect once you're there.

Even in the real deluxe and first-class properties, however, don't expect top-rate service and efficiency. The slow tropical pace is what folks mean when they talk about "island time." Also, things often don't work as well in the tropics as they do in some of the fancy resorts of California or Europe. You might even experience power failures.

Ask detailed questions when booking a room. Don't just ask to be booked into a certain hotel, but specify your likes and dislikes. There are several logistics of getting the right room in a hotel. Entertainment in Puerto Rico is often alfresco, so light sleepers obviously won't want a room directly over a steel band. In general, back rooms cost less than oceanfront rooms, and lower-floor rooms cost less than upper-floor units. Therefore, if budget is a major consideration for you, opt for the cheaper rooms. You won't have a great view, but you'll pay less. Just make sure that it isn't next to the all-night drummers.

MAP VS. AP, CP & EP?

All resorts offer a **European Plan (EP)** rate, which means you pay for the price of a room. That leaves you free to dine around at night at various other resorts or restaurants without restriction. Another plan preferred by many is the **Continental Plan (CP),** which means you get your room and a continental breakfast of juice, coffee, bread, jam, and so on, included in a set price. This plan is preferred by many because most guests don't like to "dine around" at breakfast time.

Another major option is the **Modified American Plan (MAP),** which includes breakfast and one main meal of the day, either lunch or dinner. The final choice is the **American Plan (AP),** which includes breakfast, lunch, and dinner.

At certain resorts you will save money by booking either the MAP or AP because discounts are granted. If you dine a la carte for lunch and dinner at various restaurants, your final dining bill will no doubt be much higher than if you stayed on the MAP or AP.

These plans might save you money, but if as part of your holiday you like to eat in various places, you might be disappointed. You face the same dining room every night, unless the resort you're staying at has many different restaurants on the dining plan. Often they don't. Many resorts have a lot of specialty restaurants, serving, say,

Japanese cuisine, but these more expensive restaurants are not included in MAP or AP; rather, they charge a la carte prices.

One option is to ask if your hotel has a dine-around plan. You might still keep costs in check, but you can avoid a culinary rut by taking your meals in some other restaurants if your hotel has such a plan. Such plans are rare in Puerto Rico, which does not specialize in all-inclusive resorts the way that Jamaica and some other islands do.

PUERTO RICAN GUESTHOUSES

Guesthouses are popular in Puerto Rico, and Puerto Ricans themselves usually seek them out when they travel. Ranging in size from 7 to 25 rooms, they offer a familial atmosphere. Many are on or near the beach, some have pools or sun decks, and a number serve meals.

In Puerto Rico, however, the term "guesthouse" has many meanings. Some guesthouses are like simple motels built around pools. Others have small individual cottages with their own kitchenettes, constructed around a main building in which you'll often find a bar and a restaurant serving local food. Some are surprisingly comfortable, often with private bathrooms and swimming pools. You may or may not have air-conditioning. The rooms are sometimes cooled by ceiling fans or by the trade winds blowing through open windows at night.

For value, the guesthouse can't be topped. If you stay at a guesthouse, you can journey over to a big beach resort and use its seaside facilities for only a small fee. Although bereft of frills, the guesthouses we've recommended are clean and safe for families or single women. However, the cheapest ones are not places where you'd want to spend a lot of time because of their modest furnishings.

For further information on guesthouses, contact the **Puerto Rico Tourism Company,** 666 Fifth Ave., New York, NY 10013 (© **800/ 223-6530** or 212/586-6262).

PARADORES

In an effort to lure travelers beyond the hotels and casinos of San Juan's historic district to the tranquil natural beauty of the island's countryside, the Puerto Rico Tourism Company offers *paradores puertorriqueños* (charming country inns), which are comfortable bases for exploring the island's varied attractions. Vacationers seeking a peaceful idyll can also choose from several privately owned and operated guesthouses.

Paradores & Country Inns of Puerto Rico

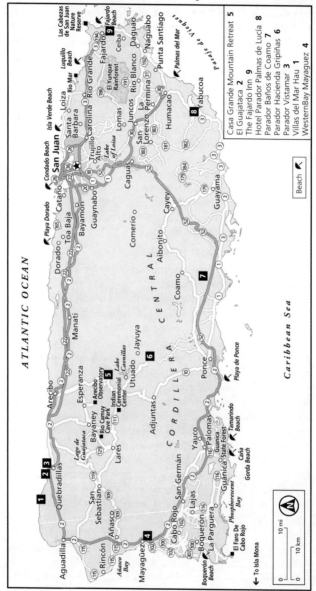

Casa Grande Mountain Retreat **5**
El Guajataca **2**
The Fajardo Inn **9**
Hotel Parador Palmas de Lucía **8**
Parador Baños de Coamo **7**
Parador Hacienda Gripiñas **6**
Parador Vistamar **3**
Villas del Mar Hau **1**
WesternBay Mayaguez **4**

Beach ◄

Using Spain's *parador* system as a model, the Puerto Rico Tourism Company established the *paradores* in 1973 to encourage tourism across the island. Each of the *paradores* is situated in a historic place or site of unusual scenic beauty, and must meet high standards of service and cleanliness. See the "Paradores & Country Inns of Puerto Rico" map on p. 41.

Some of the *paradores* are located in the mountains, and others by the sea. Most have pools, and all offer excellent Puerto Rican cuisine. Many are within easy driving distance of San Juan.

Our favorite *paradores* are all in western Puerto Rico (see chapter 9). For a plantation ambience and an evocation of the Puerto Rico of colonial times, there is the **Parador Hacienda Gripiñas** at Jayuya, some 30 miles (48km) southwest of San Juan; it is a former coffee plantation. **Parador Vistamar,** at Quebradillas, one of the largest paradores in Puerto Rico, enjoys a mountain location with beautiful gardens of tropical flowers.

VILLAS & VACATION HOMES

You can often secure good deals in Puerto Rico by renting privately owned villas and vacation homes.

Almost every villa has a staff, or at least a maid who comes in a few days a week. Villas also provide the essentials of home life, including bed linen and cooking paraphernalia. Condos usually come with a reception desk and are often comparable to life in a suite at a big resort hotel. Nearly every condo complex has a swimming pool, and some have more than one.

Private apartments are rented either with or without maid service. This is more of a no-frills option than the villas and condos. An apartment might not be in a building with a swimming pool, and it might not have a front desk to help you. Among the major categories of vacation homes, cottages offer the most freewheeling way to live. Most cottages are fairly simple, many opening in an ideal fashion onto a beach, whereas others may be clustered around a communal pool. Many contain no more than a simple bedroom, together with a small kitchen and bathroom. For the peak winter season, reservations should be made at least 5 or 6 months in advance.

Dozens of agents throughout the United States and Canada offer these types of rentals (see "Rental Agencies" below for some recommendations). You can also write to local tourist-information offices, which can advise you on vacation-home rentals.

Travel experts agree that savings, especially for a family of three to six people, or two or three couples, can range from 50% to 60% over what a hotel would cost. If there are only two in your party, these savings probably don't apply.

RENTAL AGENCIES

Agencies specializing in renting properties in Puerto Rico include:

- **A1 Vacations,** 95 Westlake Rd., Suite 205, Hardy, VA 24101 (✆ **540/721-9915;** www.a1vacations.com), in business since 1998, offers condos, villas, cottages, and vacation homes throughout the Caribbean, including many properties in Puerto Rico.
- **Hideaways Aficionado,** 767 Islington St., Portsmouth, NH 03801 (✆ **800/843-4433** or 603/430-4433; www.hideaways. com), provides a 144-page guide with illustrations of its accommodations in the Caribbean so that you can get an idea of what you're renting. Most of its villas, which can accommodate up to three couples or a large family of about 10, come with maid service. You can also ask this travel club about discounts on plane fares and car rentals.

FAST FACTS: Puerto Rico

American Express See "Fast Facts: San Juan," on p. 57.

Area Code Telephone area codes in use for Puerto Rico are **787** and **939.** Dial the area code, even for local calls.

Banks All major U.S. banks have branches in Puerto Rico; their hours are 8am to 2:30pm Monday through Friday and 9:45am to noon on Saturday.

Business Hours Regular business hours are Monday through Friday, 8am to 5pm. Shopping hours vary considerably. Regular shopping hours are Monday through Thursday and Saturday, 9am to 6pm. On Friday, stores have a long day: 9am to 9pm. Many stores also open on Sunday, 11am to 5pm.

Camera & Film It's important to protect your camera not only from theft, but also from salt water and sand; furthermore, your camera can become overheated, and any film it contains can be ruined if left in the sun or locked in the trunk of a car. See "Fast Facts: San Juan," on p. 57.

Climate   See "When to Go," earlier in this chapter.

Drugs   A branch of the Federal Narcotics Strike Force is permanently stationed in Puerto Rico, where illegal drugs and narcotics are a problem. Convictions for possession of marijuana can bring severe penalties, ranging from 2 to 10 years in prison for a first offense. Possession of hard drugs, such as cocaine or heroin, can lead to 15 years or more in prison.

Drugstores   It's a good idea to carry enough prescription medications with you to last the duration of your stay. If you're going into the hinterlands, take along the medicines you'll need. If you need any additional medications, you'll find many drugstores in San Juan and other leading cities. One of the most centrally located pharmacies in Old San Juan is the **Puerto Rican Drug Co.**, Calle San Francisco 157 (© 787/725-2202); it's open daily from 7:30am to 9:30pm.

Electricity   The electricity is 110 volts AC, as it is in the continental United States and Canada.

Embassies & Consulates   Because Puerto Rico is part of the United States, there is no U.S. embassy or consulate. Instead, there are branches of all the principal U.S. federal agencies. Canada has no embassy or consulate either. There are no special provisions or agencies catering to British travel needs in Puerto Rico, nor are there agencies serving citizens of Australia or New Zealand.

Emergencies   In an emergency, dial © **911.** Or call the local police (© **787/343-2020**), fire department (© **787/343-2330**), ambulance (© **787/343-2550**), or medical assistance (© **787/754-3535**).

Holidays   See "When to Go," earlier in this chapter.

Hospitals   In a medical emergency, call © **911. Ashford Presbyterian Community Hospital,** 1451 Ashford Ave., San Juan (© **787/721-2160**; www.presbypr.com), maintains 24-hour emergency service. Service is also provided at **Clínica Las Américas,** 400 Franklin Delano Roosevelt Ave., Hato Rey (© **787/765-1919**), and at **Río Piedras Medical Center,** Av. Américo Miranda, Río Piedras (© **787/777-3535**).

Internet Access   Public access to the Internet is available at some large-scale resorts; the staff members often provide access from their own computers. Another place to try is **Cybernet,** 1128 Ashford Ave., Condado (© **787/724-4033**;

www.cybernetcafepr.com), which is open daily 9am to 11pm. It charges $3 for 20 minutes, $5 for 35 minutes, $7 for 50 minutes, and $9 for 65 minutes.

Language English is understood at the big resorts and in most of San Juan. Out in the island, Spanish is still *número uno.*

Liquor Laws You must be 18 years of age to purchase liquor in stores or buy drinks in hotels, bars, and restaurants. Under Puerto Rican law, alcoholic beverages cannot be served in a casino.

Marriage Requirements There are no residency requirements for getting married in Puerto Rico. You need parental consent if either of you is under 18. Blood tests are required, although a test conducted in your home country within 10 days of the ceremony will suffice. A doctor must sign the license after an examination of the bride and groom. For complete details, contact the **Commonwealth of Puerto Rico Health Department,** Demographic Register, Franklin Delano Roosevelt Avenue, Hato Rey (P.O. Box 11854), San Juan, PR 00910 (© **787/728-7980**).

Newspapers & Magazines The San Juan Star, a daily English-language newspaper, has been called the *"International Herald Tribune* of the Caribbean." It concentrates extensively on news from the United States. You can also pick up copies of *USA Today* at most news kiosks. If you read Spanish, you might enjoy *El Nuevo Día,* the most popular local tabloid. Few significant magazines are published in Puerto Rico, but *Time* and *Newsweek* are available at most newsstands.

Passports **For Residents of the United States:** Since Puerto Rico is a Commonwealth, no passport is required when coming from mainland U.S.

For Residents of Canada: Passport applications are available at travel agencies throughout Canada or from the central **Passport Office,** Department of Foreign Affairs and International Trade, Ottawa, ON K1A 0G3 (© **800/567-6868;** www.ppt.gc.ca).

For Residents of the United Kingdom: To pick up an application for a standard 10-year passport (5-year passport for children under 16), visit your nearest passport office, major post office, or travel agency, or contact the **United Kingdom Passport Service** at © **0870/521-0410** or search its website at www.ukpa.gov.uk.

For Residents of Ireland: You can apply for a 10-year passport at the **Passport Office,** Setanta Centre, Molesworth Street, Dublin 2 (*Ⓒ* **01/671-1633;** www.irlgov.ie/iveagh). Those under age 18 and over 65 must apply for a 12€ 3-year passport. You can also apply at 1A South Mall, Cork (*Ⓒ* **021/ 494-4700)** or at most main post offices.

For Residents of Australia: You can pick up an application from your local post office or any branch of Passports Australia, but you must schedule an interview at the passport office to present your application materials. Call the **Australian Passport Information Service** at *Ⓒ* **61/131-232,** or visit the government website at www.smartraveller.gov.au.

For Residents of New Zealand: You can pick up a passport application at any New Zealand Passports Office or download it from their website. Contact the **Passports Office** at *Ⓒ* **0800/ 225-050** in New Zealand or 04/474-8100, or log on to www. passports.govt.nz.

Pets To bring your pet in, you must produce a health certificate from a U.S. mainland veterinarian and show proof of vaccination against rabies. Very few hotels allow animals, so check in advance.

Postal Services Because the U.S. Postal Service is responsible for handling mail in Puerto Rico, the regulations and tariffs are the same as on the mainland United States. Stamps can be purchased at any post office, all of which are open Monday through Friday from 8am to 5pm. Saturday hours are from 8am to noon (closed Sun). As on the mainland, you can purchase stamps at vending machines in airports, stores, and hotels. First-class letters to addresses within Puerto Rico, the United States, and its territories cost 39¢; postcards, 24¢. Letters and postcards to Canada both cost 60¢ for the first half-ounce. Letters and postcards to other countries cost 80¢ for the first half-ounce.

Safety See "Health & Safety," earlier in this chapter.

Smoking Antismoking regulation is less stringent here than it is on the U.S. mainland. Anyone over 18 can smoke in any bar here. Smoking is permitted in restaurants within designated sections, but not necessarily everywhere. Most hotels have smoking and nonsmoking rooms.

Taxes All hotel rooms in Puerto Rico are subject to a tax, which is not included in the rates given in this book. At casino hotels, the tax is 11%; at noncasino hotels, it's 9%. At country inns you pay a 7% tax. Most hotels also add a 10% service charge. If they don't, you're expected to tip for services rendered. When you're booking a room, it's always best to inquire about these added charges. There is no airport departure tax.

Telephone & Fax Coin-operated phones can be found throughout the island, with a particularly dense concentration in San Juan. You have to dial the area code even when it's a local call. There are two area codes in use on island—**787** and **939**. If you're calling long-distance within Puerto Rico, add a **1** before the numbers. When you're placing a call to the U.S. mainland or to anywhere else overseas, preface the number with **011**. An operator (or a recorded voice) will tell you how much money to deposit, although you'll probably find it more practical to use a calling card issued by such long-distance carriers as Sprint, AT&T, or MCI. Public phones that allow credit cards such as American Express, Visa, or Master-Card to be inserted or "swiped" through a magnetic slot are rare on the island; they're mainly found at the San Juan airport. Most phone booths contain printed instructions for dialing. Local calls are 10¢. Many Puerto Ricans buy phone cards valid for between 15 and 100 units. The 30-unit card costs $14; the 60-unit card, $28. The card provides an even less expensive and usually more convenient way of calling within Puerto Rico or to the U.S. mainland. They are for sale in most drugstores and gift shops on the island.

Most hotels can send a telex or fax for you and bill the costs to your room, and in some cases, they'll even send a fax for a nonguest if you agree to pay a charge. Barring that, several agencies in San Juan will send a fax anywhere you want for a fee. Many are associated with print shops/photocopy stands.

Time Puerto Rico is on Atlantic Standard Time, which is 1 hour later than Eastern Standard Time. Puerto Rico does not go on daylight saving time, however, so the time here is the same year-round.

Tipping Tipping is expected here, so hand over the money as you would on the U.S. mainland. That usually means 15% in restaurants, 10% in bars, and 10% to 15% for taxi drivers, hairdressers, and other services, depending on the quality of the service rendered. Tip a porter, either at the airport or at your hotel, $1 per bag. The U.S. government imposes income tax on waitstaff and other service-industry workers whose income is tip-based according to the gross receipts of their employers; therefore, if you don't tip them, those workers could end up paying tax anyway.

Water See "Health & Safety" earlier in this chapter.

Weights & Measures There's a mixed bag of measurements in Puerto Rico. Because of its Spanish tradition, most weights (meat and poultry) and measures (gasoline and road distances) are metric. But because of the U.S. presence, speed limits appear in miles per hour and liquids such as beer are sold by the ounce.

3

Getting to Know San Juan

All but a handful of visitors arrive in San Juan, the capital city. It is the political base, economic powerhouse, and cultural center of the island, and it's home to about one-third of all Puerto Ricans.

The second-oldest city in the Americas (behind Santo Domingo in the Dominican Republic), this metropolis presents two different faces. On one hand, the charming historic district, Old San Juan, is strongly reminiscent of the Spanish Empire. On the other hand, modern expressways outside the historic district cut through urban sprawl to link towering concrete buildings and beachfront hotels resembling those of Miami Beach.

Old San Juan is a 7-square-block area that was once completely enclosed by a wall erected by the Spanish with slave labor. The most powerful fortress in the Caribbean, this fortified city repeatedly held off would-be attackers. By the 19th century, however, it had become one of the Caribbean's most charming residential and commercial districts. Today it's a setting for restaurants and shops. Most of the major resort hotels are located nearby, along the Condado beachfront and at Isla Verde (see chapter 4).

1 Orientation

ARRIVING BY PLANE & GETTING INTO THE CITY

Visitors from overseas arrive at **Luis Muñoz Marín International Airport** (✆ 787/791-1014), the major transportation center of the Caribbean. The airport is on the easternmost side of the city, rather inconvenient to nearly all hotels except the resorts and small inns at Isla Verde.

The airport offers services such as a tourist-information center, restaurants, hair stylists, coin lockers for storing luggage, bookstores, banks, currency-exchange kiosks, and a bar (daily 9am–8pm) that offers Puerto Rican rums.

BY TAXI Some of the larger hotels send vans to pick up airport passengers and transport them to various properties along the

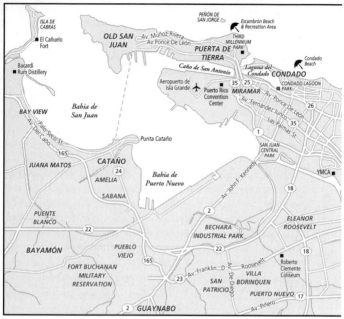

beachfront. It's wise to find out if your hotel offers this service when making a reservation. If your hotel doesn't have shuttle service between the airport and its precincts, you'll have to get there under your own steam—most likely by taxi. Dozens of taxis line up outside the airport to meet arriving flights, so you rarely have to wait. Fares can vary widely, depending on traffic conditions. Again depending on traffic, figure on about a 30-minute drive from the airport to your hotel along the Condado.

Although technically cab drivers should turn on their meters, more often than not they'll quote a flat rate before starting out. The rate system seems effective and fair, and if you're caught in impenetrable traffic, it might actually work to your advantage. The island's **Tourist Transportation Division** (© **787/999-2100**) establishes flat rates between the Luis Muñoz Marín International Airport and major tourist zones, as listed here: From the airport to any hotel in Isla Verde, the fee is $10; to any hotel in the Condado district, the charge is $14; and to any hotel in Old San Juan, the cost is $19.

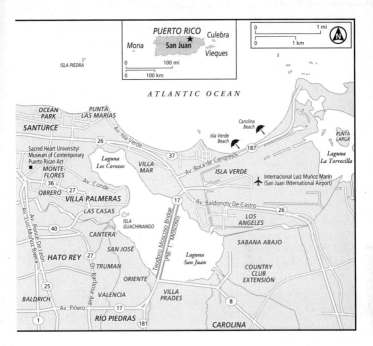

Normal tipping supplements of between 10% and 15% of that fare are appreciated.

BY MINIVAN OR LIMOUSINE   A wide variety of vehicles at the San Juan airport call themselves *limosinas* (their Spanish name). One outfit whose sign-up desk is in the arrivals hall of the international airport, near American Airlines, is the **Airport Limousine Service** (© 787/791-4745). It offers minivan service from the airport to various San Juan neighborhoods for prices that are lower than what a taxi would charge. When 5 to 10 passengers can be accumulated, the fare for transport, with luggage, is $10 per person to any hotel in Isla Verde, $11 per person to the Condado, or $12 per person to Old San Juan.

For conventional limousine service, **Bracero Limousine** (© 787/253-5466) offers cars with drivers that will meet you and your entourage at the arrivals terminal for luxurious, private transportation to your hotel. Transport to virtually anywhere in San Juan ranges from $90 to $130; transport to points throughout the island varies from $60 per hour in a sedan carrying four passengers to $80 per hour in a limousine with six passengers. Ideally, transport should be arranged in advance, so that a car and driver can be waiting for you near the arrivals terminal.

BY CAR   All the major car-rental companies have kiosks at the airport. Although it's possible to rent a car once you arrive, your best bet is to reserve one before you leave home. See the "Getting Around" section of chapter 2 for details.

To drive into the city, head west along Route 26, which becomes Route 25 as it enters Old San Juan. If you stay on Route 25 (also called Av. Muñoz Rivera), you'll have the best view of the ocean and the monumental city walls.

Just before you reach the capitol building, turn left between the Natural Resources Department and the modern House of Representatives office building. Go 2 blocks, until you reach the intersection of Paseo de Covadonga, and then take a right past the Treasury Building and park your car in the **Covadonga Parking Garage** (② 787/722-2337) on the left. The garage is open 24 hours; the first hour costs $1, the second hour 65¢, and 24 hours costs $16.

BY BUS   Those with little luggage can take the A5 bus, which runs to the center of the city.

VISITOR INFORMATION

Tourist information is available at the **Luis Muñoz Marín International Airport** (② 787/791-1014) December through April daily from 9am to 10pm; May through November daily 9am to 8pm. Another office is at **La Casita,** Pier 1, Old San Juan (② 787/722-1739), open Saturday through Wednesday 9am to 8pm, Thursday and Friday 9am to 5:30pm.

CITY LAYOUT

See the map on p. 50 for an overview of the layout of San Juan.

FINDING AN ADDRESS   Finding an address in San Juan isn't always easy. You'll have to contend not only with missing street signs and numbers, but also with street addresses that appear sometimes in English and at other times in Spanish. The most common Spanish terms for thoroughfares are *calle* (street) and *avenida* (avenue). When it is used, the street number follows the street name; for example, the El Convento hotel is located at Calle del Cristo 100, in Old San Juan. Locating a building in Old San Juan is relatively easy. The area is only 7 square blocks, so by walking around, it's possible to locate most addresses.

STREET MAPS *¿Qué Pasa?,* the monthly tourist magazine distributed free by the tourist office, contains accurate, easy-to-read maps of San Juan and the Condado that pinpoint the major attractions.

THE NEIGHBORHOODS IN BRIEF

Old San Juan   This is the most historic area in the West Indies. Filled with Spanish colonial architecture and under constant restoration, it lies on the western end of an islet. It's encircled by water; on the north is the Atlantic Ocean, and on the south and west is the tranquil San Juan Bay. Ponte San Antonio bridge connects the Old Town with "mainland" Puerto Rico. Ramparts and old Spanish fortresses form its outer walls.

Puerta de Tierra   Translated as "gateway to the land" or "gateway to the island," Puerta de Tierra lies just east of the old city walls of San Juan. It is split by Avenida Ponce de León and interconnects Old San Juan with the Puerto Rican "mainland." Founded by freed black slaves, the settlement today functions as the island's administrative center and is the site of military and government buildings, including the capitol and various U.S. naval reserves.

Miramar   Miramar is an upscale residential neighborhood across the bridge from Puerta de Tierra. Yachts anchor in its waters on the bay side of Ponte Isla Grande, and some of the finest homes in Puerto Rico are found here. It's also the site of Isla Grande Airport, where you can board flights to the islands of Vieques and Culebra.

Condado   Linked to Puerta de Tierra and Old San Juan by a bridge built in 1910, the Condado was once known as the Riviera of the Caribbean, enjoying a voguish reputation in the 1920s. Over the years the area has declined. It is now a cliché to compare it to Miami Beach. But like Miami Beach, the Condado is making major improvements, although many parts of it remain seedy and in need of restoration. The prostitutes, pimps, and drug dealers are still here, but there are many fine deluxe hotels as well. Much of the Condado architecture today is viewed as "kitsch," the way Art Deco on Miami Beach is prized. The area is especially popular with gay travelers, but straights also flock here, especially those attracted to the beaches during cruise-ship stopovers. Much of the Condado has been turned into timeshare condos.

Ocean Park   Dividing the competitive beach resort areas of the Condado and Isla Verde, Ocean Park is a beachfront residential neighborhood that's sometimes plagued by flooding, especially during hurricanes. It's completely built up today with houses that are smaller and more spread out than those in the Condado district. Beaches here are slightly less crowded than those at Condado or Isla Verde. Because several gay guesthouses are located here, some of the beaches of Ocean Park are popular with gay men.

Villa Palmeras   Villa Palmeras is a residential sector and business area of San Juan, an eastern extension of the Santurce district. Its far eastern frontier opens onto Laguna Los Corozos. On the eastern side of the water is the international airport. From the Old Town, Route 26 east takes you to this district.

Isla Verde   East of the Condado, en route to the airport, Isla Verde—technically known as the "Carolina" section of San Juan—is the chief rival of the Condado. Because much of the Condado is in need of massive rejuvenation, many of the great resorts have fled east to Isla Verde, which has better, cleaner beaches. Don't come here for history or romance. Two features put Isla Verde on the tourist map: some of San Juan's best beaches and its most deluxe, all-inclusive hotels. Isla Verde is the Las Vegas of San Juan.

Hato Rey   Situated to the south of the Martín Peña canal, this area was a marsh until landfill and concrete changed it forever. Today it is the Wall Street of the West Indies, filled with many high-rises, a large federal complex, and many business and banking offices.

Río Piedras   South of Hato Rey and Santurce, this is the site of the University of Puerto Rico. It's dominated by the landmark Roosevelt Bell Tower, named for Theodore Roosevelt, who donated the money for its construction. The main thoroughfare is Paseo de Diego, site of a popular local produce market. The Agricultural Experimental Station of Puerto Rico maintains a botanical garden that includes many tropical plants, including 125 species of palms.

Bayamon   The San Juan sprawl has reached this once-distant southwestern suburb, which was once farmland. Some 207,000 people and nearly 200 factories are now located in this large district. Bus no. 46 from the center of San Juan runs out here.

2 Getting Around

BY TAXI

Except for a handful of important, high-profile tourist routes, public taxis are metered within San Juan (or should be). Normal tipping supplements of between 10% and 15% are appreciated. Passengers traveling between most other destinations within greater San Juan are charged by meter readings. The initial charge is $2, plus 10¢ for each ⅟₁₆ mile (.1km) and 50¢ for every suitcase, with a minimum fare of $3. These rates apply to conventional *taxis turísticos,* which are usually white-painted vehicles with official logos on their doors. Owned by a medley of individual outfitters within San Juan, they maintain standards that are higher than those of the cheaper but more erratic and inconvenient *públicos.* Call the **PSC** (© 787/756-1401) to request information or to report any irregularities.

Taxis are invariably lined up outside the entrance to most of the island's hotels, and if they're not, a staff member can almost always call one for you. But if you want to arrange a taxi on your own, call the **Cooperative Major Taxi** (© 787/723-2460).

You'll have to negotiate a fare with the driver, usually at a flat rate, for trips to far-flung destinations within Puerto Rico.

BY BUS

The **Metropolitan Bus Authority** (© 787/767-7979 for route information) operates buses in the greater San Juan area. Bus stops are marked by upright metal signs or yellow posts that say PARADA. There's one bus terminal in the dock area and another at the Plaza de Colón. A typical fare is 25¢ to 50¢.

Most of the large hotels of the Condado and Isla Verde maintain air-conditioned buses that make free shuttle runs into Old San Juan. Clients are usually deposited at the Plaza de Colón. Public buses also make the run along the Condado, stopping at clearly designated bus stops placed near the major hotels. Public buses usually deposit their clients at the Plaza de Colón and the main bus terminal across the street from the Cataño ferryboat pier.

Here are some useful public bus routes: Bus no. B21 goes from the Plaza de Colón along the Condado, eventually reaching the commercial section of San Juan, Hato Rey; bus no. A7 passes from Old San Juan to the Condado and goes on to Avenida Isla Verde; and no. A5 heads for Avenida de Diego in the Condado district, then makes a long run to Isla Verde and the airport.

BY TRAIN

Tren Urbano, the first mass-transit project in the history of Puerto Rico, opened in 2005, linking San Juan to its suburbs such as Santurce, Bayamon, and Guaynabo. Costing $1.55 billion, the system provides an easy mode of transportation to the most congested areas of metropolitan San Juan. During rush hour (5–9am and 3–6pm), the train operates every 5 minutes; otherwise, it runs every 10 minutes. There is no service daily from 11pm to 5am. The fare is $1.50 one way. From the airport, it's possible to take the AMA-B40 bus to Tren Urbano, a 30-minute ride. For information, call ② 787/765-0927.

ON FOOT

This is the only way to truly explore Old San Juan. All the major attractions can easily be covered in a day. If you're going from Old San Juan to Isla Verde, however, you'll need to rely on public transportation.

BY TROLLEY

Departure points in the historic area are the Marina and La Puntilla, but you can board along the route by flagging the trolley down (wave at it and signal for it to stop) or by waiting at any of the clearly designated stopping points. Relax and enjoy the sights as the trolleys rumble through the old and narrow streets.

BY CAR

See "Getting Around," in chapter 2, for details—including some reasons you shouldn't plan to drive in Puerto Rico.

BY FERRY

The **Agua Expreso** (② 787/788-1155) connects Old San Juan with the industrial and residential community of Cataño, across the bay. Ferries depart daily every 30 minutes from 6am to 10pm. The one-way fare to Cataño is 50¢. Departures are from the San Juan Terminal at pier no. 2 in Old San Juan. However, it's best to avoid rush hours because hundreds of locals who work in town use this ferry. The ride lasts 6 minutes.

FAST FACTS: San Juan

Airport See "Arriving by Plane & Getting into the City," earlier in this chapter.

Bus Information For information about bus routes in San Juan, call (℗ **787/729-1512.**

Camera & Film **Uniphoto,** 1112 Ashford Ave., Condado ((℗ **787/722-3653**), has a full range of photographic services; open Monday through Friday 9am to 6pm, Saturday 9:30am to 6pm.

Car Rentals See "Getting Around" in chapter 2. If you want to reserve after you've arrived in Puerto Rico, call **Avis** ((℗ **800/230-5926** or 787/791-2865), **Budget** ((℗ **787/791-0600**), or **Hertz** ((℗ **800/654-3131** or 787/791-0840).

Currency Exchange The unit of currency is the U.S. dollar. Most banks provide currency exchange, and you can also exchange money at the **Luis Muñoz Marín International Airport.** See "Money," in chapter 2.

Drugstores One of the most centrally located pharmacies is **Puerto Rican Drug Co.,** Calle San Francisco 157 ((℗ **787/725-2202**), in Old San Juan. It's open daily from 7:30am to 9:30pm. **Walgreens,** 1130 Ashford Ave., Condado ((℗ **787/725-1510**), is open 24 hours.

Emergencies In an emergency, dial (℗ **911.** Or call the local police ((℗ **787/343-2020**), fire department ((℗ **787/343-2330**), ambulance ((℗ **787/343-2550**), or medical assistance ((℗ **787/754-2222**).

Eyeglasses Services are available at **Pearle Vision Express,** Plaza Las Américas Shopping Mall ((℗ **787/753-1033**). Hours are Monday through Saturday from 9am to 9pm and Sunday from 11am to 5pm.

Hospitals **Ashford Presbyterian Community Hospital,** 1451 Ashford Ave. ((℗ **787/721-2160**), maintains a 24-hour emergency room.

Police Call (℗ **787/727-7020** for the local police.

Post Office In San Juan, the **General Post Office** is at Av. Roosevelt 585 ((℗ **787/622-1799**). If you don't know your address in San Juan, you can ask that your mail be sent here "c/o General Delivery." This main branch is open Monday through Friday from 6am to 9pm, Saturday from 8am to 2pm. A letter from Puerto Rico to the U.S. mainland will arrive in about 4 days. See "Fast Facts: Puerto Rico," in chapter 2, for more information.

Restrooms You'll need to enter a hotel lobby, cafe, or restaurant to ask for access to a toilet. Fortunately, large-scale hotels will usually comply.

Safety At night, exercise extreme caution when walking along the back streets of San Juan, and don't venture onto the unguarded public stretches of the Condado and Isla Verde beaches at night. Muggers operate in these areas.

Salons Most of San Juan's large resort hotels, including the Condado Plaza, the Marriott, and the Wyndham Old San Juan, maintain hair salons.

Taxis See "Getting Around," earlier in this chapter.

Telephone & Fax Many public telephones are available at **World Service Telephone (AT&T),** Pier 1, Old San Juan (© **787/721-2520**). To send a fax, go to **Eagle Print,** 1229 F. D. Roosevelt Blvd., Puerto Nuevo (© **787/782-7830**). For more information, see "Fast Facts: Puerto Rico" on p. 43.

4

Where to Stay in San Juan

Whatever your preferences in accommodations—a beachfront resort or a place in historic Old San Juan, sumptuous luxury or an inexpensive base from which to see the sights—you can find a perfect fit in San Juan.

If you prefer shopping and historic sights to the beach, then Old San Juan might be your nest. The high-rise resort hotels lie primarily along the Condado beach strip and the equally good sands of Isla Verde. The hotels along Condado and Isla Verde attract the cruise-ship and casino crowds. The hotels away from the beach in San Juan, in such sections as Santurce, are primarily for business clients.

In addition to checking the recommendations listed here, you might want to contact a travel agent; there are package deals galore that can save you money and match you with an establishment that meets your requirements. See "Packages for the Independent Traveler" on p. 33. Before talking to a travel agent, you should refer to our comments about how to select a room in Puerto Rico. See "Tips on Accommodations" on p. 38.

Not all hotels here have air-conditioned rooms. We've pointed them out in the recommendations in this chapter. If air-conditioning is important to you, make sure "A/C" appears in the "In room" section at the end of the listing.

All hotel rooms in Puerto Rico are subject to a tax that is not included in the rates given in this book. At casino hotels, the tax is 11%; at noncasino hotels, it's 9%. At country inns you pay a 7% tax. Most hotels also add a 10% service charge. If they don't, you're expected to tip for services rendered. When you're booking a room, it's a good idea to ask about these charges.

1 Old San Juan

Old San Juan is 1½ miles (2.4km) from the beach. You should choose a hotel here if you're more interested in shopping and attractions than you are in watersports.

EXPENSIVE

El Convento ✿✿ Puerto Rico's most famous hotel came majestically back to life when it was restored and reopened in 1997, and it continues to offer some of the most charming and historic hotel experiences anywhere in the Caribbean. As one observer put it, El Convento "is an exquisitely wrought David on an island of otherwise glitzy Goliaths." Built in 1651 in the heart of the old city, it was the New World's first Carmelite convent, but over the years it played many roles, from a dance hall to a flophouse to a parking lot for garbage trucks. It first opened as a hotel in 1962.

The midsize accommodations include Spanish-style furnishings, throw rugs, paneling, and Andalusian terra-cotta floor tiles. Each unit contains two double or twin beds, fitted with fine linen. The small bathrooms, with tub/shower combinations, contain scales and second phones. For the ultimate in luxury, ask for Gloria Vanderbilt's restored suite or ask for no. 508, a corner room with panoramic views. Although the facilities here aren't as diverse as those of some resorts on the Condado or in Isla Verde, this hotel's sweeping charm and Old Town location usually compensate. A possible drawback for some is that El Convento is a 15-minute walk to the nearest beach. The so-called pool here is accessible via the fourth floor, and it measures only about 6×10 feet (1.8×3m)—very small, but personalized, charming, and endearing because of its view over the facade of the nearby cathedral. There's a Jacuzzi immediately adjacent to the pool and a big sun terrace.

Calle de Cristo 100, San Juan, PR 00901. ⓒ **800/468-2779** or 787/723-9020. Fax 787/721-2877. www.elconvento.com. 67 units. Winter $325–$420 double; off season $235–$295 double; year-round $600–$750 suite. Rates include continental breakfast. AE, DC, DISC, MC, V. Parking $10. Bus: Old Town trolley. **Amenities:** 3 restaurants; 3 bars; small rooftop plunge pool; fitness center; Jacuzzi; massage; laundry service; nonsmoking rooms; rooms for those w/limited mobility. *In room:* A/C, TV, coffeemaker, hair dryer, iron, safe, Wi-Fi.

Sheraton Old San Juan Hotel & Casino ✿ Opened in 1997, this dignified, nine-story, waterfront hotel was part of a $100-million renovation of San Juan's cruise-port facilities. The hotel has an unusual and desirable position between buildings erected by the Spanish monarchs in the 19th century and the city's busiest and most modern cruise-ship terminals. Most of the major cruise ships dock nearby, making this a worthwhile choice if you want to spend time in San Juan before boarding a ship. On days when cruise ships pull into port, the hotel's lobby and bars are likely to be jammed with passengers stretching their legs after a few days at sea.

Old San Juan Accommodations

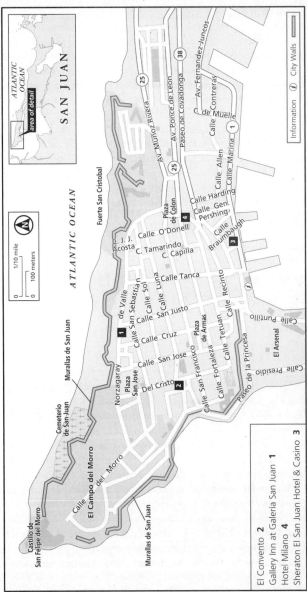

El Convento **2**
Gallery Inn at Galeria San Juan **1**
Hotel Milano **4**
Sheraton El San Juan Hotel & Casino **3**

Information ⓘ   City Walls ▭

Although the pastel building is modern, iron railings and exterior detailing convey a sense of colonial San Juan. The triangular shape of the building encircles an inner courtyard that floods light into the tasteful and comfortable bedrooms, each of which has two phone lines and a modem connection for laptop computers. Other than that, the smallish rooms lack character. Each room has a compact bathroom with a shower stall. Think of a Holiday Inn geared for business travelers. If you want Old Town character and atmosphere, head for El Convento (see above) instead. Most of the lobby level here is devoted to a mammoth casino. The upscale dining room serves perfectly fine, if unremarkable, international cuisine, with some regional specialties.

Calle Brumbaugh 100, San Juan, PR 00902. ℭ **787/721-5100.** Fax 787/721-1111. www.sheraton.com. 240 units. Winter $240–$365 double, $315–$420 suite; off season $150–$220 double, $200–$330 suite. AE, DC, DISC, MC, V. Free self-parking, valet parking $12. Bus: A7. **Amenities:** Restaurant; 3 bars; outdoor pool; fitness center; Jacuzzi; car-rental desk; business center; room service; nonsmoking rooms; rooms for those w/limited mobility; casino. *In room:* A/C, TV, dataport, minibar, coffeemaker, hair dryer, iron/ironing board, Wi-Fi.

MODERATE

Gallery Inn at Galería San Juan ⍟ *Finds*   This hotel's location and ambience are unbeatable, though the nearest beach is a 15-minute ride away. Set on a hilltop in Old Town, with a sweeping sea view, this unusual hotel contains a maze of verdant courtyards. In the 1700s it was the home of an aristocratic Spanish family. Today it's the most whimsically bohemian hotel in the Caribbean. Jan D'Esopo and Manuco Gandia created this inn out of their art studio. They cast bronze in their studio when not tending to their collection of birds, including macaws and cockatoos. The entire inn is covered with clay and bronze figures as well as other original art. We suggest booking one of the least expensive doubles; even the cheapest units are fairly roomy and attractively furnished, with good beds. Complimentary wine and cheese are served from 6 to 7pm.

Note to lovers: The honeymoon suite has a Jacuzzi on a private balcony with a panoramic view of El Morro. From the rooftop terrace, there is a 360-degree view of the historic Old Town and the port. This is the highest point in San Juan and the most idyllic place to enjoy a breeze at twilight and a glass of wine.

Calle Norzagaray 204–206, San Juan, PR 00901. ℭ **787/722-1808.** Fax 787/724-7360. www.thegalleryinn.com. 22 units, some with shower only. $225–$310 double; $410 suite. Rates include continental breakfast. AE, DC, MC, V. There are 6 free parking spaces, plus parking on the street. Bus: Old Town trolley. **Amenities:** Breakfast room. *In room:* A/C, dataport, hair dryer.

Hotel Milano   This Old Town hotel was created in April 1999 from a 1920s warehouse. You enter a wood-sheathed lobby at the lower, less desirable end of Calle Fortaleza before ascending to one of the clean, well-lit bedrooms. Despite its location in historic Old Town, there's not much charm about this place. The simple, modern rooms have cruise ship-style decor and unremarkable views. The more expensive accommodations contain small refrigerators and dataports.

The building's fifth floor (the elevator goes only to the fourth floor) contains an alfresco Italian and Puerto Rican restaurant called the Panoramic, which has views of San Juan's harbor.

Calle Fortaleza 307, San Juan, PR 00901. © 877/729-9050 or 787/729-9050. Fax 787/722-3379. www.hotelmilanopr.com. 30 units. Winter $90–$175 double; off season $75–$125 double. Rates include continental breakfast. AE, MC, V. Bus: Old Town trolley. **Amenities:** Restaurant; bar; nonsmoking rooms; rooms for those w/limited mobility. *In room:* A/C, TV, fridge, hair dryer.

2 Puerta de Tierra

Stay in Puerta de Tierra only if you have a desire to be at either the Caribe Hilton or the Normandie Hotel. When you stay in Puerta de Tierra, you're sandwiched halfway between Old San Juan and the Condado, but you're not getting the advantages of staying right in the heart of either. For the locations of hotels in Puerta de Tierra, see the "Eastern San Jan Accommodations" map in this section.

Caribe Hilton 🏨🏨🏨 *Kids*   Thanks to rivers of money poured into its radical, ongoing renovation, this deluxe hotel is one of the most up-to-date spa and convention hotels in San Juan. Because of an unusual configuration of natural barriers and legal maneuverings, the hotel has the only private beach on the island (and the only garden incorporating an antique naval installation: the semi-ruined colonial Fort San Gerónimo). Because this beachfront hotel was the first Hilton ever built outside the U.S. mainland (in 1949), the chain considers it its most historic property. The Caribe's size (17 acres/6.9ha of parks and gardens) and sprawling facilities often attract conventions and tour groups.

Rooms have been radically upgraded. Variations in price are related to the views outside and the amenities within. Each room has a larger-than-expected bathroom with a tub/shower combo as well as comfortable, tropical-inspired furniture. In the Caribe Terrace Bar, you can order the bartender's celebrated piña colada, which was once enjoyed by movie legends Joan Crawford and Errol Flynn. An ocean-front spa and fitness center is the only beachside spa in Puerto Rico.

It features such tantalizing delights as couples massages, body wraps, hydrotherapy tub treatments, and soothing cucumber sun therapies.

Next to the main hotel, a cluster of luxurious Condado Lagoon Villas have been completed at the new Paseo Caribe, which makes the Hilton the largest conglomerate of bedrooms on the island. These villas have a master bedroom, kitchen, dining room, and lots of storage space. In development for 2008 is a mini-mall with restaurants, boutiques, and a cinema lounge.

Calle Los Rosales, San Juan, PR 00901. © **800/HILTONS** or 787/721-0303. Fax 787/725-8849. www.caribe.hilton.com. 812 units. Winter $385–$400 double; off season $275–$305 double; year-round $500–$1,220 suite. Children 16 and under stay free in parent's room (maximum 4 people per room). AE, DC, DISC, MC, V. Self-parking $15; valet parking $20. Bus: B21. **Amenities:** 5 restaurants; 2 bars; outdoor pool; health club; spa; children's activities and playground; business center (6am–3am); limited room service; babysitting; laundry service; dry cleaning; nonsmoking rooms; rooms for those w/limited mobility. *In room:* A/C, TV, minibar, hair dryer, iron, safe, Wi-Fi.

Normandie Hotel   It isn't as well accessorized as its nearby competitor the Hilton, but for a clientele of mostly business travelers, it doesn't really matter. One guest, however, found the Hilton bright and festive, the Normandie "dark and haunting." The hotel first opened in 1939 and remains one of the purest examples of Art Deco architecture in Puerto Rico. Originally built for a Parisian cancan dancer by her tycoon husband, the building has a curve-sided design that was inspired by the famous French ocean liner, the *Normandie.* The gardens are not particularly extensive, and the beach is unexceptional. But several multimillion-dollar renovations have given the place a conservative, vaguely historic charm. Bedrooms are tastefully outfitted, each with a neatly tiled tub/shower bathroom. The lobby retains its original Art Deco zest, soaring upward into an atrium whose centerpiece is a bubbling aquarium.

Av. Muñoz-Rivera 499, San Juan, PR 00919. © **877/987-2929** or 787/729-2929. Fax 787/729-3083. www.normandiepr.com. 173 units. Winter $195–$250 double, $500 suite; off season $145–$205 double, $450 suite. AE, DC, MC, V. Parking $10. Bus: A5 or B21. **Amenities:** Restaurant; bar; cafe; pool; health club; room service; babysitting; laundry service; rooms for those w/limited mobility. *In room:* A/C, TV, coffeemaker, hair dryer, iron, safe, Wi-Fi.

3 Condado

Once the Condado area was filled with the residences of the very wealthy, but all that changed with the construction of the Puerto Rico Convention Center. Private villas gave way to high-rise hotel blocks, restaurants, and nightclubs. The Condado shopping area,

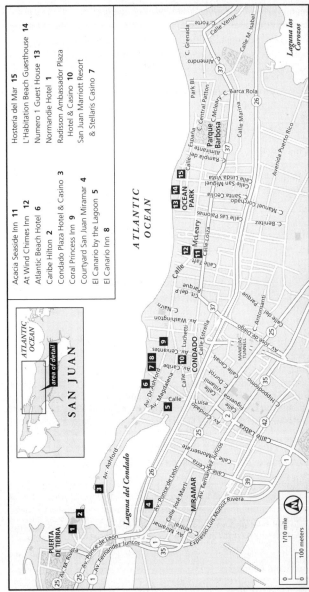

Acacia Seaside Inn **11**
At Wind Chimes Inn **12**
Atlantic Beach Hotel **6**
Caribe Hilton **2**
Condado Plaza Hotel & Casino **3**
Coral Princess Inn **9**
Courtyard San Juan Miramar **4**
El Canario by the Lagoon **5**
El Canario Inn **8**

Hosteria del Mar **15**
L'Habitation Beach Guesthouse **14**
Numero 1 Guest House **13**
Normandie Hotel **1**
Radisson Ambassador Plaza
  Hotel & Casino **10**
San Juan Marriott Resort
  & Stellaris Casino **7**

along Ashford and Magdalena avenues, has an extraordinary number of boutiques. There are good bus connections into Old San Juan, and taxis are plentiful. For the locations of hotels in Condado, see the "Eastern San Juan Accommodations" map on p. 65.

VERY EXPENSIVE

Condado Plaza Hotel & Casino ✦ *(Kids)*   This is one of the busiest hotels in Puerto Rico, with enough facilities, restaurants, and distractions to keep visitors occupied for weeks. It is the most prominent of San Juan's hotels, set on a poor strip of beachfront on the Condado. It's a favorite of business travelers, tour groups, and conventions, but it also attracts independent travelers, especially families (see "Family-Friendly Accommodations" on p. 77), because of its wide array of amenities. The Caribe Hilton is its major rival, and we still prefer it to the Condado Plaza (see above). Of the chain-related properties on the island, the Condado Plaza has evolved into the most middlebrow, with small, overcrowded pools and a narrow beach. However, this place is known for its restaurants with culinary diversity that attracts many local residents.

Each unit has a private terrace and is spacious, bright, and airy, fitted with deluxe beds, either one king-size, two doubles, or two twins. The good-size bathrooms contain tub/shower combos. The complex's best section, the Plaza Club, has 80 units (including five duplex suites), a VIP lounge reserved exclusively for the use of its guests, and private check-in/checkout service.

999 Ashford Ave., San Juan, PR 00907. ⓒ **787/721-1000.** Fax 787/721-4613. www. condadoplaza.com. 570 units. Winter $369–$560 double, $729–$1,200 suite; off season $239–$449 double, $399–$1,200 suite. AE, DC, DISC, MC, V. Self-parking $10, valet parking $15. Bus: C10 or B21. **Amenities:** 6 restaurants; 2 bars; 3 outdoor pools; 2 tennis courts; health club; spa; 3 Jacuzzis; watersports equipment; car-rental desk; business center; salon; room service; laundry service; dry cleaning; casino. *In room:* A/C, TV, minibar, coffeemaker, hair dryer, iron, safe, Wi-Fi.

San Juan Marriott Resort & Stellaris Casino ✦   It's the tallest building on the Condado, a 21-story landmark that Marriott spent staggering sums to renovate in a radically different format after a tragic fire gutted the premises in 1989. The current building packs in lots of postmodern style, and one of the best beaches on the Condado is right outside. Furnishings in the soaring lobby were inspired by Chippendale. If there's a flaw, it's the decor of the comfortable but bland bedrooms, with pastel colors that look washed out when compared to the rich mahoganies and jewel tones of the rooms in the rival Condado Plaza Hotel. They're generally spacious, with good views of the water, and each has a tiled bathroom with a tub/shower combination. We suggest having only one dinner in-house—at **Ristorante Tuscany** (p. 95).

1309 Ashford Ave., San Juan, PR 00907. © **800/228-9290** or 787/722-7000. Fax 787/722-6800. www.marriott.com. 525 units. Winter $420–$640 double, $830 suite; off season $225–$280 double, $385 suite. Suite rate includes breakfast. AE, DC, DISC, MC, V. Self-parking $14, valet parking $18. Bus: B21. **Amenities:** 2 restaurants; 3 bars; pool; 2 tennis courts; health club; Jacuzzi; sauna; tour desk; car-rental desk; business center; room service; babysitting; laundry service; dry cleaning; rooms for those w/limited mobility; casino. *In room:* A/C, TV, minibar, coffeemaker, hair dryer, iron, safe, Wi-Fi.

EXPENSIVE

Radisson Ambassador Plaza Hotel & Casino ⊛   At the eastern edge of the Condado, a short walk from the beach, the Ambassador is now competitive with its more glamorous neighbors, after a local entrepreneur poured $40 million into its restoration. Since then, it has evolved into a competent but not particularly exciting hotel. What's missing (especially at these prices) are the resort amenities associated with the Hilton, the Condado Plaza, the Ritz-Carlton, and El San Juan. This hotel also lacks the sense of whimsy and fun that's so much a part of those glitzy competitors.

Accommodations are in a pair of towers, one of which is devoted to suites. The decor is inspired variously by 18th-century Versailles, 19th-century London, imperial China, and Art Deco California. However, despite the gaudy, glitzy overlay, the hotel used to be a Howard Johnson's, a fact that's evident in the relatively small size of the standard rooms. Each unit has a balcony with outdoor furniture. The beds (twins or doubles) are fitted with fine linen, and each bathroom has generous shelf space and a tub/shower combination.

1369 Ashford Ave., San Juan, PR 00907. © **800/468-8512** or 787/721-7300. Fax 787/723-6151. www.radisson.com. 233 units. Winter $210–$275 double, $210–$320 suite; off season $189–$275 double, $210–$310 suite. Self-parking $10. AE, DC, DISC, MC, V. Bus: B21 or C10. **Amenities:** 2 restaurants; 2 bars; rooftop pool; health club; room service; babysitting; laundry service; dry cleaning; rooms for those w/limited mobility; casino. *In room:* A/C, TV, coffeemaker, hair dryer, iron, safe (in suites).

MODERATE

El Canario by the Lagoon   A relaxing, informal, European-style hotel, El Canario is in a residential neighborhood just a short block from Condado Beach. The place is a bit run-down, and staff members are not too helpful, but it charges affordable rates. The hotel is very much in the Condado styling, which evokes Miami Beach in the 1960s. The bedrooms are generous in size and have balconies.

Most of them have twin beds and a sleek and contemporary bathroom, with a shower stall and enough space to spread out your stuff. If the hotel doesn't have room for you, it can book you into El Canario Inn (see p. 70).

Calle Clemenceau 4, Condado, San Juan, PR 00907. © **800/533-2649** or 787/722-5058. Fax 787/723-8590. www.canariohotels.com. 44 units. Winter $120–$135 double; off season $95–$105 double. Rates include continental breakfast. AE, DISC, MC, V. Bus: B21 or C10. **Amenities:** Tour desk; coin-operated laundry; nonsmoking rooms. *In room:* A/C, TV, safe, Wi-Fi.

INEXPENSIVE

Acacia Seaside Inn *(Value)*   This inn, originally built as a private home in 1943 and transformed into a simple hotel in 1948, didn't become well-known until the late 1960s, when its reasonable rates began to attract families with children and college students traveling in groups. It's a stucco-covered building with vaguely Spanish-colonial detailing on a residential street lined with similar structures. Each unit has simple, slightly battered furniture and a small shower-only bathroom. There's no pool and few amenities on-site, but the beach is only a 5-minute walk away.

Calle Taft 8, Condado, San Juan, PR 00911. © **787/725-0668.** Fax 787/728-7524. 22 units (shower only). Winter $120–$140 double; off season $120 double. AE, DISC, MC, V. Parking $10. Bus: A5 or B21. **Amenities:** Sunbathing terrace. *In room:* A/C, TV, fridge.

Atlantic Beach Hotel   This is the most famous gay hotel in Puerto Rico. Housed in a five-story building with vaguely Art Deco styling, the hotel is best known for its ground-floor indoor/outdoor bar—the most visibly gay bar in Puerto Rico. It extends from the hotel lobby onto a wooden deck about 15 feet (4.6m) above the sands of Condado Beach. The units are simple cubicles with stripped-down but serviceable and clean decor. Some of the rooms are smaller than others, but few of the short-term guests seem to mind—maybe because the place can have the spirit of a house party. Each unit has a small, shower-only bathroom with plumbing that might not always be in prime condition. There's an on-again, off-again in-house restaurant and the above-mentioned bar. The space was originally conceived as a disco that thrived in the 1970s and early '80s.

Several readers have written in to lament the restrictive policy of not allowing a guest to take a visitor back to the bedrooms. One disgruntled patron wrote, "Lighten up, folks! We're big boys and can decide for ourselves who we want to bring up to our room." If you're going with a lover, fine. If you want to play with the locals, stay in another hotel. All rooms are nonsmoking.

Calle Vendig 1, Condado, San Juan, PR 00907. (C) **787/721-6900.** Fax 787/721-6917. www.atlanticbeachhotel.net. 35 units (shower only). Winter $130–$150 double; off season $90–$135 double. AE, DISC, MC, V. Bus: B21. **Amenities:** Restaurant; bar; laundry service; dry cleaning; rooms for those w/limited mobility. *In room:* A/C, TV, safe.

At Wind Chimes Inn *Kids*   This restored and renovated Spanish manor, 1 short block from the beach and 3½ miles (5.6km) from the airport, is one of the best guesthouses on the Condado. Upon entering a tropical patio, you'll find tile tables surrounded by palm trees and bougainvillea. There's plenty of space on the deck and a covered lounge for relaxing, socializing, and eating breakfast. Dozens of decorative wind chimes add melody to the daily breezes. The good-size rooms are individually decorated and some include kitchenettes; all contain ceiling fans and air-conditioning. Beds are comfortable and come in four sizes, ranging from twin to king-size. The shower-only bathrooms, though small, are efficiently laid out. Families like this place not only because of the accommodations and the affordable prices but also because they can prepare light meals here, cutting down on food costs.

1750 McLeary Ave., Condado, San Juan, PR 00911. (C) **800/946-3244** or 787/727-4153. Fax 787/728-0671. www.atwindchimesinn.com. 22 units (shower only). Winter $99–$140 double, $135–$150 suite; off season $75–$125 double, $125 suite. AE, DISC, MC, V. Parking $5. Bus: B21 or A5. **Amenities:** Bar; outdoor pool; room service; rooms for those w/limited mobility. *In room:* A/C, TV, kitchen, Wi-Fi.

Coral Princess Inn *Finds*   This is one of the best boutique hotels on the Condado, small but choice. The Art Deco building has been completely restored, with its original lines respected, and the location is only a 2-minute walk from the Condado beaches. The atmosphere is cozy and comfortable, the service personalized. The spacious bedrooms are adorned with marble, and, even though air-conditioned, each has a tropical ceiling fan along with a private bathroom with Jacuzzi tub. Each room is decorated with original paintings by Mara Torres, a well-known local artist. A continental breakfast is served in the lounge or at the swimming pool, where a constantly flowing fountain adds to the ambience. Sunbathers head for the deck where a hot tub also awaits.

1159 Magdalena Ave., Condado, PR 00907. (C) **787/977-7700.** Fax 787/722-5032. www.coralpr.com. 25 units. Winter $115–$165 double; off-season $99–$150 double. AE, DC, DISC, MC, V. Bus: 1. **Amenities:** Outdoor pool; sun deck; laundry service; nonsmoking rooms; rooms for those w/limited mobility. *In room:* A/C, TV, kitchenette (in some), fridge, hair dryer, safe (in some).

El Canario Inn *Value*   Affiliated with El Canario by the Lagoon Hotel (see above), this little bed-and-breakfast, originally built as a private home, is one of the best values along the high-priced Condado strip. The location is just 1 block from the beach (you can walk there in your bathing suit). This well-established hotel lies directly on the landmark Ashford Avenue, center of Condado action, and is close to casinos, nightclubs, and many restaurants in all price ranges. Although surrounded by megaresorts, it is a simple inn, with rather small but comfortable rooms and good maintenance by a helpful staff. Each unit has a small, tiled, shower-only bathroom. You can relax on the hotel's patios or in the whirlpool area, which is surrounded by tropical foliage. Note that the inn has no elevator.

1317 Ashford Ave., Condado, San Juan, PR 00907. © **800/533-2649** or 787/722-3861. Fax 787/722-0391. www.canariohotels.com. 25 units (shower only). Winter $119–$134 double; off season $90–$100 double. AE, DC, MC, V. Bus: B21 or C10. **Amenities:** Limited room service. *In room:* A/C, TV, safe.

4 Miramar

Miramar, a residential neighborhood, is very much a part of metropolitan San Juan, and a brisk 30-minute walk will take you where the action is. Regrettably, the beach is at least half a mile (.8km) away. For the location of this hotel in Miramar, see the "Eastern San Juan Accommodations" map on p. 65.

Courtyard San Juan Miramar *♠*   Long known as the Excelsior, this hotel has been vastly improved with massive renovations following its takeover by the Marriott people. Spread across 11 floors, the bedrooms have been overhauled with new furnishings, which are comfortable and tasteful, each with a modern bathroom with a tub/shower combo. Rooms no longer have kitchenettes, but each includes a fridge. Special attention was paid to the beds, which now have thicker mattresses, custom comforters, and fluffier pillows. Pullout sofa beds and rollaway beds are also features of the restored hotel. Guests have the choice of a first-class restaurant, Augusto, or the more informal Café Bistro de Paris.

Av. Ponce de León 801, San Juan, PR 00907. © **800/298-4274** or 787/721-7400. Fax 787/722-1787. www.courtyardsj.com. 136 units. Winter $115–$179 double, $230 suite; off season $95–$159 double, $230 suite. Children 12 and under stay free in parent's room; cribs free. AE, DC, DISC, MC, V. Bus: 1, 2, or A5. **Amenities:** 2 restaurants; outdoor pool; health club; babysitting; laundry service; rooms for those w/limited mobility. *In room:* A/C, TV, fridge, hair dryer, safe, Wi-Fi.

5 Santurce & Ocean Park

Less fashionable (and a bit less expensive) than their nearest neighbors Condado (to the west) and Isla Verde (to the east), Santurce and Ocean Park are wedged into a modern, not particularly beautiful neighborhood that's bisected by lots of roaring traffic arteries and commercial enterprises. Lots of Sanjuaneros come here to work in the district's many offices and to eat in its many restaurants. The coastal subdivision of Ocean Park is a bit more fashionable than landlocked Santurce, but with the beach never more than a 20-minute walk away, few of Santurce's residents seem to mind. For the locations of hotels in Santurce and Ocean Park, see the "Eastern San Juan Accommodations" map on p. 65.

MODERATE

Hostería del Mar ✦   Lying a few blocks from the Condado casinos and right on the beach are the white walls of this distinctive landmark. It's in a residential seaside community that's popular with locals looking for beach action on weekends. The hotel boasts medium-size oceanview rooms. Those on the second floor have balconies; those on the first floor open onto patios. The decor is invitingly tropical, with wicker furniture, good beds, pastel prints, and ceiling fans. The bathrooms are small but efficient, some with shower, some with tub only. The most popular unit is no. 201, with a king-size bed, private balcony, kitchenette, and a view of the beach; it's idyllic for a honeymoon. There's no pool, but a full-service restaurant here is known for its vegetarian, macrobiotic, and Puerto Rican plates, all freshly made. The place is simple, yet with its own elegance, and the hospitality is warm.

Calle Tapía 1, Ocean Park, San Juan, PR 00911. ℂ **877/727-3302** or 787/727-3302. Fax 787/268-0772. www.hosteriadelmarpr.com. 27 units. Winter $86–$143 double without ocean view, $189–$260 double with ocean view, $275–$289 apt; off season $69–$100 double without ocean view, $130–$165 double with ocean view, $216–$230 apt. Children 11 and under stay free in parent's room. AE, DISC, MC, V. Bus: A5. **Amenities:** Restaurant; laundry service; dry cleaning. *In room:* A/C, TV, kitchenette, coffeemaker (in some).

Numero Uno Guest House ✦✦ *(Finds*   As a translation of its name implies, this is the best of the small-scale, low-rise guesthouses in Ocean Park. It was originally built in the 1950s as a private beach house in a prestigious residential neighborhood adjacent to the wide sands of Ocean Park Beach. A massive renovation in 1999 transformed the place into the closest thing in Ocean Park to the kind of stylish boutique hotel you might find in an upscale California neighborhood. Much of this is thanks to the hardworking owner, Esther Feliciano, who cultivates within her walled compound a verdant garden replete with splashing fountains, a small swimming pool, and manicured shrubbery and palms. Stylish-looking bedrooms contain tile floors, wicker or rattan furniture, comfortable beds, and tiled, shower-only bathrooms. Some repeat clients, many of whom are gay, refer to it as their fantasy version of a private villa beside a superb and usually convivial beach. The staff can direct you to watersports emporiums nearby for virtually any tropical watersport. Whereas it lacks the staggering diversity of the big hotels of the nearby Condado or Isla Verde, some guests value its sense of intimacy and small-scale charm.

Calle Santa Ana 1, Ocean Park, San Juan, PR 00911. © 866/726-5010 or 787/726-5010. Fax 787/727-5482. www.numero1guesthouse.com. 13 units (shower only). Winter $115–$225 double, $265 apt, $225 junior suite; off season $60–$145 double, $165 apt, $165 junior suite. $20 each additional occupant of a double room. Rates include continental breakfast. AE, MC, V. Bus: A5. **Amenities:** Restaurant; bar; outdoor pool; room service; nonsmoking rooms; rooms for those w/limited mobility. *In room:* A/C, TV, dataport, minibar, hair dryer, iron/ironing board, safe.

INEXPENSIVE

L'Habitation Beach Guesthouse   This small hotel sits on a tranquil tree-lined street with a sandy beach right in its backyard. Located only a few blocks from the Condado, this inn has a laid-back atmosphere. The good-size and well-maintained bedrooms have ceiling fans, comfortable beds, and fairly simple furnishings. The most spacious rooms are nos. 8 and 9, which also open onto ocean views. Each unit has a small, tiled, shower-only bathroom. Chairs and beverage service are provided in a private beach area, and guests can enjoy breakfast alfresco. You can also eat or drink on the breezy patio overlooking the sea. Ask for one of the bar's special margaritas.

Calle Italia 1957, Ocean Park, San Juan, PR 00911. © **787/727-2499.** Fax 787/727-2599. www.habitationbeach.com. 10 units (shower only). Winter $78–$131 double; off season $65–$88 double. Extra person $20. Rates include continental breakfast. AE, DISC, MC, V. Free parking. Bus: T1. **Amenities:** Bar; laundry service. *In room:* A/C, TV, coffeemaker, safe.

6 Isla Verde: Near the Airport

Beach-bordered Isla Verde is closer to the airport than the Condado and Old San Juan. The hotels here are farther from Old San Juan than those in Miramar, Condado, and Ocean Park. It's a good choice if you don't mind the isolation and want to be near fairly

Isla Verde Accommodations

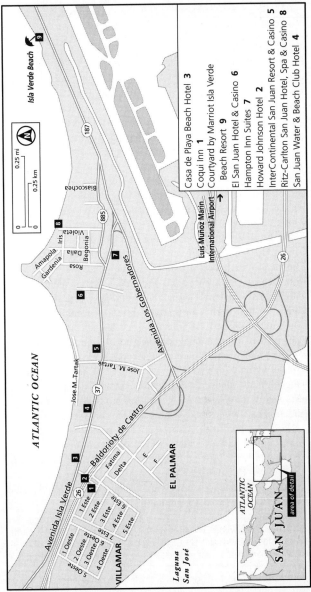

Casa de Playa Beach Hotel **3**
Coqui Inn **1**
Courtyard by Marriot Isla Verde
  Beach Resort **9**
El San Juan Hotel & Casino **6**
Hampton Inn Suites **7**
Howard Johnson Hotel **2**
InterContinental San Juan Resort & Casino **5**
Ritz-Carlton San Juan Hotel, Spa & Casino **8**
San Juan Water & Beach Club Hotel **4**

good beaches. For the locations of hotels in Isla Verde, see the map "Isla Verde Accommodations" in this section.

VERY EXPENSIVE

El San Juan Hotel & Casino *Kids*   This hotel is no longer the dazzler it once was. The Ritz-Carlton has taken the truly elite business, and the San Juan Water & Beach Club Hotel is even more sophisticated. Nonetheless, El San Juan Hotel is still a good choice for (well-to-do) families, with lots of activities for children. The beachfront hotel is surrounded by 350 palms, century-old banyans, and gardens. Its 2,100-foot (640m) sandy beach is the finest in the San Juan area. The hotel's river pool, with currents, cascades, and lagoons, evokes a jungle stream, and the lobby is the most opulent and memorable in the Caribbean. Entirely sheathed in red marble and hand-carved mahogany paneling, the public rooms stretch on almost endlessly.

The hotel was getting a little tired in its last days as a Wyndham, but massive renovations in 2007 should take care of that problem. The large, well-decorated rooms have intriguing touches of high-tech; each contains three phones and a VCR. Bedrooms are imbued with honey-hued woods and rattans and king-size or double beds. Bathrooms have all the amenities and tub/shower combos; a few feature Jacuzzis. About 150 of the units, designed as comfortable bungalows, are in the outer reaches of the garden. Known as *casitas,* they include Roman tubs, atrium showers, and access to the fern-lined paths of a tropical jungle a few steps away. A 17-story, $60-million wing with 120 suites, all oceanfront, was completed in 1998. The ultra-luxury tower features 103 one- or two-bedroom units, eight garden suites, five governor's suites, and four presidential suites.

No other hotel in the Caribbean offers such a rich diversity of dining options and such high-quality food. Japanese, Italian, Mexican, and 24-hour American/Caribbean restaurants are just a few of the options. **The Ranch** *RR* offers gargantuan portions of steak and seafood (including a famous and famously pricey lobster). Also see reviews of **La Piccola Fontana** (p. 101) and Yamato (p. 104).

Av. Isla Verde 6063, San Juan, PR 00979. © **866/317-8935** or 787/791-1000. Fax 787/791-0390. www.elsanjuanhotel.com. 382 units. Winter $359–$819 double, from $1,200 suite; off season $219–$499 double, from $1,099 suite. AE, DC, DISC, MC, V. Self-parking $10, valet parking $20. Bus: A5. **Amenities:** 8 restaurants; 4 bars; 2 outdoor pools; tennis court; health club; spa; sauna and steam room; watersports equipment/rentals; children's programs; business center; room service; massage; babysitting; laundry service; dry cleaning; rooms for those w/limited mobility;

casino. *In room:* A/C, TV/VCR, minibar, coffeemaker, hair dryer, iron/ironing board, safe, Wi-Fi.

InterContinental San Juan Resort & Casino ⊛ Thanks to an extensive $15.2-million restoration, this resort on the beach now competes with El San Juan Hotel next door, but it still doesn't overtake it. You'll get the sense of living in a sophisticated beach resort rather than a hotel where the sun rises and sets around the whims of high-rolling gamblers.

Most of the comfortable, medium-size rooms have balconies and terraces and tasteful furnishings with a lot of pizzazz. Top-floor rooms are the most expensive, even though they lack balconies. Each bathroom has a power showerhead, a deep tub, and a scale. The most desirable units are in the Plaza Club, a minihotel within the hotel that sports a private entrance, concierge service, complimentary food and beverage buffets, and suite/spa and beach facilities. Dining within any of this hotel's five restaurants merits attention, although the choice is vaster at the neighboring El San Juan Hotel. Even if you're not a guest, consider a visit to **Ruth's Chris Steak House** (p. 102), which serves the best steaks in San Juan. **Momoyama** (p. 104) is also worth a trek across town, and its sushi bar is the finest along the beachfront. However, we find the Market Cafe, with its made-to-order foods and snacks, overrated.

Av. Isla Verde 5961, Isla Verde, PR 00937. ℂ **888/424-6835** or 787/791-6100. Fax 787/253-2510. www.intercontinental.com. 402 units. Winter $299–$699 double, $799–$1,099 suite; off season $279–$379 double, $399–$1,099 suite. Children 15 and under stay free in parent's room. AE, DC, DISC, MC, V. Self-parking $12, valet parking $22. Bus: A7, M7, or T1. **Amenities:** 5 restaurants; lounge; the Caribbean's largest free-form pool; health club; whirlpool; sauna; scuba diving; limo service; business center; room service; massage; babysitting; laundry service; dry cleaning; rooms for those w/limited mobility; casino. *In room:* A/C, TV, minibar, coffeemaker, hair dryer, iron, safe, Wi-Fi.

Ritz-Carlton San Juan Hotel, Spa & Casino ⊛⊛⊛ This is one of the most spectacular deluxe hotels in the Caribbean. Set on 8 acres (3.2ha) of prime beachfront, within a 5-minute drive of the airport, it appeals to both business travelers and vacationers. The decor reflects Caribbean flavor and the Hispanic culture of the island, with artwork from prominent local artists. More visible, however, is an emphasis on continental elegance. This resort has some of the most opulent public areas anywhere, including wrought-iron balustrades and crystal chandeliers.

Beautifully furnished guest rooms open onto ocean views or the gardens of nearby condos. Rooms are very large, with excellent furnishings and fine linen. The bathrooms are exceptionally plush, with tub/shower combos, scales, bathrobes, and deluxe toiletries. Some rooms are accessible for guests with disabilities. Preferred accommodations are in the ninth-floor Ritz-Carlton Club, which has a private lounge and personal concierge staff.

The scope and diversity of dining here is second only to that at the El San Juan, and for top-shelf dining venues, the Ritz-Carlton has no equal. The hotel also has the Caribbean's largest **casino** (p. 137).

Av. de los Gobernadores (State Rd.) 6961, no. 187, Isla Verde, PR 00979. ⓒ **800/ 241-3333** or 787/253-1700. Fax 787/253-0700. www.ritzcarlton.com. 416 units. Winter $589–$819 double; off season $299–$549 double; year-round from $1,500 suite. AE, DC, DISC, MC, V. Valet parking $20. Bus: A5, B40, or C45. **Amenities:** 5 restaurants; 3 bars; nightclub; large pool; 2 tennis courts; health club; spa; children's programs; salon; room service; babysitting; laundry service; dry cleaning; rooms for those w/limited mobility; Caribbean's largest casino. In room: A/C, TV, minibar, hair dryer, safe, Wi-Fi.

San Juan Water & Beach Club Hotel ⓐⓐⓐ   A refreshing change from the megachain resorts of San Juan, this ultrachic hotel is hip and contemporary. It's the city's only boutique hotel on a beach. We find much to praise at this small and exclusive hotel because of its highly personalized and well-trained staff. Although avant-garde, the design is not daringly provocative. Behind glass are "waterfalls," even on the elevators, and inventive theatrical-style lighting is used to bring the outdoors inside. The one-of-a-kind glass art doors are from Murano, the fabled center of glassmaking outside Venice. The hotel overlooks Isla Verde's best beach area, and all the bedrooms are spacious, opening onto views of the water and containing custom-designed beds positioned to face the ocean. Bathrooms are tiled and elegant, with tub/shower combinations. Unique features are the open-air 11th-floor exotic bar, with the Caribbean's only rooftop fireplace. The pool is a level above; it's like swimming in an ocean in the sky.

Calle José M. Tartak 2, Isla Verde, Puerto Rico 00979. ⓒ **888/265-6699** or 787/ 253-3666. Fax 787/728-3610. www.waterclubsanjuan.com. 84 units. Winter $269–$330 double, $695 suite; off season $179–$239 double, $695 suite. AE, DC, DISC, MC, V. Bus: T1 or A5. **Amenities:** 2 restaurants; 2 bars; outdoor rooftop pool; fitness center; Jacuzzi; room service; dry cleaning; nonsmoking rooms; rooms for those w/limited mobility. In room: A/C, TV, minibar, hair dryer, iron, safe, Wi-Fi.

(Kids) Family-Friendly Accommodations

At Wind Chimes Inn (p. 69)   Families like this hotel not only because of the accommodations and the affordable prices, but also because they can prepare meals here, cutting down on food costs.

Courtyard by Marriott Isla Verde Beach Resort (p. 77) This is an affordable option, and the kids will enjoy the Bananas Ice Cream Parlour, the game room, and Kids' Club activities for ages 3 through 11. Summer family packages can save you money and usually include coupons for pizza and banana sundaes.

Hampton Inn Suites (p. 78)   For families seeking the kind of lodging values found on the mainland, this new hotel is highly desirable, as many of its rooms have two double beds. There's also a beautiful swimming pool in a tropical setting. Suites have microwaves and refrigerators.

El San Juan Hotel & Casino (p. 74)   This hotel, although expensive, offers more programs for children than any other hotel in Puerto Rico. Its supervised Kids' Klub provides daily activities—ranging from face painting to swimming lessons—for children 5 to 12 years of age.

EXPENSIVE

Courtyard by Marriott Isla Verde Beach Resort ⭐ (Kids)   This is affordable Caribbean at its best. Opening on Isla Verde Beach, close to the airport, the 12-story hotel has been completely refurbished, making it suitable for business travelers, families, or the random vacationer. It's a big, bustling place with many amenities and midsize and well-furnished bedrooms. Art Deco furnishings dominate, and there is plenty of comfort. The casino and lobby restaurants are filled with the sounds of Latin rhythms at night.

Boca de Cangrejos 7012, Isla Verde, PR 00979. (C) **800/791-2553** or 787/791-0404. Fax 787/791-1460. www.sjcourtyard.com. 293 units. Winter $275–$350 double, $400–$450 suite; off season $185–$260 double, $310–$360 suite. AE, DC, DISC, MC, V. Bus: M7. **Amenities:** 3 restaurants; ice-cream parlor; bar; outdoor pool; fitness center; kids' club; business center; room service; laundry service; dry cleaning; casino. *In room:* A/C, TV, minibar, hair dryer, iron, safe, Wi-Fi.

MODERATE

Hampton Inn Suites *(Kids)*   Opened in 1997, this chain hotel is set across the busy avenue from Isla Verde's sandy beachfront, far enough away to keep costs down but within a leisurely 10-minute walk of the casinos and nightlife. Two towers, with four and five floors, hold the well-maintained, well-furnished, and comfortable bedrooms. There's no restaurant on the premises and no real garden; other than a whirlpool and a swimming pool with a swim-up bar, there are few facilities or amenities. Because of its reasonable prices and location, however, this Isla Verde Inn could be a good choice. Families are especially fond of staying here despite the fact that there are no special children's programs; many of the rooms have two double beds, and suites have microwaves and refrigerators.

Av. Isla Verde 6530, Isla Verde, PR 00979. ✆ **800/HAMPTON** or 787/791-8777. Fax 787/791-8757. http://hamptoninn.hilton.com. 201 units. Winter $239 double, $259 suite; off season $189 double, $199 suite. Rates include breakfast bar. AE, DC, DISC, MC, V. Parking $5. Bus: A5 or C45. **Amenities:** Bar; outdoor pool; fitness center; whirlpool; laundry service; rooms for those w/limited mobility. *In room:* A/C, TV, fridge (in suites), microwave (in suites), coffeemaker, hair dryer, iron, Wi-Fi.

Howard Johnson Hotel *(Value)*   Rising eight stories above the busy traffic of Isla Verde, this chain hotel offers comfortable but small bedrooms, furnished simply with bland, modern furniture. They're done in typical motel style, with small but serviceable tub/shower combos. Many guests carry a tote bag to the beach across the street and then hit the bars and restaurants of the expensive hotels nearby. There's a restaurant and a pool. Though it's simple and not very personal, this is a good choice for the money.

Av. Isla Verde 4820, Isla Verde, PR 00979. ✆ **800/728-1300** or 787/728-1300. Fax 787/268-0637. www.hojo.com. 115 units. Winter $145 double; off season $115 double; year-round $189–$225 suite. AE, MC, V. Parking $6.50. Bus: A5. **Amenities:** Restaurant; outdoor pool; health club; room service; nonsmoking rooms; rooms for those w/limited mobility. *In room:* A/C, TV, coffeemaker, hair dryer, iron.

INEXPENSIVE

Casa de Playa Beach Hotel *(Finds)*   Jutting out over the sand on the mile-long (1.6km) Isla Verde beach, this bargain oasis is a find. If you're less interested in being in the center of San Juan than you are in spending time on the beach, check out this modest choice. The hotel consists of two two-story buildings, with a porch around the second floor and a small garden in front. Furnishings are modest and functional but comfortable nonetheless. Each room has a small, tidily maintained bathroom with a tiled shower. Standard but inexpensive Italian food is served at a beach bar and restaurant. The hotel doesn't have everything—no pool, no room service—but the price is hard to beat in Isla Verde.

Av. Isla Verde 4851, San Juan, PR 09979. ℂ **800/916-2272** or 787/728-9779. Fax 787/727-1334. 21 units. Winter $90 double, $170 suite; off season $80 double, $130 suite. Children 9 and under stay free in parent's room. Rates include continental breakfast. AE, DC, DISC, MC, V. Free parking. Bus: A5. **Amenities:** Restaurant; bar; laundry service. *In room:* A/C, TV, safe.

Coqui Inn   Across the busy avenue from the larger and much more expensive San Juan Grand Beach Resort & Casino, this is really two hotels in one. They stand side by side and charge the same prices. Both of them are equally comfortable, though modest. The beach is a 5-minute walk away, and each of the hotels has a pool. There are 25 rooms in one (formerly the Green Isle Inn). The other (formerly Casa Mathiesen) is only slighter larger, with 29 units. The furnishings are summery, simple, and comfortable. Each has a tiled tub/shower bathroom.

Calle Uno 36, Villamar, Isla Verde, PR 00979. ℂ **800/677-8860** or 787/726-8662. Fax 787/268-2415. www.coqui-inn.com. 54 units. Winter $89–$109 double; off season $79–$99 double. Rates include breakfast. Children under 12 stay free in parent's room. AE, DISC, MC, V. Free parking. Bus: A5. **Amenities:** Restaurant; bar; 2 small outdoor pools; laundry service; rooms for those w/limited mobility. *In room:* A/C, TV, kitchenette (in some), safe, Wi-Fi.

5

Where to Dine in San Juan

San Juan has the widest array of restaurants in the Caribbean. You can enjoy fine continental, American, Italian, Chinese, Mexican, and Japanese cuisines, to name a few. In recent years, many restaurants have shown a greater appreciation for traditional Puerto Rican cooking, and local specialties now appear on the menus of numerous restaurants. When possible, many chefs enhance their dishes with native ingredients.

Many of San Juan's best restaurants are in the resort hotels along the Condado and at Isla Verde. There has been a restaurant explosion in San Juan in the past few years, but many of the newer ones are off the beaten tourist path, and some have not yet achieved the quality found at many of the older, more traditional restaurants.

Local seafood is generally in plentiful supply, but no restaurant guarantees that it will have fresh fish every night, especially during winter, when the sea can be too turbulent for fishing. In those cases, the chef relies on fresh or frozen fish flown in from Miami. If you want fresh fish caught in Puerto Rican waters, ask your server about the catch of the day. Make sure he or she can guarantee that the fish was recently caught rather than resting for a while in the icebox.

1 Best Bets

- **Best Classic Creole Cooking:** Chef Wilo Benet at **Pikayo** is a master specialist in the *criollo* cooking of the colonial age, emphasizing the Spanish, Indian, and African elements in his unusual recipes. See p. 98.
- **Best French Cuisine:** Against a Moorish and Andalusian background, **Trois Cent Onze** serves a classic French cuisine with innovative overtones. Great attention is paid to the color, flavor, and texture of each dish. See p. 86.
- **Best for a Romantic Dinner:** Out in Miramar, **Augusto's Cuisine,** on the 15th floor of the Hotel Excelsior, offers a stunning

and panoramic view of San Juan at night. It also serves one of the best French and international cuisines in the Caribbean, backed up by an extensive wine list. See p. 97.

- **Best *Asopao:*** Soul food to Puerto Ricans, *asopao* is the regional gumbo, made in as many different ways as there are chefs on the island. Some versions are too thick to be called soup, such as the seafood variety at **La Bombonera,** in San Juan's Old Town, which is more like a stew. One popular version of *asopao* includes pigeon peas, although the one with chicken is better-known. See p. 90.

- **Best Spanish Cuisine:** You'd have to go all the way to Madrid to find Spanish food as well prepared as it is at **Ramiro's.** The chefs take full advantage of fresh island produce to create an innovative cuisine of New Creole, although its roots are firmly planted in Spain. Their fresh fish and chargrilled meats are succulent, and any dessert with the strawberry-and-guava sauce is a sure palate pleaser. See p. 94.

- **Best Local Cuisine:** Devoted to *la cocina criolla,* the term for the often starchy local cuisine, **Ajili Mójili** features food that islanders might have enjoyed in their mama's kitchens. Try such specialties as *mofongos* (green plantains stuffed with veal, chicken, shrimp, or pork) or the most classic *arroz con pollo* (stewed chicken with saffron rice) in town. See p. 93.

- **Best Italian Restaurant:** In Wyndham El San Juan Hotel & Casino, **La Piccola Fontana** takes you on a culinary tour of sunny Italy. Plate after plate of delectable northern Italian food is presented nightly—everything from grilled filets of fresh fish to succulent pastas. Service is first-rate, and the welcome warm. See p. 101.

- **Best Pizza:** At **Via Appia,** you should try the special: a delectable blend of sausages, onions, mushrooms, pepperoni, green pepper, and bubbling cheese. Or sample a pizza with meatballs or one with vegetarian ingredients. See p. 97.

- **Best Sunday Brunch:** Both locals and American visitors flock to **Palmeras** at the Caribe Hilton for its delectable all-you-can-eat Sunday brunch. Good food, glamour, and live music are combined here. The freshly prepared seafood alone is worth the set price, which includes champagne. See p. 92.

2 Old San Juan

EXPENSIVE

Aquaviva ★★ LATIN/SEAFOOD   One of the hottest restaurant tickets in Old San Juan, this is the third and final addition to a trio of stylish restaurants, each within a few steps of each other, that are owned by the same investors. The location is at the bottom of Calle Fortaleza, in Old San Juan, within a cool, turquoise-colored environment that's in welcome contrast to the saffron-and-fire-colored decor of the other members (Dragonfly on p. 87 and Parrot Club on p. 85). Presiding above the sometimes frenetic bar action and dining room hubbub of this place are replicas of three *aquaviva* (jellyfish), quivering with illumination, each painstakingly manufactured from stained glass specifically for this site.

The result verges on the chaotic, albeit in the most stylish of ways. Just when you think the bar area is packed to the point where no further clients will possibly be admitted, *boom,* a new carload of hopefuls will cram themselves in among the stylish and scantily dressed crowd. Oysters and stiff drinks are served at the bar. Flowing from the open-to-view kitchens come dishes whose ingredients derive from the watery turquoise world that inspired this restaurant's color scheme. The best examples include six different seviches, including one made with mahimahi, mango juice, and lemons, and a different version with marlin and garlic. You might opt for a heaping tower composed of fried oysters, coconut-flavored shrimp, fried octopus, and calamari. The best main courses include grilled fresh mahimahi with smoky shrimp, salsa, and coconut-poached yuca; seared medallions of halibut with a fondue of spinach and crabmeat; and a succulent version of paella garnished with seafood and pork sausage. More recent additions to the menu feature such zesty fare as lamb spareribs with a tamarindo glaze or seared tuna in a Szechuan peppercorn sauce.

Calle Fortaleza 364. (C) **787/722-0665.** Reservations not accepted. Main courses $16–$42. AE, DC, MC, V. Mon–Wed 6–11pm; Thurs–Sat 6pm–midnight; Sun 4–10pm. Bus: Old Town Trolley.

Barú ★ CARIBBEAN/MEDITERRANEAN   This is one of the most fashionable and popular of the creative and imaginative restaurants of Old San Juan, with an attractive and hard-playing clientele of beautiful people, some of whom might effectively compete for roles on *telenovelas* (Hispanic soap operas). Named after an unspoiled island off the north coast of Colombia (a personal favorite of its Colombian-born owner), Barú occupies a stately high-ceilinged space capped with massive timbers, fronted with a hyper-convivial

Old San Juan Dining

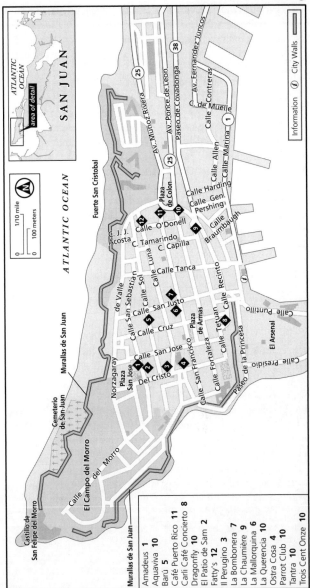

Information ⓘ   City Walls

Amadeus **1**
Aquaviva **10**
Barú **5**
Café Puerto Rico **11**
Carli Café Concierto **8**
Dragonfly **10**
El Patio de Sam **2**
Fatty's **12**
Il Perugino **3**
La Bombonera **7**
La Chaumière **9**
La Mallorquina **6**
La Querencia **10**
Ostra Cosa **4**
Parrot Club **10**
Tantra **10**
Trois Cent Onze **10**

mahogany bar, and decorated with paintings by such Colombia-born artistic luminaries as Botéro. Many dishes are deliberately conceived as something midway between an appetizer and a main-course platter, so it's hard to know how much or how many courses to order. Ask your waitperson to guide you.

Menu items include an unusual choice of five different kinds of carpaccio (tuna, halibut, salmon, beef, or Serrano ham), presented in paper-thin and very small portions that are spread out like a few sheets of tissue paper on a pretentiously large plate. Seviche of mahimahi is appropriately tart and appealingly permeated with citrus, and marinated lamb chops with a paprika and pineapple mojo sauce is flavorful. Other culinary ideas include almond-encrusted goat cheese with Jamaican jerk mango dip and yuca chips, and sliced filet mignon. Regrettably, the place is not cheap, and service is well-intentioned but disorganized as the youthful staff maneuver as best they can through the packed-in crowd. From Thursday to Saturday nights and on the first Tuesday of every month, the restaurant is transformed into a nightclub with either live bands, ranging from salsa to flamenco, or a DJ. The nightclub transformation takes place after 10pm.

Calle San Sebastián 150. ℂ 787/977-7107. Reservations required. Main courses $15–$28. AE, MC, V. Sun–Wed 6pm–midnight; Thurs–Sat 6pm–2am. Bus: Old Town Trolley.

Carli Café Concierto ℱ INTERNATIONAL   This stylish restaurant is owned by Carli Muñoz. The gold disc hanging on the wall attests to Carli's success in his previous role as a pianist for the Beach Boys. Nowadays, Carli entertains his dinner guests nightly with a combination of standards, romantic jazz, and original material on his grand piano. Diners can sit outside on the Plazoleta, where they can enjoy a panoramic view of the bay, or they can eat inside against a backdrop of a tasteful decor of terra-cotta walls and black marble tables. The chef tempts visitors with an imaginative international menu, including such delights as quail rockettes stuffed with dried fruits and sage. The filet of salmon and a mouthwatering rack of lamb are among the finest main dishes. The bar, with its mahogany and brass fittings, is an ideal spot to chill out.

Edificio Banco Popular, Calle Tetuán 206, off Plazoleta Rafael Carrión. ℂ 787/725-4927. Reservations recommended. Main courses $16–$34. AE, V. Mon–Fri 3:30–11pm; Sat 4–11:30pm. Bus: M2 or M3.

Il Perugino ℱℱ ITALIAN   Affiliated with the El Convento hotel (p. 60), this is Puerto Rico's finest Italian restaurant, serving a cuisine that at times seems inspired. Located across from the hotel, the restaurant specializes in the cuisine of Umbria, that province of Italy adjoining Tuscany. The chef and owner, Franco Seccarelli, hails from Umbria and insists that the classic dishes be authentic to his homeland. A special architectural feature of the restaurant is a converted dry well in the center that serves as a wine cellar. Service is impeccable and friendly.

Our favorite homemade pastas include black fettuccine with a shellfish ragout, or ricotta and spinach gnocchetti with fresh tomatoes. For a starter, opt for the shrimp salad with grilled zucchini, a sublime dish, as is another salad made with scallops and porcini mushrooms. Among the meat and poultry dishes, Seccarelli shines with his pheasant breast alla cacciatora and his pork filets flavored with an unusual combination of thyme and blueberries. Another dish we recently raved about was the rack of lamb with fresh herbs and a rich red-wine sauce. Desserts are also succulent and homemade.

105 Cristo St. (© 787/722-5481. Reservations recommended. Main courses $18–$36. AE, DISC, MC, V. Thurs–Sat noon–3pm; daily 6:30–11pm. Bus: Old Town trolley.

La Chaumière ♠ CLASSIC FRENCH   The classic cuisine here has a loyal following of foodies. Just steps from the famous Tapía Theater, this restaurant has cafe-style decor in a greenhouse setting. You might begin with a Marseilles-style fish soup or a hearty country pâté, then follow with a perfectly prepared rack of baby lamb Provençal, filet mignon with béarnaise sauce, magret of duckling, or Dover sole meunière. Or you might choose the tender chateaubriand for two. Old standbys include chitterling sausage with red-wine sauce, Veal Oscar, and Oysters Rockefeller.

Calle Tetuán 364. (© 787/722-3330. Reservations required. Main courses $26–$50. AE, DC, MC, V. Mon–Sat 6pm–midnight. Closed July–Aug. Bus: Old Town Trolley.

Parrot Club ♠♠♠ NUEVO LATINO/CARIBBEAN   Parrot Club is one of the most sought-after restaurants in Old San Juan. This bistro and bar serves Nuevo Latino cuisine that blends traditional Puerto Rican cookery with Spanish, Taíno, and African influences. It's set in a stately 1902 building that was originally a hair-tonic factory. Today you'll find a cheerful-looking dining room, where San Juan's mayor and the governor of Puerto Rico can sometimes be spotted, and a verdantly landscaped courtyard, where tables for at least 200 diners are scattered among potted ferns, palms, and orchids. Live music—Brazilian, salsa, or Latino jazz—is offered nightly as well as during the popular Sunday brunches.

Menu items are updated interpretations of old Puerto Rican specialties. They include seviche of halibut, salmon, tuna, and mahimahi;

delicious crabcakes; *criollo*-style flank steak; and pan-seared tuna served with a sauce made from dark rum and essence of oranges. Everybody's favorite drink is the Parrot Passion, made from lemon-flavored rum, triple sec, oranges, and passion fruit.

Calle Fortaleza 363. ℂ **787/725-7370.** Reservations not accepted. Main courses $18–$36 dinner, $12–$20 lunch. AE, DC, MC, V. Daily 11:30am–3pm and 6–11pm. Closed 2 weeks in Sept. Bus: Old Town Trolley.

Trois Cent Onze 𝄇𝄇 FRENCH   When the French/Puerto Rican owners of this place—named after its 311 address—renovated this building in 1999, they discovered some of the most beautiful Moorish-Andalusian tilework in San Juan's old town buried beneath layers of later coverings. Because of those tiles, and because of the delicate Andalusian-style iron rosette above the door, they wisely decided to retain the area's Moorish embellishments during the reconfiguration of their restaurant's decor. What you'll get today is the premier French restaurant of San Juan, replete with a zinc bar near the entrance, a soaring and richly beamed ceiling, and a decor like what you might have expected in the Casbah of old Tangiers. Your hosts are Christophe Gourdain and Zylma Perez, who are proud to recite the building's former use as the photography studio that developed many of Puerto Rico's earliest movies.

Colors, textures, and flavors combine here to produce an irresistible array of dishes. Menu items include a carpaccio of salmon marinated in citrus; sautéed sea scallops served with an almond-flavored butter sauce; mango and crabmeat salad; magret of duckling roasted with honey; and pork medallions served with caramelized onions, stewed white beans, and spicy merguez sausage. Desserts are classics; our favorite is the Grand Marnier soufflé, but you can also order a thin-crust warm apple tart with vanilla ice cream, or a chocolate mousse flavored with Puerto Rican rum.

Calle Fortaleza 311. ℂ **787/725-7959.** Reservations recommended. Main courses $19–$30. AE, DISC, MC, V. Mon–Fri noon–3pm; Mon–Sat 6–11pm. Bus: Old Town Trolley, T2, or 2.

MODERATE

Amadeus 𝄇𝄇 CARIBBEAN   Housed in a brick-and-stone building that was constructed in the 18th century by a wealthy merchant, Amadeus offers Caribbean ingredients with a nouvelle twist. The appetizers alone are worth the trip here, especially the Amadeus dumplings with guava sauce and arrowroot fritters. And try the smoked-salmon-and-caviar pizza. One zesty specialty is pork scaloppine with sweet-and-sour sauce.

Calle San Sebastián 106 (across from the Iglesia de San José). ✆ 787/722-8635.
Reservations recommended. Main courses $7.75–$25. AE, DISC, MC, V. Mon 6–10pm;
Tues–Sun noon–11pm (kitchen closes at 10pm). Bus: Old Town Trolley, M2, M3, or A5.

Dragonfly ✸✸✸ LATIN/ASIAN   At one of San Juan's hottest
restaurants, the decor has been compared to that of a bordello in old
San Francisco. You pass through the beaded curtains into a world of
red ceilings, fringed lamps, and gilded mirrors. The restaurant lies right
across the street from the Parrot Club, and these two dining enclaves
have put the newly named SoFo district (south of Calle Fortaleza in
Old Town) on the culinary map. In the bar, the preferred cigarette is
Marlboro and the most popular drink is a lethal "Dragon Punch."
Night after night Dragonfly is the fun party place in town. Along with
the latest gossip, you can enjoy live Latin jazz as background music.

This new-generation San Juan restaurant offers sexy cookery, such
as seafood seviche scooped up with yuca, and plantain chips, *chichar-
rones* (pork rinds), spicy crab cakes, and a host of other dishes, such
as marinated grilled meats. We applaud the chefs for their use of root
vegetables such as yuca. The red snapper and grouper are excellent,
and we love the pumpkin and beans of every type. The barbecued
lamb shanks are very hearty and filling. Ravioli, timbales, confits,
cassoulets—it's a dizzy array of taste temptations.

Calle Fortaleza 364. ✆ 787/977-3886. Reservations not accepted. Main courses
$8–$25. AE, MC, V. Mon–Wed 6–11pm; Thurs–Sat 6pm–midnight. Bus: A5 or T1.

El Patio de Sam AMERICAN/PUERTO RICAN   Established
in 1953, this joint has survived several generations of clients, who
came here for booze, fantastic juicy burgers, Puerto Rican food, and
dialogue. There is the unmistakable aura of pop, youth culture,
Margaritaville, and college-age drinking ethos. The setting includes
an exterior space with tables that overlook a historic statue of Ponce
de León and a well-known church, and a labyrinth of dark, smoke-
stained inner rooms with high-beamed ceilings and lots of potted
plants. Dining usually occurs in a skylit garden-style courtyard in
back where there is no view but a welcome sense of calm. In addition to those burgers, you can also order more sophisticated dishes
such as Puerto Rican–style fried pork, seviche, shellfish paella, chicken
and rice, and *churrasco* (Argentine-styled grilled meats).

Calle San Sebastián 102 (across from the Iglesia de San José). ✆ 787/723-1149.
Sandwiches, burgers, and salads $9–$10; platters $10–$15. AE, MC, V. Mon–Tues
11:30am–10pm; Thurs–Sat 11:30am–2am. Bus: Old Town Trolley.

La Mallorquina ✸ PUERTO RICAN   Founded in 1848, this old
favorite has been run by the Rojos family since 1900. If you look

carefully at the floor adjacent to the old-fashioned mahogany bar, you'll see the building's original gray-and-white marble flooring, which the owners are laboriously restoring, square foot by square foot, to its original condition. Lunches here tend to attract local office workers; dinners are more cosmopolitan and more leisurely, with many residents of the Condado and other modern neighborhoods selecting this place specifically because of its old-fashioned, old-world charm.

The food has changed little here over the decades, with special emphasis on *asopao* made with rice and either chicken, shrimp, or lobster and shrimp. *Arroz con pollo* is almost as popular. Begin with either garlic soup or gazpacho, end with flan, and you'll have eaten a meal that's authentically Puerto Rican.

Calle San Justo 207. ℂ **787/722-3261.** Reservations not accepted at lunch, recommended at dinner. Dinner main courses $15–$46 (highest price is for lobster). AE, MC, V. Mon–Sat 11:30am–10pm. Closed Sept. Bus: Old Town Trolley.

La Querencia 🅐 *Finds* PUERTO RICAN/INTERNATIONAL Because of the many desirable restaurants that flank it, it's easy to overlook the charms of this one. Set within a 400-year-old town house, it offers an appealing mixture of elegance, restraint, and urban hip, all of it factored into a long and narrow format that includes an exotic and cozy bar (painted red) near the entrance, and a more formal forest-green dining room in back. The high ceiling and formal layout evoke a salon in a colonial governor's house. Surrounding you will be a collection of antique guitars and wind instruments. Separating the two areas is a skylit courtyard with an open view of the hardworking kitchens.

You can opt to sit anywhere within this warren of rooms, but our preferences involve drinks and *tapas* in the red-painted bar area in front, surrounded by artwork and hints of Madrid during its *movida,* and candlelit meals in back. Your meal might begin delectably with a seviche of sea bass with orange zest; or sautéed shrimp with roasted pineapple, coconut flakes, and a rum-flavored vinaigrette. Main courses include a superb version of pork loin topped with cranberry sauce, served over caramelized apples, or a rack of lamb with red, black, and white bean ragout with fines herbs and puff pastry.

Calle Fortaleza 320. ℂ **787/723-0357.** Reservations recommended Sat–Sun. Main courses $16–$26. AE, DISC, MC, V. Tues–Sun 6–11pm. Bus: Old Town Trolley, T2, or 2.

Ostra Cosa 🅐🅐 *Finds* ECLECTIC/ARGENTINE This is the most artfully promoted restaurant in San Juan, with a growing clientele who swear that the ambience here is one of the most sensual and romantic in Old San Juan. It was created by a former advertising executive, Alberto Nazario, a lifestyle guru who mingles New Age thinking with good culinary techniques to promote love, devotion, and a heightened sexuality. Couples dine beneath a massive *quenepe* tree—waiters will tell you to hug the tree and make a wish—in a colonial courtyard surrounded by a 16th-century building that was once the home of the colony's governor. The atmosphere, enhanced by domesticated quail and chirping tree frogs, will make you feel far removed from the cares of the city. Featured foods are high in phosphorus, zinc, and flavor, designed to promote an "eat-up, dress-down experience." The seviche is superb, as are the grilled prawns. But it is the conch, known as Caribbean Viagra, that rates "Wow!!" or *"Ay ay ay!!!"*

Calle del Cristo 154. © 787/722-2672. Reservations recommended. Main courses $11–$32. AE, MC, V. Sun–Wed noon–10pm; Fri–Sat noon–11pm. Bus: Old Town Trolley.

Tantra ★ *Value* INDO-LATINO   This is one of the most genuinely creative restaurants in San Juan, a one-of-a-kind luminary in a dining scene that sometimes relies merely on derivations of tried-and-true themes. Set in the heart of "restaurant row" on Calle Fortaleza, it has become famous for a sophisticated fusion of Latino and South Indian cuisine. Its chef and owner, Indian-born Ramesh Pillai, oversees a blend of slow-cooked tandoori cuisine from South India with Puerto Rico–derived spices, flavors, and ingredients. All of this occurs within a warm, candlelit environment. One of the best martinis we've ever had (a version with cinnamon and cloves) is an appropriate way to begin a meal here. The best menu items include sesame *masala*-crusted sushi tuna with peanut sauce; fried coconut sesame jumbo shrimp with Indian noodles; chicken *tikka masala* with flat naan bread; and an absolutely brilliant version of tandoori chicken, one of the establishment's bestsellers. Dessert might be a cardamom-flavored flan. Even if you've already had dinner, don't overlook this place as a nightlife option.

Calle Fortaleza 356. © 787/977-8141. Reservations recommended. Main courses $13–$19. AE, MC, V. Mon–Sat noon–3am; Sun noon–12:30am. Bus: T1 or 2.

INEXPENSIVE

Café Puerto Rico CREOLE/PUERTO RICAN   On the Plaza de Colón, this restaurant offers balconies overlooking one of the most charming of Old Town squares. The setting is colonial, with beamed ceilings and tile floors, and with ceiling fans whirling overhead. The menu features hearty regional fare. Tasty options include fried fish filet, paella, and lobster cooked as you like it. Eggplant parmagiana is an excellent vegetarian option, and you might also order eye round stuffed with ham in Creole sauce. On weekends live bands play here, and the sound of romantic boleros or salsa fills the air. The cafe is an especially good value then, because you get your food and entertainment for just the price of dinner.

Calle O'Donnell 208. © **787/724-2281**. Main courses $9–$21. AE, MC, V. Mon–Sat 11:30am–11pm; Sun 11:30am–9pm . Bus: Old Town Trolley.

Fatty's JAMAICAN/WEST INDIAN   Amazingly, Puerto Rico didn't have a Jamaican restaurant until this dive opened. You'll know it's Jamaican when you see a picture of Bob Marley and the Jamaican flag displayed. Not only that, but reggae music plays in the background. The welcoming owner, "Fatty," is a great cook, turning out marvelous jerk dishes, especially chicken, fish, and shrimp. The chef is also known for curry chicken and a rice dish flavored with coconut milk. Chicken balls with curry sauce is another local favorite. Fried red snapper and conch in garlic sauce also won our hearts.

Calle O'Donnell 102. © **787/586-6925**. Main courses $7–$12. Thurs noon–3pm; Fri–Wed noon–9pm. Bus: Old Town Trolley.

La Bombonera ★★ (Value PUERTO RICAN   This place offers exceptional value in its homemade pastries, well-stuffed sandwiches, and endless cups of coffee—and it has done so since 1902. Its atmosphere evokes turn-of-the-20th-century Castille transplanted to the New World. The food is authentically Puerto Rican, homemade, and inexpensive, with regional dishes such as rice with squid, roast leg of pork, and seafood *asopao*. For dessert, you might select an apple, pineapple, or prune pie, or one of many types of flan. Service is polite, if a bit rushed, and the place fills up quickly at lunchtime.

Calle San Francisco 259. © **787/722-0658**. Reservations recommended. American breakfast $4–$10; main courses $6–$20. AE, DC, DISC, MC, V. Daily 7:30am–8pm. Bus: Old Town Trolley.

3 Puerta de Tierra

All three of the restaurants below are in the Caribe Hilton; to locate them, see the map "Eastern San Juan Dining" in this section.

Madrid-San Juan ★ SPANISH   This restaurant lies within the mega-compound known as the Caribe Hilton. Its decor, especially that of its baronial-looking dining room in back, emulates that of a gracious and rather formal *tasca* in Spain, replete with Serrano hams hanging above the bar, a roster of oil paintings (many of which are

Eastern San Juan Dining

Ajili Mójili **5**
Augusto's Cuisine **4**
Café Madrid **18**
Chayote's **3**
Cielito Lindo **7**
Don Tello **16**
Fleria **17**

José José Restaurant **10**
La Compostela **15**
Madrid-San Juan **2**
Morton's of Chicago **1**
Palmeras **1**
Pamela's **19**
Pikayo **8**

Portobello **11**
Ramiro's **6**
Ristorante Tuscany **12**
Urdin **9**
Via Appia **14**
Zabó **13**

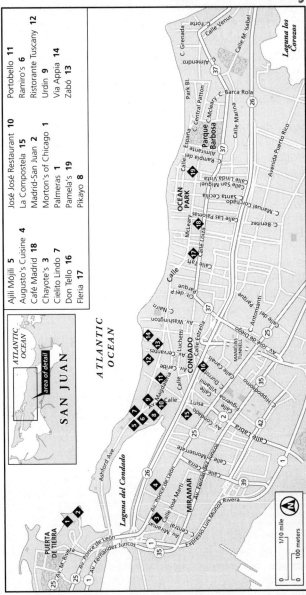

for sale), a scarlet-covered dining room that you might have imagined as a tableau within a still life by Goya, and rack upon rack of wine. There's something big, generous, and well-mannered about this place, as a quick perusal of the list of tapas (both hot and cold) and the conventional lunch or dinner menu will quickly show. Highlights include *piquillo* peppers stuffed with pulverized codfish, fried plantain with smoked salmon, codfish fritters, *fabada asturianas* (a well-seasoned and soupy version of stew that combines fava beans, sausages, and ham), fried fresh anchovies, and chorizo sausages in red-wine sauce. Main courses include breast of chicken in garlic sauce; filet mignon with Manchego cheese and Serrano ham; thin-sliced filet of beef with onions; *asopao de mariscos; mofongo* stuffed with shrimp; and halibut steak garnished with shrimp, mushrooms, and raisin sauce.

In the Caribe Hilton, Calle Los Rosales. ② 787/721-0303. Reservations recommended. Tapas $6.50–$12; main courses $21–$35. AE, DC, DISC, MC, V. Sun–Thurs noon–midnight; Fri noon–1am; Sat 6pm–midnight. Bus: B21.

Morton's of Chicago ☆☆

When it comes to steaks, Ruth's Chris Steak House in Isla Verde enjoys a slight edge, but otherwise Morton's is king of the steaks and other choice meats. The chain of gourmet steakhouses was founded in 1978 by Arnie Morton, former executive vice president of the *Playboy* empire. Beef lovers, from Al Gore to Liza Minnelli, know they'll get quality meats perfectly cooked at Morton's. Carts laden with menu options, ranging from prime midwestern beefsteaks to succulent lamb or veal chops, are wheeled around for your selection. This is a place where the bartenders make stiff drinks, and the waiters tempt you with their fresh fish, lobster, and chicken dishes. The house specialty is a 24-ounce porterhouse, and Morton's has the island's best prime rib. The vegetables here are among the freshest in the area. Appetizers include perfectly cooked jumbo shrimp with cocktail sauce and smoked Pacific salmon. For dessert, we always gravitate to one of the soufflés, such as raspberry or Grand Marnier.

In the Caribe Hilton, Calle Los Rosales. ② 787/977-6262. Reservations required. Main courses $26–$52. AE, DC, DISC, MC, V. Mon–Sat 5–11pm; Sun 5–10pm. Bus: B21.

Palmeras ☆ Kids

INTERNATIONAL   Every Sunday the Hilton's brunch captivates the imagination of island residents and U.S. visitors with its combination of excellently prepared food, glamour, and entertainment. There's a clown to keep the children amused, as well as live music on the bandstand for anyone who cares to dance. Champagne is included in the price. Food is arranged at several different stations:

Puerto Rican dishes, seafood, paella, ribs, cold cuts, steaks, pastas, and salads. Although Sunday is the most festive time to visit, Palmeras prides itself on serving the biggest and most elaborate breakfast buffet in Puerto Rico on any morning. Another lavish buffet is the Friday-night seafood fiesta. On other nights dinner is a la carte. Specialties include pastas, paellas, chicken, and cheese quesadillas, along with an array of other international food.

In the Caribe Hilton, Calle Los Rosales. ⓒ **787/721-0303.** Reservations recommended for Sun brunch and Fri night. Breakfast buffet $20 Mon–Sat, $28 Sun; lunch buffet $22 Mon–Thurs, $30 Fri–Sat. Main courses $13–$29. AE, DC, MC, V. Sun–Thurs 6am–11pm; Fri–Sat 6am–midnight. Bus: 21.

4 Condado

For the locations of Condado restaurants, see the map "Eastern San Juan Dining" on p. 91.

EXPENSIVE

Ajili Mójili ⓕⓕ PUERTO RICAN/CREOLE   This restaurant is devoted exclusively to *la cocina criolla,* the starchy, down-home cuisine that developed on the island a century ago. Though the building housing it is quite modern, you can see artful replicas of the kind of crumbling brick walls you'd expect in Old San Juan and a bar that evokes Old Spain. The staff will willingly describe menu items in colloquial English. Locals come here for a taste of the food they enjoyed at their mother's knee, like *mofongos* (green plantains stuffed with veal, chicken, shrimp, or pork), *arroz con pollo* (chicken and rice), *medallones de cerdo encebollado* (pork loin sautéed with onions), *carne mechada* (beef rib-eye stuffed with ham), and *lechón asado con maposteado* (roast pork with rice and beans). Wash it all down with an ice-cold bottle of local beer.

1006 Ashford Ave. (at the corner of Calle Joffre). ⓒ **787/725-9195.** Reservations recommended. Main courses $16–$30; lunch $12–$26. AE, DISC, MC, V. Mon–Fri noon–3pm; Mon–Thurs 6–10pm; Sat 11:45am–3:30pm; Fri–Sat 6–11pm; Sun 12:30–4pm and 6–10pm. Bus: B21.

José José Restaurant ⓕ *Finds* INTERNATIONAL   The imaginative and flavor-filled dishes at this elegant, colonial-style restaurant next to the Convention Center come as a real surprise. The cooking is warm and generous, and some of the dishes appear on no other menu in San Juan. Try, for example, the loin of ostrich in a sweet cinnamon sauce served with plantain. The lobster-and-wild-mushroom risotto tops anything we've ever sampled in San Juan. The chefs are equally adept at other seafood dishes, including a delectable broiled hake served with a tangy caper sauce. The meat dishes are imaginative as well, including beef cheeks with a garlic-laced linguini. Chef Josébreu is one of San Juan's finest chefs.

1110 Magdalena Ave. ℭ **787/725-8546.** Reservations required. Main courses $23–$35; tasting menu $60–$70. AE, MC, V. Tues–Fri noon–3pm and 6:30–10pm; Sat 6:30–10:30pm; Sun noon–6:30pm. Bus: A7 or M2.

La Compostela ℱ SPANISH   This restaurant offers formal service from a battalion of well-dressed waiters. Established by a Galician-born family, the pine-trimmed restaurant has gained a reputation as one of the best in the capital. The chef made his name on the roast peppers stuffed with salmon mousse. Equally delectable are duck with orange and ginger sauce and baby rack of lamb with fresh herbs. The shellfish grilled in brandy sauce is a sure winner. The chef also makes two different versions of paella, both savory. The wine cellar, comprising some 10,000 bottles, is one of the most impressive in San Juan.

Av. Condado 106. ℭ **787/724-6088.** Reservations required. Main courses $24–$39. AE, DC, MC, V. Mon–Fri noon–2:30pm; Mon–Sat 6:30–10:30pm. Bus: M2.

Portobello ℱ INTERNATIONAL   This restaurant offers some of the finest service on the Condado and a classic Italian cuisine, centered primarily in the north of Italy, especially Lombardy. The menu has expanded to become international, with Puerto Rican specialties and such dishes as succulent steaks or paellas. It's the domain of chef and owner Martin Acosta. His restaurant's picture windows open onto views of the Atlantic and the night lights of the Condado. Appetizers include hot seafood antipasti and Caesar and spinach salads. The Caesar salad is made tableside with real panache. For a main course, you can order one of the homemade pasta dishes or choose from such appetizing dishes as seafood supreme, *vitello* Martino (with shrimp), gnocchi with cream sauce and Parmesan, and filet mignon Monnalisa, which is flambéed at your table. In fact, almost any dish can receive a table-side flambé if you want. Good and reasonably priced wines add to the dining pleasure.

In the Diamond Palace Hotel & Casino, Av. Condado 55. ℭ **787/722-5256.** Reservations recommended. Main courses $20–$25. AE, DC, DISC, MC, V. Daily 5pm–midnight. Bus: A7.

Ramiro's ℱℱ SPANISH/INTERNATIONAL   This restaurant boasts the most imaginative menu on the Condado. Its refined "New Creole" cooking is a style pioneered by owner and chef Jesús Ramiro and his brother Oscar. You might begin with breadfruit *mille-feuille* with local crabmeat and avocado. For your main course, any fresh fish or meat can be chargrilled on request. Some recent menu specialties have included paillard of lamb with spiced root vegetables and guava sauce, charcoal-grilled Black Angus steak with shiitake mushrooms, and grilled striped sea bass with citrus sauce. Among the many homemade desserts are caramelized mango on puff pastry with strawberry-and-guava sauce and "four seasons" chocolate.

1106 Magdalena Ave. *C* **787/721-9049.** Reservations recommended off season, required in winter. Main courses $27–$39. AE, MC, V. Sun–Fri noon–3pm and 6–11pm; Sat 6–10pm. Bus: A7, T1, or M2.

Ristorante Tuscany *666* NORTHERN ITALIAN   This is the showcase restaurant of one of the most elaborate hotel reconstructions in the history of Puerto Rico, and the kitchen continues to rack up culinary awards. Notable entrees include grilled veal chops with shallots and glaze of Madeira, and grilled chicken breast in cream sauce with chestnuts, asparagus, and brandy, surrounded with fried artichokes. The seafood selections are excellent, especially the fresh red snapper sautéed in olive oil, garlic, parsley, and lemon juice. The risottos prepared al dente in the traditional northern Italian style are the finest on the island, especially the one made with seafood and herbs. The cold and hot appetizers are virtual meals unto themselves, with such favorites as grilled polenta with sausages or fresh clams and mussels simmered in herb-flavored tomato broth.

In the San Juan Marriott Resort, 1309 Ashford Av. *C* **787/722-7000.** Reservations recommended. Main courses $23–$49. AE, DC, DISC, MC, V. Daily 6–11pm. Bus: B21.

MODERATE

Most main courses in the restaurants below are at the low end of the price scale. These restaurants each have only two or three dishes that are expensive, almost invariably involving shellfish.

Urdin *66* SPANISH/INTERNATIONAL   Urdin is proud of its reputation as one of the capital's bright young restaurants. It occupies a low-slung, stucco-covered house set near a slew of competitors. Inside, a fanciful decor of postmodern, Caribbean-inspired accents and metal sculptures brings a touch of Latino New York. Popularity has brought an unexpected development to this highly visible restaurant: The bar is almost more popular than the food. Consequently, you're likely to find the bar area jam-packed every day between 6 and 10pm. Cliquish, heterosexual, and fashionable, some of this crowd eventually gravitates toward the tables. Yes, that was Ricky Martin we spotted here one evening.

Filled with authentic Spanish flavor that's not necessarily geared to the palates of timid diners, the food is innovative, flavorful, strong, and earthy. For starters, there are baby eels Bilbaina-style and Castilian lentil soup. Main courses include fresh filet of salmon in mustard sauce, filet of fish "Hollywood style" (with onions, raisins, and mango slices, served in white-wine sauce), and rack of lamb with orange sauce. One always-pleasing dish is *piquillo* peppers stuffed with seafood mousse and black-olive sauce. Savvy locals finish their meal with a slice of sweet-potato cheesecake. The staff can put a damper on (if they're sulky) or enhance (if they're welcoming) a meal here.

1105 Magdalena Ave. ℂ 787/724-0420. Reservations recommended. Main courses $16–$29. AE, MC, V. Mon–Fri 11am–3pm and 6–10:30pm; Sat 6–10:30pm. Bus: A7.

Zabó ☆ AMERICAN/PUERTO RICAN/STEAK   This restaurant enjoys citywide fame, thanks to its blend of bucolic charm and superb innovative food. It's set in a dignified villa that provides some low-rise dignity in a sea of skyscraping condos. The creative force here is owner and chef/culinary director Paul Carroll, who built the place from its origins as a simple deli into one of the most sought-after restaurants on the Condado. Menu items fuse the cuisines of the Mediterranean, the Pacific Rim, and the Caribbean into a collection that includes dishes such as blinis stuffed with medallions of lobster with ginger, thyme, and beurre blanc; carpaccio of salmon with mesclun salad and balsamic vinegar; and baked chorizo stuffed with mushrooms, sherry, paprika, and cheddar. The black-bean soup is among the very best in Puerto Rico, served with parboiled cloves of garlic marinated in olive oil that melt in your mouth like candy.

Calle Candina 14 (entrance is via an alleyway leading from Ashford Ave. between Washington and Cervantes). ℂ 787/725-9494. Reservations recommended. Snacks $6; main courses $15–$35. AE, MC, V. Mon–Fri 11am–3pm; Tues–Wed 6–10pm; Thurs–Fri 6–11pm; Sat 7–11pm. Bus: A7.

INEXPENSIVE

Cielito Lindo *Value* MEXICAN   One of the most likable things about this restaurant is the way it retains low prices and an utter lack of pretension, despite the expensive Condado real estate that surrounds it. Something about it might remind you of a low-slung house in Puebla, Mexico, home of owner Jaime Pandal, who maintains a vigilant position from a perch at the cash register. Walls are outfitted with an intriguing mix of Mexican arts and crafts and ads for popular tequilas and beer. None of the selections have changed since the restaurant was founded, a policy that long-term clients find reassuring. The place is mobbed, especially on weekends, with those looking for heaping portions of well-prepared, standardized Mexican food. Examples include fajitas of steak or chicken; strips of filet steak sautéed with green peppers and onions, covered with tomatoes and spicy gravy; enchiladas of chicken or cheese, covered with cheese and served with sour cream; and several kinds of tacos.

1108 Magdalena Ave. ℂ **787/723-5597.** Reservations recommended for dinner. Main courses $10–$20. AE, MC, V. Mon–Wed 11am–10pm; Thurs–Fri 11am–11pm; Sat–Sun 5–11pm. Bus: B21 or C10.

Via Appia ✪ PIZZA/ITALIAN   A favorite of Sanjuaneros visiting Condado for the day, Via Appia offers food that's sometimes praiseworthy. Its pizzas are the best in the neighborhood. The chef's signature pizza, Via Appia, is a savory pie made with sausages, onions, mushrooms, pepperoni, green peppers, cheese, and spices. Vegetarians also have a pizza to call their own (made with whole-wheat dough, eggplant, mushrooms, green peppers, onions, tomatoes, and cheese). There's even a pizza with meatballs. Savory pasta dishes, including baked ziti, lasagna, and spaghetti, are also prepared with several of your favorite sauces. All of this can be washed down with sangria. During the day, freshly made salads and sandwiches are also available.

1350 Ashford Ave. ℂ **787/725-8711.** Pizza and main courses $9–$16. AE, MC, V. Daily 11am–11pm. Bus: B21 or C10.

5 Miramar

For the locations of restaurants in Miramar, see the map "Eastern San Juan Dining" on p. 91.

Augusto's Cuisine ✪✪✪ FRENCH/INTERNATIONAL   With its European flair, this is one of the most elegant and glamorous restaurants in Puerto Rico. Austrian-born owner/chef Augusto Schreiner, assisted by a partly French-born staff, operates from a gray-and-green dining room set on the lobby level of a 15-story hotel in Miramar. Menu items are concocted from strictly fresh ingredients, including such dishes as lobster risotto; rack of lamb with aromatic herbs and fresh garlic; an oft-changing cream-based soup of the day (one of the best is corn and fresh oyster soup); and a succulent version of medallions of veal Rossini style, prepared with foie gras and Madeira sauce. The wine list is one of the most extensive on the island.

In the Hotel Excelsior, Av. Ponce de León 801. ℂ 787/725-7700. Reservations recommended. Main courses $24–$38. AE, MC, V. Tues–Fri noon–3pm; Tues–Sat 7–10pm. Bus: T1.

Chayote's ✦ PUERTO RICAN/INTERNATIONAL   The cuisine of this restaurant is among the most innovative in San Juan. It draws local business leaders, government officials, and celebs like Sylvester Stallone and Melanie Griffith. It's an artsy, modern, basement-level bistro in a surprisingly obscure hotel (the Olimpo). The restaurant changes its menu every 3 months, but you might find appetizers like a yuca turnover stuffed with crabmeat and served with mango and papaya chutney, or ripe plantain stuffed with chicken and served with fresh tomato sauce. For a main dish, you might try red-snapper filet with citrus vinaigrette made of passion fruit, orange, and lemon. An exotic touch appears in the pork filet seasoned with dried fruits and spices in tamarind sauce and served with green banana and taro-root timbale. To finish off your meal, there's nothing better than the mango flan served with macerated strawberries.

In the Olimpo Hotel, Av. Miramar 603. ℂ 787/722-9385. Reservations recommended. Main courses $24–$48. AE, MC, V. Tues–Fri 11:30am–2:30pm; Tues–Sat 6:30–10:30pm. Bus: B5.

6 Santurce & Ocean Park

For the locations of restaurants in Santurce and Ocean Park, see the map "Eastern San Juan Dining" on p. 91.

VERY EXPENSIVE

Pikayo ✦✦✦ PUERTO RICAN/CAJUN   This is an ideal place to go for the new generation of Puerto Rican cookery, with a touch of Cajun thrown in for spice and zest. Starkly minimalist, it has a lighting scheme whose tones change from reds to blues to yellows throughout the course of your dinner. And a large TV screen shows, through closed circuitry, the culinary rituals transpiring minute-by-minute within the restaurant's kitchen. This place not only keeps up with the latest culinary trends, but it often sets them, thanks to the inspired guidance of owner and celebrity chef Wilo Benet. Formal but not stuffy, and winner of more culinary awards than virtually any other restaurant in Puerto Rico, Pikayo is a specialist in the *cocina criolla* of the colonial age, emphasizing the Spanish, Indian, and African elements in its unusual recipes. Appetizers include a dazzling array of taste explosions: Try shrimp spring rolls with peanut *sofrito* sauce; crab cake with aioli; or perhaps a ripe plantain, goat-cheese, and onion tart. Main course delights feature charred rare yellowfin tuna with onion *escabeche* and red-snapper filet with sweet-potato purée served with foie gras butter. Our favorite remains the grilled shrimp with polenta and barbecue sauce made with guava.

Museum of Art of Puerto Rico, Av. José de Diego 299. ℂ **787/721-6194.** Reservations recommended. Main courses $28–$54; fixed-price menus $85. AE, DC, MC, V. Tues–Sun noon–3pm; Tues–Sat 6–11pm. Bus: M2, A7, or T1.

EXPENSIVE

Pamela's ℛ CARIBBEAN FUSION/VEGETARIAN   A sense of cachet and style is very pronounced at this restaurant, a fact that's somewhat surprising considering its out-of-the-way location. Part of its allure derives from a sophisticated blend of Caribbean cuisines that combines local ingredients with Puerto Rican flair and a sense of New York style. Menu items include a salad that marries vine-ripened and oven-roasted tomatoes, each drizzled with a roasted garlic–and-cilantro vinaigrette; club sandwiches stuffed with barbecued shrimp and cilantro-flavored mayonnaise; plantain-encrusted crab cakes with a spicy tomato-herb emulsion; and grilled island-spiced pork loin served with guava glaze and fresh local fruits. Beer and any of a wide array of party-colored drinks go well with this food.

In the Numero Uno Guest House, Calle Santa Ana 1, Ocean Park. ℂ **787/726-5010.** Reservations recommended. Sandwiches and salads at lunch $10–$16; main course platters $22–$29. AE, MC, V. Daily noon–3pm and 6–10pm. Bus: A5.

MODERATE

Fleria ℛ *Finds* GREEK   Lying on the border of Condado near the Ocean Park beaches, this discovery is the domain of owner-chef Theo Ladia-Apostalahis, who brings a touch of the Mediterranean to the Caribbean. Artists, writers, and politicians, even beachcombers, come here not only to enjoy the good food but to unwind. The decor consists of blue walls, high ceilings, and a display of paintings of Greek monuments, ruins, and gods. There is a wood replica of the Acropolis. At night, burning candles make the mood more romantic.

The hosts present a white board listing the Greek specialties of the day, each dish explained and questions answered. Scrumptious appetizers include an olive pâté or fava beans served with freshly baked bread to soak up the olive oil. Each main dish is accompanied by a delicious Greek salad and a fresh vegetable. Some of the menu's delights include chicken breast stuffed with feta cheese and spinach and grilled mahimahi. Lamb is prepared in five different ways and, of course, you expect moussaka to be the chef's specialty.

Calle Loiza 1754, Santurce. ☎ 787/268-0010. Main courses $14–$22. Tues–Fri noon–3pm and 5–10pm; Sun noon–10pm. Bus: 1.

INEXPENSIVE

Café Madrid *(Finds)* PUERTO RICAN   Come here to escape from the gloss and sheen of big-city, big-money tourism. Local residents promote this simple diner for its sense of workaday conviviality and low, low prices. Located on a narrow but busy street in a congested commercial neighborhood of Ocean Park, this joint has a battered facade with plastic lettering—signs that the inside is going to be very tacky. At first glance, that's partially true. But if you retain a sense of humor, you might begin to appreciate the Formica bar tops, rows of mismatched refrigerators, big-lettered menus over sizzling deep-fat fryers, and the kinds of industrial accessories that Andy Warhol might have appreciated or even collected. It's been the domain of the Molina family since the 1930s, and the food has changed very little since then. Examples include roasted pork, sold either as a full-size meal platter or stuffed into a sandwich; several kinds of *asopao* and *carne frita* (fried meat); lasagna; and lots of empanadas. Roasted chicken, the signature dish, is a perpetual favorite.

Calle Loíza 100 (at the corner of Calle Las Flores). ☎ 787/728-5250. Reservations not accepted. Breakfast platters $3.25–$12; sandwiches $3–$6; lunch and dinner main courses $6–$11. MC, V. Daily 6am–10pm. Bus: B5 or T1.

Don Tello *(Finds)* PUERTO RICAN   Right at the Santurce Market Square (Plaza del Mercado), this is a family-run restaurant serving an authentic *criollo* cuisine. All the locals call the owners, Jorge and Rosin, by their first names. In a casual atmosphere, diners dress informally, eat well, and don't pay a lot of money for the privilege. The service is excellent, and the ingredients are fresh and well-prepared. The fish tastes among the freshest in San Juan. We've enjoyed the filet of sea bass in a plantain sauce, or a well-seasoned whole roasted sea bass. Grilled filet of mahimahi is another one of our favorites, as is the grilled filet of hake. You can also enjoy the traditional *asopao* of Puerto Rico, made with chicken, shrimp, lobster, or shellfish. A savory chicken stew is also served, as is a tender filet of steak roasted with onions.

Dos Hermanos 180, Santurce. ☎ 787/724-5752. Reservations required. Main courses $7–$19. AE, DISC, MC, V. Tues–Wed 11am–5pm; Thurs–Sat 11am–9pm; Sun noon–5pm. Bus: 1, 5, or 21.

7 Isla Verde

VERY EXPENSIVE

BLT Steak ★★★ STEAK The award-winning chef Laurent Touroundel has opened his first restaurant in the Caribbean, a first-class steakhouse in a luxe hotel. Food enjoyed at a critically acclaimed New York–based restaurant can now be eaten in San Juan. An innovative and passionate chef, Touroundel is known for his modern decor, a sumptuous yet simply prepared cuisine, and his polished service. Woods in a palette of chocolate brown and even supple suede paneling add to the masculine decor—that and the Makassar ebony tables and the deep caramel-colored banquettes.

Begin with such succulent appetizers as lobster salad or shrimp cocktail, moving on to such house specialties as hanger steak or braised short ribs. The chef prepares the best veal chop in town (14 oz.) and also cooks a porterhouse for two. The herb-marinated American Kobe skirt steak is the best of its kind we've enjoyed in Puerto Rico. Fish and shellfish also are included—such delights as spiced swordfish or sautéed Dover sole. We especially like the sauces that can be ordered with the fish, including cilantro-laced mayonnaise or ginger ketchup. Like any good steakhouse, the cooks pay special attention to their fresh vegetables, featuring grilled asparagus or creamy spinach. Desserts are all the childhood favorites: carrot cake, lemon meringue pie, strawberry sundae, and banana bread pudding.

In the Ritz-Carlton San Juan Hotel, Spa & Casino, Av. de los Gobernadores (State Rd. 6961) 187, Isla Verde. ✆ **787/253-1700.** Reservations required. Main courses $28–$98. AE, DC, MC, V. Tues–Sun 6–11pm. Bus: A5, B40, or C45.

La Piccola Fontana ★★★ NORTHERN ITALIAN Right off the luxurious Palm Court in the Wyndham El San Juan Hotel, this restaurant takes classic northern Italian cuisine seriously and delivers plate after plate of delectable food nightly. From its white linen to its classically formal service, it enjoys a fine reputation. The food is straightforward, generous, and extremely well-prepared. You'll dine in one of two neo-Palladian rooms whose wall frescoes depict Italy's ruins and landscapes. Menu items range from the appealingly simple—such as grilled filets of fish or grilled veal chops—to more elaborate dishes, such as tortellini San Daniele, made with veal, prosciutto, cream, and sage; and linguine *scogliere,* with shrimp, clams, and other seafood. Grilled medallions of filet mignon are served with braised arugula, Parmesan cheese, and balsamic vinegar.

In Wyndham El San Juan Hotel & Casino, Av. Isla Verde 6063. ℂ **787/791-0966.** Reservations required. Main courses $20–$40. AE, DC, MC, V. Daily 6–10:30pm. Bus: A5.

Ruth's Chris Steak House ⭐⭐ STEAK This Puerto Rican branch of one of the most famous steakhouse chains in the world presents macho food, especially steaks that are among the best beef dishes in San Juan. It obsessively focuses on big drinks and big steaks, grilled in the simplest possible way—usually just with salt, pepper, and a brush-over of butter. These are served within two dark blue, mahogany-trimmed dining rooms, separated by a saloon-style bar.

You might begin with barbecued shrimp, mushrooms stuffed with crabmeat, or seared ahi tuna. Or you might opt for a salad as an appetizer. Portions are large and very filling. Steaks are the finest from the U.S. cattle country. Examples include rib-eyes, veal chops, porterhouse, New York strips, and filet mignons. There's also roasted chicken, lobster, and a fresh catch of the day.

In the InterContinental San Juan Resort & Casino, Av. Isla Grande 187. ℂ **787/791-6100.** Reservations recommended. Main courses $22–$40. AE, DC, MC, V. Sun–Thurs 6–10pm; Fri–Sat 6–11pm. Bus: M7.

EXPENSIVE

Tangerine ⭐⭐ EURO-ASIAN This is the ultimate in chic Isla Verde dining, and it just happens to lie adjacent to the street-level reception area of the San Juan Water & Beach Club Hotel (p. 76). Minimalist, postmodern, and angular, and outfitted in monochromatic colors that include steel gray and navy blue, it has a prominent bar area in back, bubbling waterfalls, big-windowed views of the tropical landscapes outside, and an occasional and rather whimsical reference to the orange-colored fruit that gave the place its name. Lighting radiates gently outward from the kind of ultra-glam fixtures that make ordinary-looking people look good and beautiful people look fabulous. Menu items include appetizers (the restaurant rather coyly refers to them as "foreplay") such as crispy Vietnamese lobster rolls with mango-based sweet chile and avocado-minted melon relish, and citrus-cured yellowfin tuna tartare. For a main course, try cassia-smoked breast of chicken with sweet garlic potato purée; and Asian-herbed crusted Colorado lamb chops with garlic-flavored mashed potatoes and a sauce made from goat cheese, pulverized cucumbers, plum-flavored sake, and yogurt. Dessert might be a lemon-lime crème brûlée.

Calle José M. Tartak 2. ℂ **787/728-3666.** Reservations required. Main courses $23–$42. AE, DC, MC, V. Daily 6:30–11pm. Bus: T1 or A5.

Isla Verde Dining

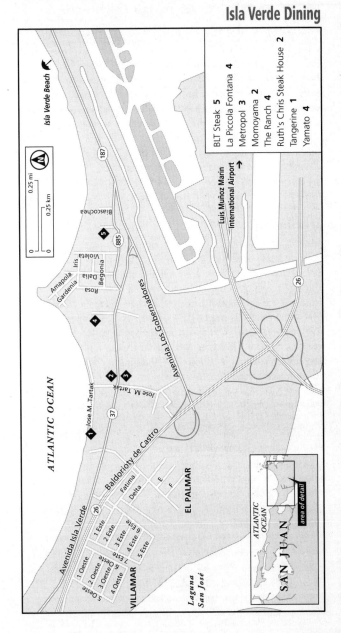

BLT Steak **5**
La Piccola Fontana **4**
Metropol **3**
Momoyama **2**
The Ranch **4**
Ruth's Chris Steak House **2**
Tangerine **1**
Yamato **4**

Yamato ⓖ JAPANESE The artfully simple decor at Yamato shows the kind of modern urban minimalism that you might expect in an upscale California restaurant. Separate sections offer conventional seating at tables; at a countertop within view of a sushi display; or at seats around a hot grill where chefs shake, rattle, and sizzle their way through a fast but elaborate cooking ritual. Many visitors eat at least some sushi with an entree such as beef sashimi with *tataki* sauce, shrimp tempura with noodle soup, filet mignon or chicken with shrimp or scallops, or several kinds of rice and noodle dishes. A more formal dress code is required.

In El San Juan Hotel & Casino, Av. Isla Verde 6063. ⓒ **787/791-1000.** Reservations required. Sushi $2.50–$6 per piece; sushi and *teppanyaki* dinners $25–$41. AE, DC, DISC, MC, V. Daily 6pm–midnight. Bus: A5.

MODERATE

Momoyama ⓖ JAPANESE Few other restaurants in Isla Verde are as indelibly associated with one dish: sushi pizza. The subject of rave reviews, it's made by deep-frying compressed rice into something akin to a pizza shell, which is layered with rows of salmon or tuna and garnished with fish roe, shaved ginger, and make-your-eyes-water wasabi. If you prefer your food cooked, you can head for one of several *teppanyaki* tables, where food is fast-cooked in front of you as part of a highly theatrical culinary show. Choices include chicken teriyaki with shrimp, soy-and-ginger chicken with filet mignon, and several kinds of tempura.

In the InterContinental San Juan Resort & Casino, Av. Isla Grande 187. ⓒ **787/791-8883.** Reservations recommended. Fixed-price lunches $12–$22; lunch and dinner main courses $23–$47. AE, MC, V. Mon–Fri noon–3pm and 5:30–11:30pm; Sat 5:30pm–midnight; Sun 1–11pm. Bus: M7.

The Ranch AMERICAN/STEAK The posh El San Juan Hotel scores an unlikely success with this irreverent, tongue-in-cheek eatery on its top (10th) floor. You'll be greeted with a hearty "Howdy, partner" and the jangling of spurs from a crew of denim-clad cowboys as you enter a replica of a corral in the North American West. Banquettes and bar stools are upholstered in faux cowhide; the decor is appropriately macho and rough-textured, and even the cowgirls on duty are likely to lasso anyone they find particularly appealing. The cowboys sing as they serve your steaks, barbecued ribs, country-fried steaks, Tex-Mex fajitas, and enchiladas. Food that's a bit less beefy includes seared red snapper with a cilantro-laced *pico de gallo* sauce. Especially succulent are soft-shell crabs layered in a pyramid with blue and yellow tortillas. And if you want to buy a souvenir pair of cowboy spurs, you'll find an intriguing collection of Western accessories and uniforms for sale outside. Consider beginning your meal with any of 20 kinds of tequila cocktails at the Tequila Bar, which lies a few steps away, on the same floor.

In Wyndham El San Juan Hotel & Casino, Av. Isla Verde 6063. © 787/791-1000. Reservations recommended at dinner Fri–Sat. Main courses $15–$35. AE, DC, DISC, MC, V. Tues–Thurs 4:30–11pm; Fri–Sat 4:30pm–midnight. Bus: A5.

INEXPENSIVE

Metropol CUBAN/PUERTO RICAN/INTERNATIONAL   This is part of a restaurant chain known for serving the island's best Cuban food, although the chefs prepare a much wider range of dishes. Metropol is the happiest blend of Cuban and Puerto Rican cuisine we've ever had. The black bean soup is among the island's finest, served in the classic Havana style with a side dish of rice and chopped onions. Endless garlic bread accompanies most dinners, including Cornish game hen stuffed with Cuban rice and beans, or perhaps marinated steak topped with a fried egg (reportedly Castro's favorite). Smoked chicken and chicken-fried steak are also heartily recommended; portions are huge. Plantains, yuca, and all that good stuff accompany most dishes. Finish with a choice of thin or firm custard. Most dishes are at the low end of the price scale.

Club Gallistico, Av. Isla Verde. © 787/791-4046. Main courses $10–$30. AE, MC, V. Daily 11:30am–10:30pm. Bus: C41, B42, or A5.

6

Exploring San Juan

The Spanish began to settle in the area now known as Old San Juan around 1521. At the outset, the city was called Puerto Rico ("Rich Port"), and the whole island was known as San Juan.

The streets are narrow and teeming with traffic, but a walk through Old San Juan—in Spanish, *el Viejo* San Juan—makes for a good stroll. Some visitors have likened it to a "Disney park with an Old World theme." Fast food and junk stores mar a lot of the beauty. Nonetheless, it's the biggest and best collection of historic buildings, stretching back 5 centuries, in all the Caribbean. You can tour it in less than a day. In this historic 7-square-block area of the western side of the city, you can see many of Puerto Rico's main tourist attractions and do some shopping along the way.

On the other hand, you might want to plop down on the sand with a drink or get outside and play. "Diving, Fishing, Tennis & Other Outdoor Pursuits," later in this chapter, describes the beaches and sports in the San Juan area.

SUGGESTED ITINERARIES
In case you would like to drag yourself away from the beach, here are some suggestions for how to see San Juan.

If You Have 1 Day
To make the most of a short stay, head straight for Old San Juan for an afternoon of sightseeing and shopping. Definitely schedule a visit to El Morro Fortress. Try to spend 2 hours at Condado Beach. In the evening, enjoy Puerto Rican cuisine at a local restaurant, dance to some salsa music, and enjoy at least one rum punch before the sun comes up.

If You Have 2 Days
On your first day, spend the morning shopping and sightseeing in Old San Juan. Plan visits to El Morro and San Juan Cathedral, and then relax on Condado Beach for the rest of the day. Enjoy a Puerto Rican dinner and some local music before calling it a night.

On your second day, spend the morning exploring El Yunque rainforest, a lush 28,000-acre (11,331ha) site east of San Juan.

Old San Juan Attractions

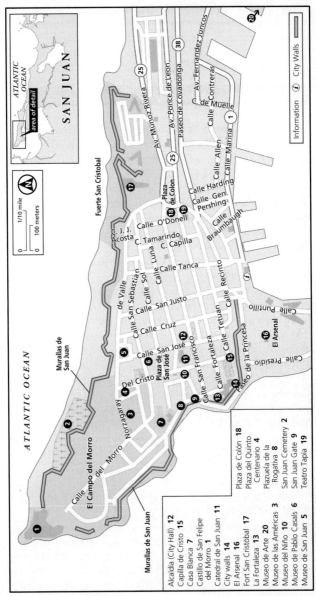

ATLANTIC OCEAN

SAN JUAN

ATLANTIC OCEAN

area of detail

0   1/10 mile
0   100 meters

Murallas de San Juan

Fuerte San Cristóbal

El Campo del Morro

Calle del Morro

Calle Norzagaray

Del Cristo

Plaza de San José

Calle San Sebastián

Calle de Valle

Calle Sol

Calle Luna

Calle San Justo

Calle Cruz

Calle San Francisco

Calle Fortaleza

Calle Tetuan

Calle Recinto

Paseo de la Princesa

El Arsenal

Calle Presidio

Calle Puntilla

C. J. J. Acosta

C. Tamarindo

C. Capilla

Calle Tanca

Calle O'Donell

Plaza de Colon

Calle Harding

Calle Gen. Pershing

Calle I Braumbaugh

Calle Marina

Calle Allen

C. de Muelle

Av. Ponce de León

Av. Muñoz Rivera

Av. Fernández Juncos

Paseo de Covadonga

Calle de Contreras

38

25

25

20

1

Information   (i) City Walls

Alcaldía (City Hall) **12**
Capilla de Cristo **15**
Casa Blanca **7**
Castillo de San Felipe del Morro **1**
Catedral de San Juan **11**
City walls **14**
El Arsenal **16**
Fort Cristóbal **17**
La Fortaleza **13**
Museo de Arte **20**
Museo de las Américas **3**
Museo del Niño **10**
Museo de Pablo Casals **6**
Museo de San Juan **5**
Plaza de Colón **18**
Plaza del Quinto Centenario **4**
Plazuela de la Rogativa **8**
San Juan Cemetery **2**
San Juan Gate **9**
Teatro Tapia **19**

Spend 2 or 3 hours at nearby Luquillo Beach, the finest beach in Puerto Rico. Buy lunch from an open-air kiosk. Return to San Juan for the evening and attend either a folk-culture show (if available) or a Las Vegas–style revue. Visit the casinos for some late-night action.

1 Seeing the Sights

FORTS

Castillo de San Felipe del Morro ⟨★⟩ *(Kids)*   Called "El Morro," this fort stands on a rocky promontory dominating the entrance to San Juan Bay. Constructed in 1540, the original fort was a round tower, which can still be seen deep inside the lower levels of the castle. More walls and cannon-firing positions were added, and by 1787, the fortification attained the complex design you see today. This fortress was attacked repeatedly by both the English and the Dutch.

The U.S. National Park Service protects the fortifications of Old San Juan, which have been declared a World Heritage Site by the United Nations. With some of the most dramatic views in the Caribbean, you'll find El Morro an intriguing labyrinth of dungeons, barracks, vaults, lookouts, and ramps. Historical and background information is provided in a video in English and Spanish. The nearest parking is the underground facility beneath the Quincentennial Plaza at the Ballajá barracks (Cuartel de Ballajá) on Calle Norzagaray. Sometimes park rangers lead hour-long tours for free, although you can also visit on your own. With the purchase of a ticket here, you don't have to pay the admission for Fort San Cristóbal (see below) if you visit during the same day.

Before going into the citadel, you can visit the new $2-million **San Juan National Historic Site** (© 787/729-6960), which is open June through November daily from 9am to 5pm and December through May daily 9am to 6pm, charging $3 for adults, $2 for seniors, and $1 for children 13 to 17 (free for children 12 and under). The center is connected via two tunnels to **Fort San Cristóbal,** and was created from a strategic military base used in World War II. Visitors view a 12-minute film about the fortifications. A photo exhibit, a gift shop, and other exhibits are of interest.

At the end of Calle Norzagaray. © 787/729-6960. Admission $3 adults, $1 seniors and kids 13–17, free for children 12 and under. June–Nov daily 9am–5pm; Dec–May daily 9am–6pm. Bus: A5, B21, or B40.

Fort San Cristóbal ⟨★⟩   This huge fortress, begun in 1634 and reengineered in the 1770s, is one of the largest ever built in the

Juan García Troche. The parcel of land was given to Ponce de León as a reward for services rendered to the Crown. Descendants of the explorer lived in the house for about 2½ centuries, until the Spanish government took it over in 1779 for use as a residence for military commanders. The U.S. government also used it as a home for army commanders. On the first floor, the **Juan Ponce de León Museum** is furnished with antiques, paintings, and artifacts from the 16th through the 18th centuries. In back is a garden with spraying fountains, offering an intimate and verdant respite.

Calle San Sebastián 1. ✆ **787/724-4102.** Admission $2. Tues–Sat 9am–noon and 1–4:30pm. Bus: Old Town Trolley.

El Arsenal   The Spaniards used a shallow craft to patrol the lagoons and mangroves in and around San Juan. Needing a base for these vessels, they constructed El Arsenal in the 19th century. It was at this base that they staged their last stand, flying the Spanish colors until the final Spaniard was removed in 1898, at the end of the Spanish-American War. Changing art exhibitions are held in the building's three galleries.

La Puntilla. ✆ **787/723-3068.** Free admission. Wed–Sun 8:30am–4:30pm. Bus: Old Town Trolley.

La Fortaleza   The office and residence of the governor of Puerto Rico is the oldest executive mansion in continuous use in the Western Hemisphere, and it has served as the island's seat of government for more than 3 centuries. Its history goes back even further than that to 1533, when construction began on a fortress to protect San Juan's Spanish settlers during raids by Carib tribesmen and pirates. The original medieval towers remain, but as the edifice was subsequently enlarged into a palace, other modes of architecture and ornamentation were also incorporated, including baroque, Gothic, neoclassical, and Arabian. La Fortaleza has been designated a national historic site by the U.S. government. Informal but proper attire is required.

Calle Fortaleza 52, overlooking San Juan Harbor. ✆ **787/721-7000,** ext. 2358. Free admission. Mon–Fri 9am–4pm (40-min. English and Spanish tours of the gardens and building every half-hour). Bus: Old Town Trolley.

Teatro Tapía   Standing across from the Plaza de Colón, this is one of the oldest theaters in the Western Hemisphere, built about 1832. In 1976 a restoration returned the theater to its original appearance. Much of Puerto Rican theater history is connected with the Tapía, named after the island's first prominent playwright, Alejandro Tapía y

Rivera (1826–82). Various productions—some musical—are staged here throughout the year, representing a repertoire of drama, dance, and cultural events.

Av. Ponce de León. ✆ 787/721-0180. Access limited to ticket holders at performances (see "San Juan After Dark," later in this chapter). Bus: B8 or B21.

HISTORIC SQUARES

In Old San Juan, **Plaza del Quinto Centenario (Quincentennial Plaza)** overlooks the Atlantic from atop the highest point in the city. A striking and symbolic feature of the plaza, which was constructed as part of the 1992–93 celebration of the 500th anniversary of the discovery of the New World, is a sculpture that rises 40 feet (12m) from the plaza's top level. The monumental sculpture in black granite and ceramics symbolizes the earthen and clay roots of American history and is the work of Jaime Suarez, one of Puerto Rico's foremost artists. From its southern end, two needle-shaped columns point skyward to the North Star, the guiding light of explorers. Placed around the plaza are fountains, other columns, and sculpted steps that represent various historic periods in Puerto Rico's 500-year heritage.

Sweeping views extend from the plaza to El Morro Fortress at the headland of San Juan Bay and to the Dominican Convent and San José Church, a rare New World example of Gothic architecture. Asilo de Beneficencia, a former indigents' hospital dating from 1832, occupies a corner of El Morro's entrance and is now the home of the Institute of Puerto Rican Culture. Adjacent to the plaza is the Cuartel de Ballajá, built in the mid–19th century as the Spanish army headquarters and still the largest edifice in the Americas constructed by Spanish engineers; it houses the Museum of the Americas.

Centrally located, Quincentennial Plaza is one of modern Puerto Rico's respectful gestures to its colorful and lively history. It is a perfect introduction for visitors seeking to discover the many rich links with the past in Old San Juan.

Once named St. James Square, or Plaza Santiago, **Plaza de Colón** in the heart of San Juan's Old Town is bustling and busy, reached along the pedestrian mall of Calle Fortaleza. The square was renamed Plaza de Colón to honor the 400th anniversary of the explorer's so-called discovery of Puerto Rico. Of course, it is more politically correct today to say that Columbus explored or came upon an already inhabited island. He certainly didn't discover it. But when a statue here, perhaps the most famous on the island, was erected atop a high pedestal, it was clearly to honor Columbus, not to decry his legacy.

SIGHTSEEING TOURS

If you want to see more of the island but you don't want to rent a car or manage the inconveniences of public transportation, perhaps an organized tour is for you.

Castillo Sightseeing Tours & Travel Services, Calle Laurel 2413, Punta Las Marías, Santurce (© 787/728-2297; www.castillotours. com), maintains offices at some of the capital's best-known hotels, including the Caribe Hilton and San Juan Marriott Resort. Using six of their own air-conditioned buses, with access to others if demand warrants it, the company's tours include pickups and drop-offs at hotels as an added convenience.

One of the most popular half-day tours departs most days of the week between 8:30 and 9am, lasts 4 to 5 hours, and costs $45 to $65 per person. Leaving from San Juan, it tours along the north-eastern part of the island to El Yunque. The company also offers a city tour of San Juan that departs daily around 1pm. The 4-hour trip costs $40 per person and includes a stop at the Bacardi Rum Factory. The company also operates full-day snorkeling tours to the reefs near the coast of a deserted island off Puerto Rico's eastern edge aboard one of two sail- and motor-driven catamarans. With lunch, snorkeling gear, and piña coladas included, the full-day (7:45am–5pm) excursion goes for $79 per person.

Few cities of the Caribbean lend themselves so gracefully to walking tours. You can embark on these on your own, stopping and shopping en route.

ESPECIALLY FOR KIDS

Puerto Rico is one of the most family-friendly islands in the Caribbean, and many hotels offer family discounts. Programs for children are also offered at a number of hotels, including day and night camp activities and babysitting services. Trained counselors at these camps supervise children as young as 3 in activities ranging from nature hikes to tennis lessons, coconut carving, and sand-sculpture contests. Teenagers can learn to hip-hop dance Latino-style with special salsa and merengue lessons, learn conversational Spanish, indulge in watersports, take jeep excursions, or scuba dive in some of the best diving locations in the world.

The best kiddies program is offered at **El San Juan Hotel & Casino** (p. 74), where camp activities are presented to children between the ages of 5 and 12. Counselors design activities according to the interests of groups of up to 10 children. Kids Klub members receive a T-shirt, membership card, and three Sand Dollars for use in the game room or at a poolside restaurant. The daily fee of $40 includes lunch.

Children should love **El Morro Fortress** (see "Forts," earlier in this chapter) because it looks just like the castles they have seen on TV and at the movies. On a rocky promontory, El Morro is filled with dungeons and dank places and also has lofty lookout points for viewing San Juan Harbor.

Luis Muñoz Marín Park has the most popular children's playground in Puerto Rico. It's filled with landscaped grounds and recreational areas—lots of room for fun in the sun.

Museo del Niño (Children's Museum) *Kids*   In the late 1990s, the city of San Juan turned over one of the most desirable buildings in the colonial zone—a 300-year-old villa directly across from the city's cathedral—to a group of sociologists and student volunteers. Jointly, they created the only children's museum in Puerto Rico. Through interactive exhibits, children learn simple lessons, such as the benefits of brushing teeth or recycling aluminum cans, or the value of caring properly for pets. Staff members include lots of student volunteers who play either one-on-one or with small groups of children. Nothing here is terribly cerebral, and nothing will necessarily compel you to return. But it does provide a play experience that some children will remember for several weeks.

Calle del Cristo 150. ℂ 787/722-3791. Admission $5, $7 children 15 and under. Tues–Thurs 9am–3:30pm; Fri 9am–5pm; Sat–Sun 12:30–5pm. Bus: Old Town Trolley.

Time Out Family Amusement Center *Kids*   This is the most popular venue for family outings in Puerto Rico. On weekends, seemingly half the families in the city show up. It has a large variety of electronic games for children and adults alike, but there are no rides.

Plaza de las Américas, Las Américas Expwy. at Roosevelt Ave., Hato Rey. ℂ 787/ 753-0606. Free admission (activities $1–$8). Mon–Thurs 9:30am–10pm; Fri–Sat 9am–11pm; Sun 9am–10pm. Bus: B21 from Old San Juan.

2 Diving, Fishing, Tennis & Other Outdoor Pursuits

Active vacationers have a wide choice of things to do in San Juan, from beaching to windsurfing. The beachside hotels, of course, offer lots of watersports activities (see chapter 4).

THE BEACHES

Some public stretches of shoreline around San Juan are overcrowded, especially on Saturday and Sunday; others are practically deserted. If you find that secluded, hidden beach of your dreams, proceed with caution. On unguarded beaches you'll have no way to protect yourself or your valuables should you be approached by a robber or mugger, which has been known to happen. For more information about the island's many beaches, call the **Department of Sports & Recreation** at © 787/728-5668.

All beaches in Puerto Rico, even those fronting the top hotels, are open to the public. Public bathing beaches are called *balnearios* and charge for parking and for use of facilities, such as lockers and showers. Beach hours in general are 9am to 5pm in winter, to 6pm off season. Major public beaches in the San Juan area have changing rooms and showers.

Famous with beach buffs since the 1920s, **Condado Beach** ⓇⓇ put San Juan on the map as a tourist resort. Backed up by high-rise hotels, it seems more like Miami Beach than any other beach in the Caribbean. From parasailing to sailing, all sorts of watersports can be booked at kiosks along the beach or at the activities desk of the hotels. There are also plenty of outdoor bars and restaurants. People-watching is a favorite sport along these golden strands.

A favorite of Sanjuaneros themselves, **Isla Verde Beach** ⓇⓇ is also ideal for swimming, and it, too, is lined with high-rise resorts à la Miami Beach. Many luxury condos are on this beachfront. Isla Verde has picnic tables, so you can pick up the makings of a lunch and make it a day at the beach. This strip is also good for snorkeling because of its calm, clear waters, and many kiosks will rent you equipment. Isla Verde Beach extends from the end of Ocean Park to the beginning of a section called Boca Cangrejos. The best beach at Isla Verde is at the Wyndham Hotel El San Juan. Most sections of this long strip have separate names, such as El Alambique, which is often the site of beach parties, and Punta El Medio, bordering the Ritz-Carlton, also a great beach and very popular, even with the locals. If you go past the luxury hotels and expensive condos behind the Luis Muñoz Marín International Airport, you arrive at the major public beach at Isla Verde. Here you'll find parking, showers, fast-food joints, and watersports equipment. The sands here are whiter than those of the Condado, and they are lined with coconut palms, sea-grape trees, and even almond trees, all of which provide shade from the fierce noonday sun.

One of the most attractive beaches in the Greater San Juan area is **Ocean Park Beach** ⓇⓇ, a mile (1.6km) of fine gold sand in a neighborhood east of Condado. This beach attracts both young people and a big gay crowd. Access to the beach at Ocean Park has been limited recently, but the best place to enter is from a section called El Ultimo Trolley. This area is ideal for volleyball, paddleball, and other games. The easternmost portion, known as Punta Las Marías, is best for windsurfing. The waters at Ocean Park are fine for swimming, although they can get rough at times.

Rivaling Condado and Isla Verde beaches, **Luquillo Beach** is the grandest in Puerto Rico and one of the most popular. It's 30 miles (48km) east of San Juan, near the town of Luquillo (see "Luquillo Beach" on p. 146).

SPORTS & OTHER OUTDOOR PURSUITS

BIKE RENTALS   The best places to bike are along Ashford Avenue (in Condado), Calle Loiza (between Condado and Ocean Park), and Avenida Baldorioty de Castro (in Santurce). Other streets in this area may be too congested. Similarly, because of the traffic, biking in Old San Juan is not recommended.

CRUISES   For the best cruises of San Juan Bay, go to **Caribe Aquatic Adventures** (see "Scuba Diving," below). Bay cruises start at $25 per person.

DEEP-SEA FISHING ⚓   Deep-sea fishing is top-notch here. Allison tuna, white and blue marlin, sailfish, wahoo, dolphin fish (mahimahi), mackerel, and tarpon are some of the fish that can be caught in Puerto Rican waters, where 30 world records have been broken. Charter arrangements can be made through most major hotels and resorts.

Benítez Fishing Charters can be contacted directly at P.O. Box 9066541, Puerto de Tierra, San Juan, PR 00906 (© **787/723-2292** until 9pm). The captain offers a 45-foot (14m) air-conditioned deluxe Hatteras called the *Sea Born.* Fishing tours for parties of up to six cost $585 for a half-day excursion, $758 for a 6-hour excursion, and $968 for a full day, with beverages and all equipment included.

GOLF   A 45-minute drive east from San Juan on the northeast coast takes you to Palmer and its 6,145-yard (5,619m) **Westin Rio Mar Golf Course** ⚓ (© **787/888-6000**). Inexperienced golfers prefer this course to the more challenging and more famous courses at Dorado (see chapter 7), even though trade winds can influence your game along the holes bordering the water, and occasional fairway flooding can present some unwanted obstacles. Greens fees are $165 for hotel guests, $190 for nonguests. A gallery of 100 iguanas also adds spice to your game at Rio Mar.

HORSE RACING   Great thoroughbreds and outstanding jockeys compete year-round at **El Comandante,** Calle 65 de Infantería, Rte. 3 Km 15.3, at Canóvanas (© **787/724-6060**), Puerto Rico's only racetrack, a 20-minute drive east of the center of San Juan. Post time varies from 2:45 to 5:30pm on Monday, Wednesday, Friday, Saturday, and Sunday. Entrance to the clubhouse costs $3; no admission is charged for the grandstand.

RUNNING   The cool, quiet morning hours before 8am are a good time to jog through the streets of Old San Juan. Head for the wide thoroughfares adjacent to El Morro and then San Cristóbal, whose walls jut upward from the flat ground. You might join Puerto Rico's governor, a dedicated runner, in making several laps around the seafront Paseo de la Princesa at the base of his home, La Fortaleza.

If you don't mind heading out into the island a bit from your base in Old San Juan, you might opt for a run through the palm trees of the Parque Central, near Calle Cerra and Route 2 in Santurce. Condado's Ashford Avenue is a busy site for morning runners as well.

SCUBA DIVING   In San Juan, the best outfitter is **Caribe Aquatic Adventures,** P.O. Box 9024278, San Juan Station, San Juan, PR 00902 (© **787/281-8858**), which operates a dive shop in the rear lobby of the Normandie Hotel that's open daily from 8am to 4pm. The company offers diving certification from both PADI and NAUI as part of 40-hour courses priced at $465 each. A resort course for first-time divers costs $135. Also offered are local daily dives in the waters close to San Juan, as well as the option of traveling farther afield into waters near the reefs of Puerto Rico's eastern shore. If time permits, we recommend a full-day dive experience; if time is limited, try one of the many worthy dive sites that lie closer to San Juan and can be experienced in a half-day.

SNORKELING   Snorkeling is better in the outlying portions of the island than in overcrowded San Juan. But if you don't have time to explore greater Puerto Rico, you'll find that most of the popular beaches, such as Luquillo and Isla Verde, have pretty good visibility and kiosks that rent equipment. Snorkeling equipment generally rents for $15. If you're on your own in the San Juan area, one of the best places is the San Juan Bay marina near the Caribe Hilton.

Watersports desks at the big San Juan hotels at Isla Verde and Condado can generally make arrangements for instruction and equipment rental, and can also lead you to the best places for snorkeling, depending on where you are in the sprawling metropolis. If

---

Tips Swimmers, Beware

You have to pick your spots carefully if you want to swim
along Condado Beach. The waters along the Condado Plaza
Hotel are calmer than in other areas because of a coral break-
water. The beach near the Marriott is not good for swimming
because of rocks and an undertow.

---

your hotel doesn't offer such services, you can contact **Caribe
Aquatic Adventures** (see "Scuba Diving," above), which caters to
both snorkelers and scuba divers. You can also rent equipment from
Caribbean School of Aquatics, Taft 1, Suite 10F, San Juan (© 787/
728-6606).

SPAS & FITNESS CENTERS   If a spa figures into your holiday
plans, the grandest and largest such facility in San Juan is found at
Ritz-Carlton San Juan Hotel, Spa & Casino ⊕, Av. de los Gobernadores 6961, no. 187, Isla Verde (© 787/253-1700). You get it all
here: the luxury life, with state-of-the-art massages, body wraps and
scrubs, facials, manicures, pedicures, and a salon guaranteed to
make you look like a movie star. In an elegant marble-and-stone setting, there are 11 rooms for pampering, including hydrotherapy and
treatments custom-tailored for individual needs. The spa also features a 7,200-square-foot (669-sq.-m) outdoor swimming pool.

The Ritz-Carlton facility is the only spa in the Caribbean to offer
the exotic and ritualistic treatments known to spa lovers around the
world as the **Balinese Massage** and the **Javanese Lulur.** The fragrant
Balinese Massage uses compression, skin-rolling, wringing, and per-
cussion and thumb-walking to "de-stress" the most uptight guests.
The Lulur originated centuries ago in the royal palaces of Central
Java as part of a ritual for royal brides-to-be. The Lulur was performed daily to beautify, soften, and "sweeten" the bride's skin.
Today women and men alike enjoy it.

The only resort spa that challenges the Ritz-Carlton is the run-
ner-up, the newly launched Olas Spa at the **Carib Hilton,** Calle Los
Rosales (© 787/721-0303). The spa offers everything from traditional massages to more exotic body and water therapies, using such
products as honey, cucumber, sea salts, seaweed, or mud baths. You
can choose your delight among the massages, including one called
"Rising Sun," a traditional Japanese form of massage called shiatsu
that uses pressure applied with hands, elbows, and knees on specific

body points. Among body wraps is one known as Firm Away, a super-firming, brown-and-green-algae body cocoon therapy for a soft, toned, and smooth skin.

The Hilton Spa has the town's best program for hair treatments, including some for thinning hair and "tired perm." It also has a state-of-the-art fitness center with Universal and Nautilus weight machines, aerobics and yoga classes, treadmills, aerobicycles, loofah body polishes, and facials.

After the extravaganza of these two spas, it's a bit of a comedown at the other leading resorts. **The Plaza Spa** at the Condado Plaza Hotel & Casino, 999 Ashford Ave. (✆ **787/721-1000**), features Universal weight-training machines, video exercycles, a sauna, whirlpools, and a spa program of facials and massage. We'd recommend this mainly for people who want only minor spa or fitness-center facilities during their stay, and not for those who want to make a spa the number-one goal of their stay in San Juan.

El San Juan Hotel & Casino, Av. Isla Verde 6063 (✆ **787/791-1000**), offers a stunning panoramic view of San Juan that almost competes with the facilities. You'll find full amenities, including fitness evaluations, supervised weight-loss programs, aerobics classes, a sauna, a steam room, and luxury massages. A daily fee for individual services is assessed if you want special treatment or care.

If your hotel doesn't have a gym or health club of its own, consider working the kinks out of your muscles at **International Fitness** ✦, 1131 Ashford Ave. Condado (✆ **787/721-0717**). It's air-conditioned, well-equipped, and popular with residents of the surrounding high-rent district. Entrance costs $10 per visit, $35 for 5 days, or $45 for a week. Hours are Monday through Thursday from 5am to 10pm, Friday from 5am to 9pm, Saturday from 9am to 7pm, and Sunday 10am to 3pm.

TENNIS   Most of the big resorts have their own tennis courts for the use of guests. There are 12 public courts, lighted at night, at **San Juan Central Municipal Park,** at Calle Cerra (exit on Rte. 2; ✆ **787/722-1646**), open Monday through Thursday 7am to 10pm, Friday 7am to 9pm, and Saturday and Sunday 7am to 6pm. Fees are $3 per hour from 7am to 6pm, and $4 per hour from 6 to 10pm.

WINDSURFING   The most savvy windsurfing advice and equipment rental is available at **Velauno,** Calle Loíza 2430, Punta Las Marías in San Juan (✆ **787/728-8716**). A 1-day rental costs $75, 3 days $150, and 1 week $225. This is the second-biggest full-service headquarters for windsurfing in the United States. The staff here will guide you to the best windsurfing, which is likely to be the Punta Las Marías in the Greater San Juan metropolitan area. Other spots on the island for windsurfing include Santa Isabel, Guánica, and La Parguera in the south; Jobos and Shacks in the northwest, and the island of Culebra off the eastern coast.

3 Shopping

Because Puerto Rico is a U.S. commonwealth, U.S. citizens don't pay duty on items brought back to the mainland. And you can still find great bargains in Puerto Rico, where the competition among shopkeepers is fierce. Even though the U.S. Virgin Islands are duty-free, you can often find far lower prices on many items in San Juan than on St. Thomas.

The streets of Old Town, such as Calle San Francisco and Calle del Cristo, are the major venues for shopping. Malls in San Juan are generally open Monday through Saturday from 9am to 9pm, Sunday from 11am to 5pm. Regular stores in town are usually open Monday through Saturday from 9am to 6pm. In Old San Juan, many stores are open on Sunday, too.

Native handicrafts can be good buys, including needlework, straw work, ceramics, hammocks, and papier-mâché fruits and vegetables, as well as paintings and sculptures by Puerto Rican artists. Among these, the carved wooden religious idols known as *santos* (saints) have been called Puerto Rico's greatest contribution to the plastic arts and are sought by collectors. For the best selection of *santos,* head for Galería Botello (see "Art," below), Olé (p. 127), or Puerto Rican Arts & Crafts (p. 127).

Puerto Rico's biggest and most up-to-date shopping mall is **Plaza Las Américas,** in the financial district of Hato Rey, right off the Las Américas Expressway. This complex, with its fountains and modern architecture, has more than 200 mostly upscale shops. The variety of goods and prices is roughly comparable to that of large stateside malls.

Unless otherwise specified, the following stores can be reached via the Old Town Trolley.

ART

Butterfly People   Butterfly People is a gallery and cafe in a handsomely restored building in Old San Juan. Butterflies, sold here in artfully arranged boxes, range from $20 for a single mounting to thousands of dollars for whole-wall murals. The butterflies are preserved and will last forever. The dimensional artwork is sold in limited editions and can be shipped worldwide. Most of these butterflies come from farms around the world, some of the most beautiful hailing from Indonesia, Malaysia, and New Guinea. Tucked away within the same premises is **Malula Antiques.** Specializing in tribal art from the Moroccan sub-Sahara and Syria, it contains a sometimes-startling collection of primitive and timeless crafts and accessories. Calle Cruz 257. ℭ 787/723-2432.

The Canvas Gallery   This is one of the most interesting art galleries we've seen in San Juan, with the kinds of paintings you'd expect at a major gallery in Madrid or New York, and very few hints of anything vaguely associated with the tourist trade. Paintings on display here are sometimes moved upstairs to add to the nightlife ambience in Olio (p. 133), a lounge under the same management. Paintings at the Canvas Gallery begin at $1,800. Recinto Sur 305. ℭ 787/977-1080.

Galería Botello   A contemporary Latin American art gallery, Galería Botello is a living tribute to the late Angel Botello, one of Puerto Rico's most outstanding artists. Born after the Spanish Civil War in a small village in Galicia, Spain, he fled to the Caribbean and spent 12 years in Haiti. His paintings and bronze sculptures, evocative of his colorful background, are done in a style uniquely his own. This *galería* is his former colonial mansion home, which he restored himself. Today it displays his paintings and sculptures, showcases the works of many outstanding local artists, and offers a large collection of Puerto Rican antique *santos.* Calle del Cristo 208. ℭ 787/723-9987.

Sun 'n Sand   This is the best store in San Juan for Haitian art and artifacts. Its walls are covered with framed versions of primitive Haitian landscapes, portraits, crowd scenes, and whimsical visions of jungles where lions, tigers, parrots, and herons take on quasi-human personalities and forms. Most paintings range from $35 to $350, although you can usually bargain them down a bit. Look for the brightly painted wall hangings crafted from sheets of metal. Also look for satirical metal wall hangings, brightly painted, representing the *tap-taps* (battered public minivans and buses) of Port-au-Prince. They make amusing and whimsical souvenirs of a trip to the Caribbean. Calle Fortaleza 152. ℭ 787/722-1135.

BOOKS

Bell, Book & Candle   For travel guides, maps, and beach-reading material, head here. It is a large, general-interest bookstore that carries fiction and classics in both Spanish and English, plus a huge selection of postcards. Av. José de Diego 102, Santurce. ✆ **787/728-5000.** Bus: A5.

Librería Cronopios   This is the leading choice in the Old Town, with the largest selection of titles. It sells a number of books on Puerto Rican culture, as well as good maps of the island. Calle San José 255. ✆ **787/724-1815.**

CARNIVAL MASKS

La Calle   Every Puerto Rican knows that the best, and cheapest, place to buy brightly painted carnival masks *(caretas)* is in Ponce, where the tradition of making them from papier-mâché originated. But if you can't spare the time for a side excursion to Ponce, this store in Old San Juan stocks one of the most varied inventories of *caretas* in the Puerto Rican capital. Depending on their size and composition (some include coconut shells, gourds, and flashy metal trim), they range from $10 to $2,500 each. Side-by-side with the pagan-inspired masks, you'll find a well-chosen selection of paintings by talented local artists, priced from $250 to $2,800 each. Calle Fortaleza 105. ✆ **787/725-1306.**

CLOTHING & BEACHWEAR

Mrs. and Miss Boutique   The most visible article available within this shop is "the magic dress," for $150. Crafted in Morocco of a silky-looking blend of rayon and cotton, it comes in 10 different colors or patterns and can be worn 11 different ways. (A saleswoman will show you how.) The shop also stocks sarongs for $9 and long dresses, sometimes from Indonesia, that begin at only $25. Calle Fortaleza 154. ✆ **787/724-8571.**

Nono Maldonado   Named after its owner, a Puerto Rico–born designer who worked for many years as the fashion editor of *Esquire* magazine, this is one of the most fashionable and upscale haberdasheries in the Caribbean. Selling both men's and women's clothing, it contains everything from socks to dinner jackets, as well as ready-to-wear versions of Maldonado's twice-a-year collections. Both ready-to-wear and couture are available here. 1112 Ashford Ave. ✆ **787/721-0456.** Bus: A7.

Polo Ralph Lauren Factory Store *Value*   It's as stylish and carefully orchestrated as anything you'd expect from one of North

Fun Fact   Grotesque Masks

The most popular of all Puerto Rican crafts are the frightening *caretas*—papier-mâché masks worn at island carnivals. Tangles of menacing horns, fang-toothed leering expressions, and bulging eyes of these half-demon, half-animal creations send children running and screaming to their parents. At carnival time, they are worn by costumed revelers called *vegigantes*. *Vegigantes* often wear bat-winged jumpsuits and roam the streets either individually or in groups.

The origins of these masks and carnivals may go back to medieval Spain and/or tribal Africa. A processional tradition in Spain, dating from the early 17th century, was intended to terrify sinners with marching devils in the hope that they would return to church. Cervantes described it briefly in *Don Quixote*. Puerto Rico blended this Spanish procession with the masked tradition brought by slaves from Africa. Some historians believe that the Taínos were also accomplished mask makers, which would make this a very ancient tradition indeed.

The predominant traditional mask colors were black, red, and yellow, all symbols of hellfire and damnation. Today, pastels are more likely to be used. Each *vegigante* sports at least two or three horns, although some masks have hundreds of horns, in all shapes and sizes. Mask making in Ponce, the major center for this craft, and in Loíza Aldea, a palm-fringed town on the island's northeastern coast, has since led to a renaissance of Puerto Rican folk art.

The premier store selling these masks is **La Calle** (p. 124). Masks can be seen in action at the three big masquerade carnivals on the island: the Ponce Festival in February, the Festival of Loíza Aldea in July, and the Día de las Máscaras at Hatillo in December.

America's leading clothiers. Even better, its prices are often 35% to 40% less than in retail stores on the U.S. mainland. You can find even greater discounts on irregular or slightly damaged garments, but inspect them carefully before buying. The store occupies two floors of a pair of colonial buildings, with one upstairs room devoted to home furnishings. Calle del Cristo 201. ℭ 787/722-2136.

W. H. Smith   This outlet sells mostly women's clothing, everything from bathing suits and beach attire to jogging suits. For men, there are shorts, bathing suits, and jogging suits. There's also a good selection of books and maps. In the Condado Plaza Hotel, 999 Ashford Ave. ℭ **787/721-1000,** ext. 2094.

COFFEE & SPICES

Spicy Caribbee   This shop has the best selection of Puerto Rican coffee, which is gaining an increasingly good reputation among aficionados. Alto Grande is the grandest brand. Other favorite brands of Puerto Rican coffee are Café Crema, Café Rico, Rioja, and Yaucono—in that order. The shop also has Old Town's best array of hot spicy sauces of the Caribbean. Calle Cristo 154. ℭ **787/725-4690.**

DEPARTMENT STORES

Marshalls   This store, part of the U.S. discount chain, is one of our favorite department stores in the whole Caribbean. Thousands of Sanjuaneros also consider it their favorite shopping expedition as well. A few dedicated born-to-shop advocates pop in virtually every day to see what new items have gone on sale. At Plaza de Armas, across from the City Hall, expect to see a massive array—at cut-rate prices—of designer clothes, housewares, home furnishings, and shoes, plus a variety of other merchandise. Calle Rafael Cordero 154. ℭ **787/722-3020.**

GIFTS & HANDICRAFTS

Atmosphere   Inventory within this exotic-looking gift-and-housewares store derives from countries with rich traditions in handicrafts. That includes Indonesia (especially Bali), Turkey, India, Mexico, Peru, and Puerto Rico. Come here with ideas about how to decorate, say, an outdoor veranda for warm-weather hangouts. Calle del Cristo 205. ℭ **787/977-2225.**

Bared & Sons *(Value)*   Now in its fourth decade, this is the main outlet of a chain of at least 20 upper-bracket jewelry stores in Puerto Rico. It has a worthy inventory of gemstones, gold, diamonds, and wristwatches on the street level, which does a thriving business with cruise-ship passengers. But the real value of this store lies one floor up, where a monumental collection of porcelain and crystal is on display in claustrophobic proximity. It's a great source for hard-to-get and discontinued patterns (priced at around 20% less than at equivalent stateside outlets) from Christofle, Royal Doulton, Wedgwood, Limoges, Royal Copenhagen, Lalique, Lladró, Herend, Baccarat, and Daum. San Justo 206 (at the corner of Calle Fortaleza). ✆ 787/724-4811.

Bóveda   This long, narrow space is crammed with exotic jewelry, clothing, greeting cards with images of life in Puerto Rico, some 100 handmade lamps, antiques, Mexican punched tin and glass, and Art Nouveau reproductions, among other items. Calle del Cristo 209. ✆ 787/725-0263.

Centro Nacional de Artes Populares y Artesanías   This store, now located at the Museum of Raices Africanas, a superb repository of native crafts, sells crafts of high-quality work. Centro Nacional scans the islands for artisans who still practice time-treasured crafts and do so with considerable skill. The prices aren't cheap, but the work merits the tab. Casa de los Contrafuertes, Plaza San José. ✆ 787/721-6866.

El Alcázar   Here you can find decorative items from almost any part of the world, maybe even remote Tibet. It's like wandering into your grandfather's attic—assuming that he was an ancient mariner with a taste for the exotic. The treasure trove of merchandise is always changing, so drop in for a surprise. Calle San José 103. ✆ 787/723-1229.

Olé   Browsing this store is a learning experience. Even the standard Panama hat takes on new dimensions. Woven from fine-textured *paja* grass and priced from $20 to $1,000, depending on the density of the weave, the hats are all created the same size, then blocked—by an employee on-site—to fit the shape of your head. Dig into this store's diverse inventory to discover a wealth of treasures— hand-beaten Chilean silver, Peruvian Christmas ornaments, Puerto Rican *santos*—almost all from Puerto Rico or Latin America. Calle Fortaleza 105. ✆ 787/724-2445.

Puerto Rican Arts & Crafts   Set in a 200-year-old colonial building, this unique store is one of the premier outlets on the island for authentic artifacts. Of particular interest are papier-mâché carnival masks from Ponce, whose grotesque and colorful features were originally conceived to chase away evil spirits. Taíno designs inspired by ancient petroglyphs are incorporated into most of the sterling silver jewelry sold here. There's an art gallery in back, with silk-screened serigraphs by local artists. The outlet has a gourmet Puerto Rican food section with items like coffee, rum, and hot sauces for sale. A related specialty of this well-respected store involves the exhibition and sale of modern replicas of the Spanish colonial tradition of *santos,* which are carved and sometimes polychromed representations of the Catholic saints and the infant Jesus. Priced from $45 to $1,100 each and laboriously carved by artisans in private studios around the island, they're easy to pack in a suitcase because the largest one measures only a foot (.3m) from halo to toe. Calle Fortaleza 204. ✆ 787/725-5596.

Xian Imports   Set within a jumbled, slightly claustrophobic setting, you'll discover porcelain, sculptures, paintings, and Chinese furniture, much of it antique. Island decorators favor this spot as a source for unusual art objects. Calle de la Cruz 153. ✆ 787/723-2214.

JEWELRY

Barrachina's   The birthplace, in 1963, of the piña colada (an honor co-claimed by the staff at the Caribe Hilton), Barrachina's is a favorite of cruise-ship passengers. It offers one of the largest selections of jewelry, perfume, cigars, and gifts in San Juan. There's a patio for drinks where you can order (what else?) a piña colada. There is also a Bacardi rum outlet (bottles cost less than stateside but cost the same as at the Bacardi distillery), a costume jewelry department, a gift shop, and a section for authentic silver jewelry, plus a restaurant. Calle Fortaleza 104 (between calles del Cristo and San José). ✆ 787/725-7912.

Emerald Isles   This jewelry boutique in the Old Town is smaller than other entities that specialize in colored gemstones, but because of its much lower overheads, its prices can sometimes be more reasonable. It specializes in Colombian emeralds, set into silver or gold settings already, or waiting for you to select one. But as long as you're in the shop, look also at the unusual inventories of contemporary reproductions of pre-Columbian Aztec jewelry, some of it gold-plated and richly enameled. Many of these pieces sell for around $50 each, and some of them are genuinely intriguing. Calle Fortaleza 105. ✆ 787/977-3769.

Joseph Manchini   This shop displays the works of its namesake, the shop's owner. He conceives almost anything you'd want in gold, silver, and bronze. Some of Old Town's most imaginative rings, bracelets, and chains are displayed here. If you don't like what's on sale, you can design your own jewelry, including pieces made from sapphires, emeralds, and rubies. Calle Fortaleza 101. ✆ 787/722-7698.

Joyería Riviera   This emporium of 18-karat gold and diamonds is the island's leading jeweler. Adjacent to Plaza de Armas, the shop has an impeccable reputation. Its owner, Julio Abislaiman, stocks his store from such diamond centers as Antwerp, Tel Aviv, and New York. This is the major distributor of Rolex watches in Puerto Rico. Prices in the store range from $150 into the tens of thousands of dollars—at these prices, it's a good thing you can get "whatever you want," according to the owner. Calle Fortaleza 257. ℂ **787/725-4000**.

Piercing Pagoda   There's nothing Puerto Rican or glamorous about this branch of a large U.S. chain. But if you're in the market for a gold or silver chain, or perhaps a pendant or set of earrings, the sales here could be worth a detour. Be alert that some displays feature 10-karat gold rather than the more preferable, and expensive, 14- or 18-karat. F. D. Roosevelt Ave. ℂ **787/706-0634**.

LACE & LINENS

Linen House   This unpretentious store specializes in table linens, bed linens, and lace, and has the island's best selection. Some of the most delicate pieces are expensive, but most are moderate in price. Inventories include embroidered shower curtains that sell for around $35 each, and lace doilies, bun warmers, place mats, and tablecloths that seamstresses took weeks to complete. Some astonishingly lovely items are available for as little as $30. The aluminum/pewter serving dishes have beautiful Spanish colonial designs. Prices here are sometimes 40% lower than those on the North American mainland. Calle Fortaleza 250. ℂ **787/721-4219**.

LEATHER & EQUESTRIAN ACCESSORIES

Lalin Leather Shop   Although it lies in an out-of-the-way suburb (Puerto Nuevo), about 2 miles (3.2km) south of San Juan, this is the best and most comprehensive cowboy and equestrian outfitter in Puerto Rico, probably in the entire Caribbean. Here you'll find all manner of boots, cowboy hats, and accessories. More important, however, is the wide array of saddles and bridles, some from Colombia, some from Puerto Rico, priced from a cost-conscious $159 to as much as $3,100. Even the highest-priced items cost a lot less than their U.S. mainland equivalents, so if you happen to have a horse or pony on the U.S. mainland, a visit here might be worth your while. If you decide to make the rather inconvenient pilgrimage, you won't be alone. Regular clients come from as far away as Iceland, the Bahamas, and New York. Everything can be shipped. Av. Piñero 1617, Puerto Nuevo. ℂ **787/781-5305**.

MALLS

Belz Factory Outlet World The largest mall of its kind in Puerto Rico, and the Caribbean as well, opened in 2001 in Canóvanas, east of San Juan en route to El Yunque. Totally enclosed and air-conditioned, it re-creates the experience of strolling through the streets of Old San Juan, sans the traffic and heat. Five interconnected buildings comprise the mall, with dozens of stores from Nike to Gap, from Dockers to Levis to Maidenform, from Samsonite to Guess, and from Papaya to Geoffrey Beene. Av. de los Gobernadores (State Rd.) 18400, no. 3, Barrio Pueblo, Canóvanas. ✆ **787/256-7040**.

MARKETS

Plaza del Mercado de Santurce If you'd like an old-fashioned Puerto Rican market, something likely to be found in a small South American country, visit this offbeat curiosity. In a West Indian structure, the central market is filled with "botanicas" hawking everything from medicinal herbs to Puerto Rican bay rum. Here is your best chance to pick up some patchouli roots. What are they used for? In religious observances and to kill unruly cockroaches. Some little cantinas here offer very typical Puerto Rican dishes, including roast pork, and you can also order the best mango-banana shakes on the island. Calle Dos Hermanos at Calle Capitol, Santurce. ✆ **787/723-8022**. Bus: B5.

4 San Juan After Dark

As in a Spanish city, nightlife begins very late, especially on Friday and Saturday nights. Hang out until the late, late afternoon on the beach, have dinner around 8pm (9 would be even more fashionable), and then the night is yours. The true party animal will rock until the broad daylight.

THE PERFORMING ARTS

Centro de Bellas Artes In the heart of Santurce, the Performing Arts Center is a 6-minute taxi ride from most of the Condado hotels. It contains the Festival Hall, Drama Hall, and the Experimental Theater. Some of the events here will be of interest only to Spanish speakers; others attract an international audience. Av. Ponce de León 22. ✆ **787/724-4747**, or 787/725-7334 for the ticket agent. Tickets $40–$200; 50% discounts for seniors. Bus: 1.

Teatro Tapía Standing across from Plaza de Colón and built about 1832, this is one of the oldest theaters in the Western Hemisphere (see "Historic Sights," earlier in this chapter). Productions, some musical, are staged throughout the year and include drama, dances, and cultural events. You'll have to call the box office (Mon–Fri 9am–6pm) for specific information. Av. Ponce de León. ✆ 787/721-0180. Tickets $20–$30, depending on the show. Bus: B8 or B21.

THE CLUB & MUSIC SCENE

Babylon Modeled after an artist's rendition of the once-notorious city in Mesopotamia, this nightclub is designed in the form of a circle, with a central dance floor and a wraparound balcony where onlookers and voyeurs—a 25-to-45-year-old age group—can observe the activities on the floor below. As one patron put it, "Here's where gringos can shake their bon-bons with San Juan's old guard." Equipped with one of the best sound systems in the Caribbean, its location within the most exciting hotel in San Juan allows guests the chance to visit the hotel's bars, its intricately decorated lobby, and its casino en route. Open Thursday through Saturday from 10pm until 3am. In El San Juan Hotel & Casino, Av. Isla Verde 6063, Isla Verde. ✆ 787/791-1000. Cover $15–$25, free for guests of El San Juan Hotel. Bus: A5.

Club Laser Set in the heart of the Old Town, this disco is especially crowded when cruise ships pull into town. Once inside, you can wander over the three floors of its historic premises, listening to whatever music happens to be hot in New York at the time, with lots of additional Latino merengue and salsa thrown in as well. Depending on the night, the age of the crowd varies, but in general it's the 20s, 30s, and even 40s set. The club is usually open Friday through Sunday from 10pm until 5am. Calle del Cruz 251 (near the corner of Calle Fortaleza). ✆ 787/725-7581. Cover $10–$15 (no cover for women before midnight on Sat). Bus: Old Town Trolley.

Hacienda Country Club This glitzy scene unfolds after a 25-minute drive out of San Juan on the signposted road to Caguas. You can't miss the club along the highway. Live musicians entertain here in an alfresco setting surrounded by mountains. A mainly 20-to-30-year-old crowd is attracted to this club, which is evocative of a club where Ricky Ricardo might have appeared in the 1950s. The cover depends on the entertainment being offered. Sometimes some of the hottest Latin groups in the Caribbean appear here. Hours and days vary. Caguas. ✆ 787/747-9692. Cover $15–$30.

Houlihan's This is a casual hangout, a member of the U.S. chain of restaurants, and a good place to hear merengue, Spanish rock music, and salsa. Houlihan's also serves reasonably priced food, with main courses costing $8 to $23. Open Sunday through Thursday 11:30am to 10pm, and Friday through Saturday 11:30am to midnight. Galería Paseos Mall, Gran Bulevar Paseos 100. ✆ 787/723-8600.

Lupi's You can hear some of the best Spanish rock at this Mexican pub and restaurant. It is a current hot spot, with typical South of the Border decoration and such familiar dishes as fajitas, nachos, and burritos. A wide range of people of all ages are attracted to the place, although after 10pm patrons in their 20s and 30s predominate. Live rock groups perform after 11pm. In addition to the nightly rock bands, karaoke is played on Friday. Open daily 11am to 2am. Rte. 187 Km 1.3, Isla Verde. ✆ 787/253-1664. Bus: A5.

Rumba This club is small and cramped, but so photogenically hip that it was selected as the site for the filming of many of the crowd scenes within *Dirty Dancing: Havana Nights.* Set immediately adjacent to the also-recommended restaurant Barú, with which it's not associated, it's known within San Juan's underground nightlife circuit as one of the places to hang. Expect beautiful people and a sense of cutting-edge Hispanic hip. Open Tuesday through Sunday 9pm to 4am. Calle San Sebastián 152. ✆ 787/725-4407. Cover $15. Bus: M2, M3, or A5.

THE BAR SCENE

Unless otherwise stated, there is no cover charge at the following bars.

Cigar Bar The Palm Court Lobby at the elegant El San Juan boasts an impressive cigar bar, with a magnificent repository of the finest stogies in the world. Although the bar is generally filled with visitors, some of San Juan's most fashionable men—and women, too—can be seen puffing away in this chic rendezvous while sipping cognac. Open daily 6pm to 3am. El San Juan Hotel & Casino, Av. Isla Verde 6063, Isla Verde. ✆ 787/791-1000. Bus: A5.

El Patio de Sam Except for the juicy burgers, we're not so keen on the food served here anymore (and neither are our readers), but we still like to visit Old Town's best-known watering hole, one of the most popular late-night joints with a good selection of beers. Live entertainment is presented here Monday through Saturday. This is a fun joint—that is, if you dine somewhere else before coming here. Open daily noon to 1am. Calle San Sebastián 102. ✆ 787/723-1149. Bus: Old Town Trolley.

Fiesta Bar   This bar lures a healthy mixture of local residents and hotel guests, usually the post-35 set. The margaritas are appropriately salty, the rhythms are hot and Latin, and the free admission usually helps you forget any losses you might have suffered in the nearby casinos. Thursday through Sunday nights, you can hear some of the best salsa and merengue music in San Juan here. Open daily from noon to 4am. In the Condado Plaza Hotel & Casino, 999 Ashford Ave. ✆ 787/721-1000. Bus: B21 or A5.

Kudeta 🏠🏠   The hottest bar in San Juan today is this three-floor town house, which jumps at midnight Thursday through Saturday in Old Town. With your honey or your hunk on your arm, head for the open-air third floor where bottle service is required. This is where the young, the restless, and the beautiful congregate. Once inside the door downstairs, you scale a tunnel-like stairway heading for the action. That action is fueled by the most "explosive martinis" in town. Dare you try something called "Chemical Warfare?" We actually prefer the Library on the second floor, with its techno DJ. Instead of books, this library has bottles on its shelves. Hours of closing vary, but expect to see dawn's early light. Calle Fortaleza 314. ✆ 787/721-3548. Cover $10. Bus: Old Town Trolley.

María's   Forget the tacky decorations. This is the town's most enduring bar, a favorite local hangout and a prime target for Old Town visitors seeking Mexican food and sangria. The atmosphere is fun, and the tropical drinks include piña coladas and frosts made of banana, orange, and strawberry, as well as the Puerto Rican beer Medalla. Open daily 10:30am to 3am (closes at 4am Fri–Sat). Calle del Cristo 204. ✆ 787/721-1678. Bus: Old Town Trolley.

Olio   Set on the upper floor of an antiques building near the cruise-ship docks, this is the most trendy, most appealing, and most hip bar in San Juan. Because there's no area that's specifically designated inside as a dance floor, it defines itself as a "lounge." By that, owner Jancy Rodriguez defines his "living room" as a labyrinth of artfully minimalist rooms with comfortable seating, a changing array of dramatic oil paintings *(olio)* on loan from the art gallery (Canvas) downstairs, and a mixture of bright lights and shadow that makes anyone look years younger. Tucked into an alcove, there's a sushi bar to alleviate those ultra-late-night hunger pangs, and onyx bartops that are lit from beneath to create zebra-striped but tawny-colored patterns. The music is trance and house music that's either very loud or so loud that it's almost unbearable, but if you can overlook that (rather silly) quirk, you can have a lot of fun at this place. Although the place opens, at least theoretically, at 10pm, it doesn't begin to jump till after midnight. Open nightly until 5am. Recinto Sur 305. ℂ 787/977-1082. Cover $10 for men; women enter free. Bus: Old Town Trolley.

Palm Court   This is the most beautiful bar on the island—perhaps in the entire Caribbean. Most of the patrons are hotel guests, but well-heeled locals make up at least a quarter of the business at this fashionable rendezvous. Set in an oval wrapped around a sunken bar area, amid marble and burnished mahogany, it offers a view of one of the world's largest chandeliers. After 7pm Monday through Saturday, live music, often salsa and merengue, emanates from an adjoining room (El Chico Bar). Open daily 6pm to 3am. In El San Juan Hotel & Casino, Av. Isla Verde 6063, Isla Verde. ℂ **787/791-1000.** Bus: A5.

Shannon's Irish Pub   Ireland and its ales meet the tropics at this pub with a Latin accent. A sports bar with TV monitors and high-energy rock 'n' roll, it's the regular watering hole of many university students. There's live music Wednesday through Sunday—everything from rock to jazz to Latin. There are pool tables, and a simple cafe serves inexpensive lunches Monday to Friday. A $3 cover charge is sometimes imposed for a special live performance. Open daily 11:30am to 1am (closes at 2:30am Fri–Sat). Calle Bori 496, Río Piedras. ℂ **787/281-8466.**

Wet Bar/Liquid   Two chic new drinking spots operate out of San Juan's finest boutique hotel, The Water Club. The main bar, Liquid, is a large area downstairs at the hotel. It's quickly become one of San Juan's most fashionable hangouts for both chic locals and a medley of visitors in all age groups. With its glass walls overlooking the ocean, it features Latino music. The best bar for watching the sun set over San Juan is the Wet Bar on the 11th floor, featuring jazz music and the Caribbean's only rooftop fireplace for those nippy nights in winter when you want to drink outside. The sensuous decor here includes striped zebrawood stools, futons, pillowy sofas, and hand-carved side tables. The walls feature Indonesian carved teak panels. Wet Bar open Thursday through Saturday 7pm to 1am; Liquid Bar 6pm to 1am. In the San Juan Water and Beach Club Hotel, Calle Tartak 2. ℂ **787/728-3666.** Bus: A5.

Zabó   Among San Juan's young, restless, and unattached, this place is more famous for its bar than its restaurant. The bar is divided into two separate spaces, the more popular being a cottage-like outbuilding on the grounds of a turn-of-the-20th-century villa.

There's lots of charm here, from the attractive crowd, stiff drinks such as Cosmopolitans and martinis, and live music every Wednesday and Thursday night 8 to 11:45pm. Some nights, depending on the operating hours of the restaurant, the bar crowd moves into the restaurant's entrance vestibule, a cozy spot for mingling. Open Tuesday and Wednesday 6 to 10pm, Thursday 6 to 11pm, and Friday and Saturday 7 to 11pm. Calle Candina 14 (entrance is via an alleyway on Ashford Ave.). ✆ **787/725-9494.** Bus: 21.

HOT NIGHTS IN GAY SAN JUAN

Straight folks are generally welcome in each of these gay venues, and many local couples show up for the hot music and dancing. Local straight boys who show up to cause trouble are generally ushered out quickly. Unless otherwise stated, there is no cover.

Beach Bar This is the site of a hugely popular Sunday-afternoon gathering, which gets really crowded beginning around 4pm and stretches into the wee hours. There's an open-air bar protected from rain by a sloping rooftop, and a space atop the sea wall with a panoramic view of the Condado beachfront. Drag shows on Sunday take place on the terrace. Open daily 11am to 1am or later. On the ground floor of the Atlantic Beach Hotel, Calle Vendig 1. ✆ **787/721-6900.** Bus: B21.

Cups Set in a Latino tavern, this place is valued as the only place in San Juan that caters almost exclusively to lesbians. Men of any sexual persuasion aren't particularly welcome. The scene reminds many lesbians of a tropical version of one of the bars they left behind at home. Entertainment such as live music or cabaret is presented Wednesday at 9pm and Friday at 10pm. Open Wednesday through Saturday 7pm to 4am. Calle San Mateo 1708, Santurce. ✆ **787/268-3570.**

Eros This two-level nightclub caters exclusively to the city's growing gay population. Patterned after the dance emporiums of New York, but on a smaller scale, the club has cutting-edge music and bathrooms that are among the most creative in the world. Here, wall murals present fantasy-charged, eroticized versions of ancient Greek and Roman gods. Regrettably, only 1 night a week (Wed) is devoted to Latin music; on other nights, the music is equivalent to what you'd find in the gay discos of either Los Angeles or New York City. Open Wednesday through Saturday 10pm to 5am. Av. Ponce de León 1257, Santurce. ✆ **787/722-1131.** Cover $5–$10. Bus: 1.

Junior's Bar *Finds* Lying on a secluded and poorly lighted street in Santurce, about a 5-block walk from the more famous gay mecca

Eros (see above), Junior's Bar seems little-known to most visitors. It's mainly a place where resident gays go to hang out, talk to each other, and order drinks. Most of the music comes from the jukebox. Drag queens (Sat–Sun) and male strippers (Mon–Fri) are a standard feature. There is no cover, but you are required to fulfill a two-drink minimum. Open daily from 8pm until 5am. Av. Condado 613 (off Av. Ponce de León), Santurce. ✆ **787/723-9477.** Bus: B21.

Teatro   Originally built in the early 1960s as a movie theater, and known to many locals as Asylum, this is one of the best-known of San Juan's gay and lesbian discos. With laser beams, artful lighting, a warren of stairs and hallways, and a panoramic balcony (site of a bar outfitted, Moroccan-style, like something you'd have expected in the Casbah), it tries to evoke the heady days of New York's Studio 54, sometimes with mixed results. Crowds here are young and—at least at first glance—notoriously fickle, sometimes staying away in droves until the impossibly late hipster-ish hour of 1am. Despite a highly visible police presence, in squad cars with klieg lights flashing, that likes to hang out in front of this place, we nonetheless highly recommend taxiing to and from a point directly in front during the impossibly late hours when it's jumping. Dance music presented inside, much to the regret of anyone who loves Latin dance music, is relentlessly committed to reggae, house, hip-hop, and garage. Open Thursday and Sunday 9pm to 6am, Friday 9:30pm to 6am, Saturday 10pm to 7am. Av. Ponce de León 1420. ✆ **787/722-1130.** Cover charge after 11:30pm $6–$25 per person, depending on the night, the crowd, and whatever celebrity DJ or live band is appearing at the time.

Tía María's Liquor Store   This is not a liquor store, but a bar that caters to both locals and visitors. As one habitué informed us, "During the day, all the local boys claim they're straight. But stick around until after midnight." The place has a very welcoming and unpretentious attitude, attracting both men and women. Don't come here for entertainment, but to hang out with the locals. Open Monday through Thursday and Sunday 11am to midnight, Friday and Saturday 11am to 2am. Av. José de Diego 326 (near the corner of Av. Ponce de León), Santurce. ✆ **787/724-4011.** Bus: B1.

CASINOS

Many visitors come to Puerto Rico on package deals and stay at one of the posh hotels at the Condado or Isla Verde just to gamble.

Nearly all the large hotels in San Juan/Condado/Isla Verde offer casinos, and there are other large casinos at some of the bigger resorts outside the metropolitan area. The atmosphere in the casinos is casual, but still you shouldn't show up in bathing suits or shorts. Most of the casinos open around noon and close at 2, 3, or 4am. Guest patrons must be at least 18 years old to enter.

The casino generating all the excitement today is the 18,500-square-foot (1,719-sq.-m) **Ritz-Carlton Casino,** Avenue of Governors, Isla Verde (© 787/253-1700), the largest casino in Puerto Rico. It combines the elegant decor of the 1940s with tropical fabrics and patterns. This is one of the plushest and most exclusive entertainment complexes in the Caribbean. You almost expect to see Joan Crawford—beautifully frocked, of course—arrive on the arm of Clark Gable. It features traditional games such as blackjack, roulette, baccarat, craps, and slot machines.

One of the splashiest of San Juan's casinos is at the **Sheraton Old San Juan Hotel & Casino,** Calle Brumbaugh 100 (© 787/721-5100), where five-card stud competes with some 240 slot machines and roulette tables. You can also try your luck at the **El San Juan Hotel & Casino** (one of the most grand), Av. Isla Verde 6063 (© 787/791-1000), or the **Condado Plaza Hotel & Casino,** 999 Ashford Ave. (© 787/721-1000). You do not have to flash passports or pay any admission fees.

COCKFIGHTS

A brutal sport not to everyone's taste, cockfights are legal in Puerto Rico. The most authentic are in Salinas, a town on the southern coast with a southwestern ethos, where the fights take place in *galleras* (cockfighting rings). But you don't have to go all the way to Salinas to see a match. About three fights per week take place at the **Coliseo Gallístico,** Av. Isla Verde 6600, at the corner of Los Gobernadores (© 787/791-6005 for schedule and tickets; Tues–Thurs 4–10pm, Sat 2–9pm), where seats cost $10, $12, $20, or $35. The best time to attend cockfights is between January and May, when more fights are scheduled.

7

Near San Juan

Within easy reach of San Juan's cosmopolitan bustle are superb attractions and natural wonders. With San Juan as your base, you can explore the island by day and return in time for a final dip in the ocean and an evening on the town. Other places near San Juan, such as the Hyatt resort at Dorado, are destinations unto themselves.

About 90 minutes west of San Juan is the world's largest radar/radio telescope, **Arecibo Observatory.** After touring this awesome facility, you can travel west to nearby **Río Camuy** for a good look at marvels below ground. Here you can plunge deep into the subterranean beauty of a spectacular cave system carved over eons by one of the world's largest underground rivers.

Just 35 miles (56km) east of San Juan is the Caribbean National Forest, the only tropical rainforest in the U.S. National Park system. Named by the Spanish for its anvil-shaped peak, **El Yunque** receives more than 100 billion gallons of rainfall annually. If you have time for only one side trip, this is the one to take. Waterfalls, wild orchids, giant ferns, towering *tabonuco* trees, and sierra palms make El Yunque a photographer's and hiker's paradise. Pick up a map and choose from dozens of trails graded by difficulty, including El Yunque's most challenging—the 6-mile (9.7km) El Toro Trail to the peak. At El Yunque is El Portal Tropical Center, with 10,000 square feet (929 sq. m) of exhibit space, plazas, and patios. This facility greatly expands the recreational and educational programs available to visitors. La Coca Falls and an observation tower are just off Route 191.

Visitors can combine a morning trip to El Yunque with an afternoon of swimming and sunning on tranquil **Luquillo Beach.** Soft white sand, shaded by coconut palms and the blue sea, makes this Puerto Rico's best and best-known beach. Take a picnic or, better yet, sample local specialties from the kiosks.

1 Arecibo & Camuy ⭑

GETTING THERE

Arecibo Observatory lies a 1¼-hour drive west of San Juan, outside the town of Arecibo. From San Juan, head west along four-lane Route 22 until you reach the town of Arecibo. At Arecibo, head south on Route 10; the 20-mile (32km) drive south on this four-lane highway is almost as interesting as the observatory itself. From Route 10, follow the signposts along a roller-coaster journey on narrow two-lane roads. Still following the signposts, you take routes 626 and 623, crossing the lush Valley of Río Tanamá until you reach Route 625, which will lead you to the entrance to the observatory.

On the same day you visit the Arecibo Observatory, you can also visit the Río Camuy caves. The caves also lie south of the town of Arecibo. Follow Route 129 southwest from Arecibo to the entrance of the caves, which are at Km 18.9 along the route, north of the town of Lares. Like the observatory, the caves lie approximately 1½ hours west of San Juan.

EXPLORING THE AREA

Dubbed "an ear to heaven," **Arecibo Observatory** ⭑, Route 625, Barrio Esperanza, Arecibo, PR 00612 (✆ **787/878-2612;** www.naic. edu), contains the world's largest and most sensitive radar/radio telescope. The telescope features a 20-acre (8.1ha) dish, or radio mirror, set in an ancient sinkhole. It's 1,000 feet (305m) in diameter and 167 feet (51m) deep, and it allows scientists to monitor natural radio emissions from distant galaxies, pulsars, and quasars, and to examine the ionosphere, the planets, and the moon using powerful radar signals. Used by scientists as part of the Search for Extraterrestrial Intelligence (SETI), this is the same site featured in the movie *Contact* with Jodie Foster. This research effort speculates that advanced civilizations elsewhere in the universe might also communicate via radio waves. During some high-season periods, the daily maximum of 1,500 visitors is reached before around 11am. We urge interested visitors to get there as soon as possible on the morning of your visit to avoid the possibility of disappointment in the event of an early cutoff.

Unusually lush vegetation flourishes under the giant dish, including ferns, wild orchids, and begonias. Assorted creatures like mongooses, lizards, and dragonflies have also taken refuge there. Suspended in outlandish fashion above the dish is a 600-ton platform that resembles a space station.

This is not a site where you'll be launched into a *Star Wars* journey through the universe. You are allowed to walk around the platform, taking in views of this gigantic dish. At the Angel Ramos Foundation Visitor Center, you are treated to interactive exhibitions on the various planetary systems, introduced to the mystery of meteors, and educated about intriguing weather phenomena.

Tours are available at the observatory daily from 9am to 4pm. The cost is $4 for adults, $2 for children and seniors. There's a souvenir shop on the grounds. Plan to spend about 1½ hours at the observatory.

Parque de las Cavernas del Río Camuy (Río Camuy Caves) ℛℛℛ, Route 129 (© **787/898-3100**), contains the third-largest underground river in the world. It runs through a network of caves, canyons, and sinkholes that have been cut through the island's limestone base over the course of millions of years. Known to the pre-Columbian Taíno peoples, the caves came to the attention of speleologists in the 1950s; they were led to the site by local boys already familiar with some of the entrances to the system. The caves were opened to the public in 1986. Visitors should allow about 1½ hours for the total experience.

Visitors first see a short film about the caves and then descend into the caverns in open-air trolleys. The trip takes you through a 200-foot-deep (61m) sinkhole and a chasm where tropical trees, ferns, and flowers flourish, along with birds and butterflies. The trolley then goes to the entrance of Clara Cave of Epalme, one of 16 caves in the Camuy caves network, where visitors begin a 45-minute walk, viewing the majestic series of rooms rich in stalagmites, stalactites, and huge natural "sculptures" formed over the centuries.

The caves are open Wednesday through Sunday from 8am to 3pm. Tickets cost $12 for adults, $7 for children 4 to 12, and $6 for seniors. Parking is $3 to $5 depending on the size of the car. For more information, phone the park.

WHERE TO DINE
The closest place for food is the **Casa Grande Mountain Retreat** (p. 181) in Utuado, a little mountain town south of Arecibo.

2 Dorado ℛ
18 miles (29km) W of San Juan

Dorado—the name itself evokes a kind of magic. For years the resort was the site of two luxurious Hyatt hotels, which are now closed to the general public. But, even though these resorts are no longer here, the famous white-sand beaches of Dorado remain. Accommodations today are rather limited, but you can visit just for the beaches, even on a day trip from San Juan.

The site was originally purchased in 1905 by Dr. Alfred T. Livingston, a Jamestown, New York, physician, who developed it as a 1,000-acre (405ha) grapefruit-and-coconut plantation. Dr. Livingston's daughter, Clara, widely known in aviation circles as a friend of Amelia Earhart, owned and operated the plantation after her father's death. It was she who built an airstrip here.

GETTING THERE

If you're driving from San Juan, take Highway 2 west and then get on Route 693 north to Dorado (trip time: 40 min.).

SPORTS & OTHER OUTDOOR PURSUITS

GOLF The Robert Trent Jones Sr.–designed courses at the **Dorado Beach Golf Club** ✸✸ (✆ 787/796-8961) match the finest anywhere. The two original courses, known as east and west (✆ 787/796-8961 for tee times), were carved out of a jungle and offer tight fairways bordered by trees and forests, with lots of ocean holes. The somewhat newer and less noted north and south courses, now called the Plantation Club (✆ 787/796-1234 for tee times at all courses), feature wide fairways with well-bunkered greens and an assortment of water traps and tricky wind factors. Each is a par-72 course. The longest is the south course, at 7,047 yards (6,444m). Greens fees, including golf carts, cost $193 per golfer in the morning, lowered to $94 after 1pm. Club rentals go for $59. There are two pro shops— one for the north and south courses and one for the east and west courses, each with a bar and snack-style restaurant. Both are open daily from 7am until around 5:30pm.

WINDSURFING & OTHER WATERSPORTS The best place for watersports on the island's north shore is along the well-maintained beachfront of La Cienda del Mar, near the 10th hole of the east golf course. Here, **Blue Dolphin Water Sports** (✆ 787/796-3000) offers 1-hour **windsurfing lessons** for $65 each; board rentals are included. Well-supplied with a wide array of Windsurfers, including some designed specifically for beginners and children, the school benefits from the almost-uninterrupted flow of the north shore's strong, steady winds and an experienced crew of instructors. A **snorkeling** trip is $40 per day for two people. Snorkeling is $15 per hour or $25 per day.

WHERE TO STAY

Embassy Suites Dorado del Mar Beach & Golf Resort ✦

This beachfront property in Dorado lies less than 2 miles (3.2km) from the center of Dorado and within easy access from the San Juan airport. It is the only all-suite resort in Puerto Rico, and it has been a success since its opening in 2001. The dark mustard-brown property offers two-room suites with balconies and 38 two-bedroom condos.

The suites are spread over seven floors, each spacious and furnished in a Caribbean tropical motif, with artwork and one king-size bed or two double beds. Most of them have ocean views. Each condo has a living room, kitchen, whirlpool, and balcony.

Although the accommodations are suites or condos, one bedroom in a condo can be rented as a double room (the rest of the condo is shut off). Likewise, it's also possible for two people to rent one bedroom in a condo, with the living room and kitchen facilities available (the other bedroom is closed off). Because condos contain two bedrooms, most of them are rented to parties of four.

The hotel attracts many families because of its very spacious accommodations. It also attracts golfers to its Chi Chi Rodriguez signature par-72 18-hole golf course, set against a panoramic backdrop of mountains and ocean.

201 Dorado del Mar Blvd., Dorado, PR 00646. © **800-EMBASSY** or 787/796-6125. Fax 787/796-6145. www.embassysuitesdorado.com. 174 units. $145–$220 double; $179–$259 suite; $235–$345 1-bedroom condo; $259–$465 2-bedroom condo. AE, DC, DISC, MC, V. **Amenities:** 3 restaurants; bar grill; pool; golf; limited room service; massage; laundry service; dry cleaning; rooms for those w/limited mobility. *In room:* A/C, TV, kitchenette, hair dryer, iron, safe, wet bar.

WHERE TO DINE

El Ladrillo ✦ SPANISH/STEAK

In 1975 Tata and Tato, the restaurant's owners, opened their original eatery with four tables in the center of Dorado. Today, greatly expanded and in another location, they still specialize in the best meats in the area, including fresh U.S. prime Angus beef and lamb, as well as sirloin, T-bones, and filet mignons, each grilled to order. Even foodies from San Juan drive out here to sample these meats and the freshly caught seafood from island waters, including Puerto Rican–style shrimp and lobster stews and even a *zarzuela,* a delicious blend of various seafood stewed with wine and laced with herbs. For appetizers, try the plantain soup or the octopus cocktail. The decor is in the regional style, and the food is fresh and beautifully prepared, each dish containing a lot of flavor and the proper seasoning. The wine cellar is small but well-chosen for distinctive flavors. At the bar you can enjoy a cigar accompanied by one of the best cognacs.

Méndez Vigo 334, Dorado. ℭ **787/796-2120.** Reservations recommended. Main courses $15–$55. AE, MC, V. Sun–Fri noon–11pm; Sat 5–11pm.

Zen Gardens ⚑ ASIAN/SUSHI   On the grounds where the Rockefellers once romped, the best sushi bar and Asian restaurant west of San Juan now operates. There are two dining areas: one where you can order a la carte, and another where the skilled chefs cook the menu in front of you. The sushi bar is closed on Sunday, however. This is a particularly relaxing place to dine, and the chefs seem to produce an endless succession of enticing dishes. Don't be surprised if you end up eating more than you planned. A variety of classical sushi and other delicacies are served with courtesy and professionalism. Dishes range from tuna and salmon sashimi to tempura fish cake. Pickled ginger and wasabi are always provided for added flavor. Meat and poultry dishes are prepared with equal skill, including well-flavored beef dishes and duck with teriyaki orange sauce.

Cerromar Hotel & Country Club, Hwy. 693, Dorado. ℭ **787/796-1173.** Reservations recommended. Main courses $17–$33. AE, MC, V. Mon–Sat 6–10:30pm; Sun 1–9:30pm.

3 El Yunque ⚑⚑⚑

25 miles (40km) E of San Juan

El Yunque rainforest, a 45-minute drive east of San Juan, is a major attraction in Puerto Rico. Part of the Caribbean National Forest, this is the only tropical forest in the U.S. National Forest Service system. The 28,000-acre (11,331ha) preserve was given its status by President Theodore Roosevelt. Today the virgin forest remains much as it was in 1493, when Columbus first sighted Puerto Rico.

GETTING THERE
From San Juan, road signs direct you to Route 3, which you follow east to the intersection of Route 191, a two-lane highway that heads south into the forest. Take 191 for 3 miles (4.8km), going through the village of Palmer. As the road rises, you will have entered the Caribbean National Forest. You can stop in at El Portal Tropical Forest Center to pick up information (see below).

VISITOR INFORMATION
El Portal Tropical Forest Center, Route 191, Río Grande (ℭ **787/ 888-1880**), an $18-million exhibition and information center, has

10,000 square feet (929 sq. m) of exhibition space. Three pavilions offer exhibits and bilingual displays. The center is open daily from 9am to 5pm; it charges an admission of $3 for adults and $1.50 for children under 12.

El Yunque is the most popular spot in Puerto Rico for hiking; for a description of our favorite trails, see "Hiking Trails," below. The **Department of Natural Resources Forest Service** (© 787/724-8774) administers some aspects of the park, although for the ordinary hiker, more useful information may be available at **El Yunque Catalina Field Office** (© 787/888-1880), near the village of Palmer, beside the main highway at the forest's northern edge. The staff can provide material about hiking routes and, with 10 days' notice, help you plan overnight tours in the forest. If you reserve in advance, the staff will also arrange for you to take part in 2-hour group tours. These tours are conducted daily every hour on the hour from 10:30am to 3:30pm; they cost $5 for adults and $3 for children under 12.

EXPLORING EL YUNQUE

Encompassing four distinct forest types, El Yunque is home to 240 species of tropical trees, flowers, and wildlife. More than 20 kinds of orchids and 50 varieties of ferns share this diverse habitat with millions of tiny tree frogs, whose distinctive cry of *coquí* (pronounced "ko-*kee*") has given them their name. Tropical birds include the lively, greenish-blue, red-fronted Puerto Rican parrot, once nearly extinct and now making a comeback. Other rare animals include the Puerto Rican boa, which grows to 7 feet (2.1m). (It is highly unlikely that you will encounter a boa. The few people who have are still shouting about it.)

El Yunque is the best of Puerto Rico's 20 forest preserves. The forest is situated high above sea level, with El Toro its highest peak. You can be fairly sure you'll be showered upon during your visit, since more than 100 billion gallons of rain fall here annually. However, the showers are brief and there are many shelters. On a quickie tour, many visitors reserve only a half-day for El Yunque. But we think it's unique and deserves at least a daylong outing.

HIKING TRAILS   The best hiking trails in El Yunque have been carefully marked by the forest rangers. Our favorite, which takes 2 hours for the round-trip jaunt, is called **La Mina & Big Tree Trail,** and it is actually two trails combined. The La Mina Trail is paved and signposted. It begins at the picnic center adjacent to the visitor center and runs parallel to La Mina River. It is named for gold once discovered on the site. After you reach La Mina Falls, the Big Tree Trail begins (also signposted). It winds a route through the towering trees of Tabonuco Forest until it approaches Route 191. Along the trail you might spot such native birds as the Puerto Rican woodpecker, the tanager, the screech owl, and the bullfinch.

Those with more time might opt for **El Yunque Trail,** which takes 4 hours round-trip to traverse. This trail—signposted from El Caimitillo Picnic Grounds—takes you on a steep, winding path. Along the way you pass natural forests of sierra palm and *palo colorado* before descending into the dwarf forest of Mount Britton, which is often shrouded in clouds. Your major goal, at least for panoramic views, will be the lookout peaks of Roca Marcas, Yunque Rock, and Los Picachos. On a bright, clear day, you can see all the way to the eastern shores of the Atlantic.

DRIVING THROUGH EL YUNQUE   If you're not a hiker but you appreciate rainforests, you can still enjoy El Yunque. You can drive through the forest on Route 191, which is a tarmac road. This trail goes from the main highway of Route 3, penetrating deep into El Yunque. You can see ferns that grow some 120 feet (37m) tall, and at any minute you expect a hungry dinosaur to peek between the fronds, looking for a snack. You're also treated to lookout towers offering panoramic views, waterfalls, picnic areas, and even a restaurant.

WHERE TO STAY

Ceiba Country Inn *(Finds*   If you're looking for an escape from the hustle and bustle of everyday life, this is the place for you. This small, well-maintained bed-and-breakfast is located on the easternmost part of Puerto Rico, near the Roosevelt Roads U.S. naval base (you must rent a car to reach this little haven in the mountains). El Yunque is only 15 miles (24km) away, and San Juan is 40 miles (64km) to the west. The rooms are on the bottom floor of a large, old family home, and each has a private shower-only bathroom. They are decorated in a tropical motif with flowered murals on the walls, painted by a local artist. For a quiet evening cocktail, you might want to visit the small lounge on the second floor.

Rte. 977 Km 1.2 (P.O. Box 1067), Ceiba, PR 00735. (C) **787/885-0471.** Fax 787/885-0471. prinn@juno.com. 9 units (shower only). $85 double. Rate includes breakfast. AE, DISC, MC, V. Free parking. **Amenities:** Patio for outdoor entertainment; bar (guests only). *In room:* A/C, ceiling fan, fridge.

WHERE TO DINE

We recommend the dining and drinking facilities at the Westin Rio Mar (see "Luquillo Beach," below), which sits very close to the entrance to El Yunque.

4 Luquillo Beach (★(★(★

31 miles (50km) E of San Juan

Luquillo Beach is the island's best and most popular public stretch of sand. From here, you can easily explore El Yunque rainforest (see section 3, above). "Luquillo" is a Spanish adaptation of *Yukiyu,* the god believed by the Taínos to inhabit El Yunque.

GETTING THERE

If you are driving, pass the San Juan airport and follow the signs to Carolina. This leads to Route 3, which travels east toward the fishing town of Fajardo, where you'll turn north to Las Croabas. To reach the Westin, the area's major hotel, follow the signs to El Yunque and then the signs to the Westin.

A hotel limousine (℡ **787/888-6000**) from the San Juan airport costs $235 per carload to the Westin Rio Mar Beach Golf Resort. A taxi costs approximately $80. Hotel buses make trips to and from the San Juan airport, based on the arrival times of incoming flights; the cost is $60 per person, each way, for transport to El Conquistador; $60 per person, round trip, to the Westin.

HITTING THE BEACH

Luquillo Beach (★(★(★, Puerto Rico's finest beach, is palm-dotted and crescent-shaped, opening onto a lagoon with calm waters and a wide, sandy bank. It's very crowded on weekends but much better during the week. There are lockers, tent sites, showers, picnic tables, and food stands that sell a sampling of the island's *frituras* (fried fare), especially cod fritters and tacos. The beach is open daily from 9am to 6pm.

You can also snorkel and skin-dive (see below) among the living reefs with lots of tropical fish. Offshore are coral formations and spectacular sea life—eels, octopuses, stingrays, tarpon, big puffer fish, turtles, nurse sharks, and squid, among other sea creatures.

SCUBA DIVING & SNORKELING

The best people to take you diving are at the **Dive Center** at the Westin Rio Mar Beach Golf Resort & Spa (℡ **787/888-6000**). This is one of the largest dive centers in Puerto Rico, a PADI five-star facility with two custom-designed boats that usually take no more than six to 10 divers. Snorkeling costs $75 for a half-day. The center also offers a full-day snorkeling trip, including lunch and drinks, for $95 per adult, $79 for children under 10. Fishing trips are available daily from 7 to 11am and 1 to 5pm and cost between $450 and $1,000, depending on the length of time you fish. For scuba divers, a two-tank dive costs $135 to $185.

WHERE TO STAY

Paradisus Puerto Rico ★ (Kids)   Although common in other islands such as Jamaica, this sprawling resort is the first all-inclusive to open in Puerto Rico. It lies a 40-minute drive east of San Juan and to the immediate west of Luquillo Beach. The resort opens onto the pristine white sands of Coco Beach. A wide variety of accommodations await guests. Many prefer one of the large and elegant suites installed in a total of 20 two-story bungalows, whereas others opt for a garden villa set in the midst of a lush garden and containing a private terrace and swimming pool. For the ultimate retreat, there are a dozen individual honeymoon suites with a cozy Jacuzzi for two. Guest rooms open onto views of the ocean or golf course. Contemporary styling is used throughout, with much use made of custom-designed mahogany furnishings. All accommodations come with a first-class, tiled bathroom with tub or shower. The public rooms are inspired by styles that range from Africa to Japan, and art used to decorate the resort ranges from Taíno Indian to modern. Of the array of on-site restaurants, we'd cast our vote for **Romantico,** a French restaurant, since it serves the best cuisine.

Rte. 968 Km 5.8, Coco Beach, PR 00745. © **800/336-3542** or 787/809-1770. Fax 787/809-1785. www.puertoricoparadisus.com. 525 units. $673–$1,000 suite; $1,100–$1,350 villa. AE, DC, DISC, MC, V. **Amenities:** 6 restaurants; 4 bars; 2 outdoor pools; 3 tennis courts; health club; spa; dive shop; watersports; children's programs (ages 4–12); car-rental desk; business center; room service; laundry service; dry cleaning; nonsmoking rooms; rooms for those w/limited mobility; casino; showroom dance club. *In room:* A/C, TV, minibar, coffeemaker, hair dryer, safe, Wi-Fi.

Westin Rio Mar Beach Golf Resort & Spa ★★★ (Kids)   Marking Westin's debut in the Caribbean, this $180-million, 481-acre (195ha) resort lies on a relatively uncrowded neighbor (Rio Mar Beach) of the massively popular Luquillo Beach, a 5-minute drive away. It was designed to compete with the Hyatt hotels at Dorado and El Conquistador, with which it's frequently compared. It's the freshest and best property in the area.

Landscaping includes several artificial lakes situated amid tropical gardens. More than 60% of the guest rooms look out over palm trees to the Atlantic. Other units open onto the mountains and forests of nearby El Yunque (just a 15-min. drive away). Throughout, the style is Spanish hacienda with nods to the surrounding jungle, incorporating unusual art and sculpture that alternates with dark woods, deep colors, rounded archways, big windows, and tile floors. In the bedrooms, muted earth tones, wicker, rattan, and painted wood furniture add to the ambience. Bedrooms are spacious, with balconies or terraces, plus tub/shower combos in the spacious bathrooms.

The resort encompasses the Rio Mar Country Club, site of two important golf courses: the Ocean Course, designed by George and Tom Fazio as part of the original resort, and the slightly more challenging River Course, the first Greg Norman–designed course in the Caribbean.

For diversity of cuisine, the only hotel in Puerto Rico that outpaces it is El Conquistador Resort (p. 190). The resort also has a 7,000-square-foot (650-sq.-m) casino.

6000 Rio Mar Blvd. (19 miles/31km east of Luis Muñoz Marín International Airport, with entrance off Puerto Rico Hwy. 3), Río Grande, PR 00745. ☎ 888/627-8556 or 787/888-6000. Fax 787/888-6320. www.westinriomar.com. 600 units. $399–$599 double; from $549 suite. AE, DC, DISC, MC, V. **Amenities:** 8 restaurants; 5 bars; 3 outdoor pools; 2 golf courses; 13 tennis courts; health club; spa; watersports; nearby horseback riding; children's programs; business center; room service; laundry service; dry cleaning; rooms for those w/limited mobility; casino. *In room:* A/C, TV, minibar, coffeemaker, hair dryer, iron, safe.

WHERE TO DINE

Brass Cactus *(Finds* AMERICAN/REGIONAL   On a service road adjacent to Route 3 at the western edge of Luquillo, within a boxy-looking concrete building that's in need of repair, is one of the town's most popular bar/restaurants. Permeated with a raunchy, no-holds-barred spirit, this amiable spot has thrived since the early 1990s, when it was established by an Illinois-born bartender who outfitted the interior with gringo memorabilia. Drinks are stiff and the crowd looks tougher than it is, tending to calm down whenever food and drink are brought out. Menu items include king crab salad; tricolor tortellini laced with chicken and shrimp; several kinds of sandwiches and burgers; and platters of *churrasco,* T-bone steaks, chicken with tequila sauce, barbecued pork, and fried mahimahi.

In the Condominio Complejo Turismo, Rte. 3 Marginal. ☎ **787/889-5735.** Sandwiches $7.95–$11; main courses $7.95–$26. MC, V. Sun–Thurs 11am–11pm; Fri–Sat 11am–midnight.

Palio ✪ ITALIAN   Richly decorated and evoking some of the splendor of the Palio, the famous horse race that's held every year within Siena, Italy's del Campo, this is the most upscale and best-recommended restaurant in the neighborhood. It's also the premier dining showcase of the also-recommended Westin Rio Mar, the region's largest and splashiest hotel.

You'll enter a richly decorated environment shaped like a half-oval, with views that sweep out over the sea, and framed with arches and deep blues and reds that evoke the Italian Renaissance. The cuisine is excellent, deeply reflective of the traditional tenets of Tuscan cooking. The menu changes frequently, but among the most popular of the traditional standards is *gamberi con funghi,* consisting of sautéed jumbo shrimp with spinach, mushrooms, and garlic in a lemon-flavored white-wine sauce; *osso buco Milanese,* veal shank braised with vegetables and served with saffron-flavored risotto; and a superb version of *zuppa di pesce* made with mussels, clams, lobster, shrimp, scallops, and spicy tomato broth. Any of the pastas can be prepared as either full or half portions.

In the Westin Rio Mar Beach Golf Resort & Spa. © **787/888-6000.** Reservations recommended. Main courses $26–$45. AE, DC, MC, V. June–Oct Tues–Sat 6–11pm; Nov–May daily 6–11pm.

Sandy's Seafood Restaurant & Steak House ✪ *Value* SEAFOOD/ STEAKS/PUERTO RICAN   The concrete-and-plate-glass facade is less obtrusive than that of other restaurants in town, and the cramped, Formica-clad interior is far from stylish. Nonetheless, Sandy's is one of the most famous restaurants in northeastern Puerto Rico, thanks to the wide array of luminaries—U.S. and Puerto Rican political figures, mainstream journalists, beauty pageant winners, and assorted slumming rich—who travel from as far away as San Juan to dine here. Set about a block from the main square of the seaside resort of Luquillo, it was founded in 1984 by Miguel Angel, aka Sandy.

Platters, especially the daily specials, are huge—so copious, in fact, that they're discussed with fervor by competitors and clients alike. The best examples include fresh shellfish, served on the half-shell; *asopao;* four kinds of steak; five different preparations of chicken, including a tasty version with garlic sauce; four kinds of gumbos; paellas; a dozen preparations of lobster; and even jalapeño peppers stuffed with shrimp or lobster.

Calle Fernández García 276. © **787/889-5765.** Reservations recommended. Main courses $6–$20; lunch special (Mon–Fri 11am–2:30pm) $5. AE, MC, V. Daily 11am–10pm.

8

Ponce & Mayagüez

For those who want to see a less urban side of Puerto Rico, Ponce, on the south shore, and Mayagüez, on the west coast, make good centers for sightseeing. From either Ponce or Mayagüez you can take a side trip to historic San Germán, Puerto Rico's second-oldest city and site of the oldest church in the New World.

Founded in 1692, Ponce is Puerto Rico's second-largest city, and it has received much attention because of its inner-city restoration. It is home to the island's premier art gallery.

Puerto Rico's third-largest city, Mayagüez, is a port city on the west coast. It might not be as architecturally remarkable as Ponce, but it's a fine base for exploring and enjoying some very good beaches.

Mayagüez and Ponce also attract beach lovers. Playa de Ponce, for example, is far less crowded than the beaches along San Juan's coastal strip. The area also lures hikers to Puerto Rico's government national forest reserves, the best of which lie outside Ponce and include Guánica State Forest and the Carite Forest Reserve, as well as the Toro Negro Forest Reserve.

One of the biggest adventure jaunts in Puerto Rico, a trip to Mona Island, can also be explored from the coast near Mayagüez.

1 Ponce ★★

75 miles (121km) SW of San Juan

"The Pearl of the South," Ponce was named after Loíza Ponce de León, great-grandson of Juan Ponce de León. Founded in 1692, Ponce is today Puerto Rico's principal shipping port on the Caribbean. The city is well-kept and attractive. A suggestion of a provincial Mediterranean town lingers in the air.

Timed to coincide with 1992's 500th anniversary celebration of Christopher Columbus's voyage to the New World, a $440-million renovation brought new life to this once-decaying city. The streets are lit with gas lamps and lined with neoclassical buildings, just as they were a century ago. Horse-drawn carriages clop by, and strollers walk along sidewalks edged with pink marble. Thanks to the restoration,

Ponce

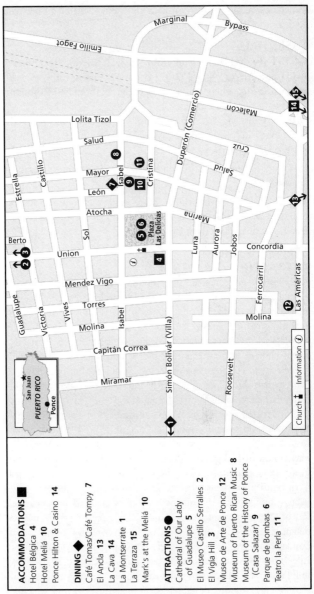

ACCOMMODATIONS ■
Hotel Bélgica **4**
Hotel Meliá **10**
Ponce Hilton & Casino **14**

DINING ◆
Café Tomas/Café Tompy **7**
El Ancla **13**
La Cava **14**
La Montserrate **1**
La Terraza **15**
Mark's at the Meliá **10**

ATTRACTIONS ●
Cathedral of Our Lady
  of Guadalupe **5**
El Museo Castillo Serralles **2**
El Vigía Hill **3**
Museo de Arte de Ponce **12**
Museum of Puerto Rican Music **8**
Museum of the History of Ponce
  (Casa Salazar) **9**
Parque de Bombas **6**
Teatro la Perla **11**

Ponce now recalls the turn of the 20th century, when it rivaled San Juan as a wealthy business and cultural center.

ESSENTIALS

GETTING THERE Flying from San Juan to Ponce five times a day, **Cape Air** (© **800/352-0714;** www.flycapeair.com), a small regional carrier, offers flights for between $115 and $150 round-trip. Flight time is 25 minutes.

If you're driving, take Route 1 south to Highway 52, then continue south and west to Ponce. Allow at least 1½ hours.

GETTING AROUND The town's inner core is small enough that everything can be visited on foot. Taxis provide the second-best alternative.

VISITOR INFORMATION Maps and information can be found at the **tourist office,** Edificio Jose Dapena (© **787/841-8160**). It's open daily from 9am to 5pm.

SEEING THE SIGHTS
ATTRACTIONS IN PONCE

Most visitors go to Ponce to see the city's architectural restoration. Calle Reina Isabel, one of the city's major residential streets, is a virtual textbook of the different Ponceño styles, ranging from interpretations of European neoclassical to Spanish colonial. The neoclassical style here often incorporates balconies, as befits the warm climate, and an extensive use of pink marble. The "Ponce Creole" style, a term for Spanish colonial, includes both exterior and interior balconies. The interior balconies have a wall of tiny windows that allow sunlight into the patio.

With partial funding from the governments of Puerto Rico and Spain, Ponce has restored more than 600 of its 1,000 historic buildings. Many are on streets radiating from the stately **Plaza Las Delicias (Plaza of Delights).** On calles Isabel, Reina, Pabellones, and Lolita Tizol, electrical and telephone wires have been buried, replica 19th-century gas lamps have been installed, and sidewalks have been trimmed with the distinctive locally quarried pink marble. Paseo Atocha, one of Ponce's main shopping streets, is now a delightful pedestrian mall with a lively street festival on the third Sunday of every month. Paseo Arias, or Callejón del Amor (Lovers' Alley), is a charming pedestrian passage between two 1920s bank buildings, Banco Popular and Banco Santander, on Plaza Las Delicias, where outdoor cafe tables invite lingering. Two monumental bronze lions by Spanish sculptor Victor Ochoa guard the entrance to the old section of the city.

In addition to the attractions listed below, the **weekday market-place** at calles Atocha and Castillo is colorful and open Monday through Friday from 8am to 5pm. Perhaps you'll want to simply sit in the plaza, watching the Ponceños at one of their favorite pastimes—strolling about town.

Cathedral of Our Lady of Guadalupe   In 1660 a rustic chapel was built on this spot on the western edge of the Plaza Las Delicias, and since then fires and earthquakes have razed the church repeatedly. In 1919 a team of priests collected funds from local parishioners to construct the Doric- and Gothic-inspired building that stands here today. Designed by architects Francisco Porrato Doría and Francisco Trublard in 1931, and featuring a pipe organ installed in 1934, it remains an important place for prayer for many. The cathedral, named after a famous holy shrine in Mexico, is the best-known church in southern Puerto Rico.

Calle Unión/Concordia. ✆ **787/842-0134.** Free admission. Mon–Fri 6am–12:30pm; Sat–Sun 6am–noon and 3–8pm.

El Museo Castillo Serralles 👁   Two miles (3.2km) north of the center of town is the largest and most imposing building in Ponce, constructed high on El Vigía Hill (see below) during the 1930s by the Serralles family, owners of a local rum distillery. One of the architectural gems of Puerto Rico, it is the best evidence of the wealth produced by the turn-of-the-20th-century sugar boom. Guides will escort you through the Spanish Revival house with Moorish and Andalusian details. Highlights include panoramic courtyards, a baronial dining room, a small cafe and souvenir shop, and a series of photographs showing the tons of earth that were brought in for the construction of the terraced gardens.

El Vigía 17. ✆ **787/259-1774.** Admission $6 adults; $3 students, seniors, and children. Tues–Sun 9:30am–5pm. Free trolley leaving from Plaza Las Delicias de Ponce.

El Vigía Hill   The city's tallest geologic feature, El Vigía Hill (300 ft./91m) dominates Ponce's northern skyline. Its base and steep slopes are covered with a maze of 19th- and early-20th-century development. When you reach the summit, you'll see the soaring Cruz del Vigía (Virgin's Cross). Built in 1984 of reinforced concrete to replace a 19th-century wooden cross in poor repair, this modern 100-foot (30m) structure bears lateral arms measuring 70 feet

(21m) long and an observation tower (accessible by elevator), from which you can see all of the natural beauty surrounding Ponce.

The cross commemorates Vigía Hill's colonial role as a deterrent to contraband smuggling. In 1801, on orders from Spain, a garrison was established atop the hill to detect any ships that might try to unload their cargoes tax-free along Puerto Rico's southern coastline.

At the north end of Ponce. Take a taxi from the Plaza Las Delicias; the ride will cost about $4.

Museo de Arte de Ponce 𝕗𝕗𝕗   Donated to the people of Puerto Rico by Luis A. Ferré, a former governor, this museum has the finest collection of European and Latin American art in the Caribbean. The building itself was designed by Edward Durell Stone (who also designed the John F. Kennedy Center for the Performing Arts in Washington, D.C.) and has been called the "Parthenon of the Caribbean." Its collection represents the principal schools of American and European art of the past 5 centuries. Among the nearly 400 works on display are exceptional pre-Raphaelite and Italian baroque paintings. Visitors will also see artworks by other European masters, as well as Puerto Rican and Latin American paintings, graphics, and sculptures. Both the Whitney Museum in New York and the Louvre in Paris have borrowed from its collection. Temporary exhibitions are also mounted here.

Av. de Las Américas 23–25. ℭ **787/848-0505.** www.museoarteponce.org. Admission $5 adults, $2.50 children under 12. Daily 10am–5pm. Follow Calle Concordia from Plaza Las Delicias 1½ miles (2.4km) south to Av. de Las Américas.

Museum of Puerto Rican Music   This museum showcases the development of Puerto Rican music, with displays of Indian, Spanish, and African musical instruments that were played in the romantic *danza,* the favorite music of 19th-century Puerto Rican society, as well as the more African-inspired *bomba* and *plena* styles. Also on view are memorabilia of composers and performers.

Calle Isabel 50. ℭ **787/848-7016.** Free admission. Tues–Sun 8:30am–midnight.

Museum of the History of Ponce (Casa Salazar)   Opened in the Casa Salazar in 1992, this museum traces the history of the city from the time of the Taíno peoples to the present. Interactive displays help visitors orient themselves and locate other attractions. The museum has a conservation laboratory, library, souvenir-and-gift shop, cafeteria, and conference facilities.

Casa Salazar ranks close to the top of Ponce's architectural treasures. Built in 1911, it combines neoclassical and Moorish details, while displaying much that is typical of the Ponce decorative style: stained-glass windows, mosaics, pressed-tin ceilings, fixed jalousies, wood or iron columns, porch balconies, interior patios, and the use of doors as windows.

Calle Reina Isabel 51–53 (at Calle Mayor). ℂ **787/844-7071**. Free admission. Tues–Sun 8:30am–5pm.

Parque de Bombas   Constructed in 1882 as the centerpiece of a 12-day agricultural fair intended to promote the civic charms of Ponce, this building was designated a year later as the island's first permanent headquarters for a volunteer firefighting brigade. It has an unusual appearance—it's painted black, red, green, and yellow. A tourist-information kiosk is situated inside the building (see "Visitor Information," above).

Plaza Las Delicias. ℂ **787/284-4141**. Free admission. Daily 9:30am–6pm.

Teatro la Perla   This theater, built in the neoclassical style in 1864, remains one of the most visible symbols of the economic prosperity of Ponce during the mid–19th century. Designed by Juan Bertoli, an Italian-born resident of Puerto Rico who studied in Europe, it was destroyed by an earthquake in 1918, and rebuilt in 1940 according to the original plans; it reopened to the public in 1941. It is noted for acoustics so clear that microphones are unnecessary. The theater is the largest and most historic in the Spanish-speaking Caribbean. Everything, from plays to concerts to beauty pageants, takes place here.

At calles Mayor and Christina. ℂ **787/843-4080**.

NEARBY ATTRACTIONS

Hacienda Buena Vista   Built in 1833, this hacienda preserves an old way of life, with its whirring waterwheels and artifacts of 19th-century farm production. Once it was one of the most successful plantations in Puerto Rico, producing coffee, corn, and citrus. It was a working coffee plantation until the 1950s, and 86 of the original 500 acres (202ha) are still part of the estate. The rooms of the hacienda have been furnished with authentic pieces from the 1850s.

Rte. 123, Barrio Magüeyez Km 16.8 (a 30-min. drive north of Ponce, in the small town of Barrio Magüeyez, between Ponce and Adjuntas). ℂ **787/812-5027** or 787/722-5882. Tours $7 adults, $4 children 5–11, free for children under 5. Reservations required. 1½-hr. English and Spanish tours Wed–Sun at 8:30 and 10:30am, 1:30 and 3:30pm; English-only tour at 1:30pm.

Tibes Indian Ceremonial Center   Bordered by the Río Portuguéz and excavated in 1975, this is the oldest cemetery in the

Antilles. It contains some 186 skeletons, dating from A.D. 300, as well as pre-Taíno plazas from A.D. 700. The site also includes a re-created Taíno village, seven rectangular ball courts, and two dance grounds. The arrangement of stone points on the dance grounds, in line with the solstices and equinoxes, suggests a pre-Columbian Stonehenge. Here you'll also find a museum, an exhibition hall that presents a documentary about Tibes, a cafeteria, and a souvenir shop.

Rte. 503 Km 2.2, Tibes (2 miles/3.2km north of Ponce). © **787/840-2255.** Admission $3 adults, $2 children. Guided tours in English and Spanish are conducted through the grounds. Tues–Sun 9am–4pm.

HIKING & BIRD-WATCHING IN GUANICA STATE FOREST ☆☆

Heading directly west from Ponce, along Route 2, you reach **Guánica State Forest** ☆☆ (© **787/821-5706**), a setting that evokes Arizona or New Mexico. Here you will find the best-preserved subtropical ecosystem on the planet. UNESCO has named Guánica a World Biosphere Reserve. Some 750 plants and tree species grow in the area.

The Cordillera Central cuts off the rain coming in from the heavily showered northeast, making this a dry region of cactuses and bedrock, a perfect film location for old-fashioned Western movies. It's also ideal country for birders. Some 50% of all of the island's terrestrial bird species can be seen in this dry and dusty forest. You might even spot the Puerto Rican emerald-breasted hummingbird. A number of migratory birds often stop here. The most serious ornithologists seek out the Puerto Rican nightjar, a local bird that was believed to be extinct. Now it's estimated that there are nearly a thousand of them.

To reach the forest, take Route 334 northeast of Guánica, to the heart of the forest. There's a ranger station here that will give you information about hiking trails. The booklet provided by the ranger station outlines 36 miles (58km) of trails through the four forest types. The most interesting is the mile-long (1.6km) **Cueva Trail,** which gives you the most scenic look at the various types of vegetation. You might even encounter the endangered bufo lemur toad, once declared extinct but found to still be jumping in this area.

Within the forest, El Portal Tropical Forest Center (near the entrance to the forest) offers 10,000 square feet (929 sq. m) of exhibition space and provides visitor information.

CARITE FOREST RESERVE ✿

In southeastern Puerto Rico, lying off the Ponce Expressway near Cayey, **Carite Forest Reserve** ✿ is a 6,000-acre (2,428ha) reserve with a dwarf forest that was produced by the region's high humidity and moist soil. From several peaks, there are panoramic views of Ponce and the Caribbean Sea. On one peak is Nuestra Madre, a Catholic spiritual meditation center that permits visitors to stroll the grounds. Fifty species of birds live in the Carite Forest Reserve, which also has a large natural pool called Charco Azul. A picnic area and campgrounds are shaded by eucalyptus and royal palms. The forest borders a lake of the same name. Drive east from Ponce along Route 52 until you near the town of Cayey, where the entrance to the forest reserve is signposted.

TORO NEGRO FOREST RESERVE ✿✿✿ & LAKE GUINEO ✿

North of Ponce via Route 139, **Toro Negro Forest Reserve** ✿✿✿ lies along the Cordillera Central, the cloud-shrouded panoramic route that follows the Cordillera Central as it goes from the southeast town of Yabucoa all the way to Mayagüez on the west coast. This 7,000-acre (2,833ha) park, ideal for hikers, straddles the highest peak of the Cordillera Central in the very heart of Puerto Rico. A forest of lush trees, the reserve also contains the headwaters of several main rivers.

The lowest temperatures recorded on the island—some 40°F (4°C)—were measured at **Lake Guineo** ✿, the island's highest lake, which lies within the reserve. The best trail to take here is a short, paved, and wickedly steep path on the north side of Route 143, going up to the south side of Cerro de Punta, which at 4,390 feet (1,338m) is the highest peak in Puerto Rico. Allow about half an hour for an ascent up this peak. Once at the top, you'll be rewarded with Puerto Rico's grandest view, sweeping across the lush interior from the Atlantic to the Caribbean coasts. Other peaks in the reserve also offer hiking possibilities.

BEACHES & OUTDOOR ACTIVITIES

Ponce is a city—not a beach resort—and should be visited mainly for its sights. There is little here in the way of organized sports, but a 10-minute drive west of Ponce will take you to **Playa de Ponce** ✿✿, a long strip of white sand opening onto the tranquil waters of the Caribbean. This beach is usually better for swimming than the Condado in San Juan.

Because the northern shore of Puerto Rico fronts the often-turbulent Atlantic, many snorkelers prefer the more tranquil southern coast, not only off Ponce, but also off **La Parguera** (see the "Western Puerto Rico & the Southwest Coast" map on p. 171). On the beaches around Ponce, water lovers can go snorkeling right off the beach, and it isn't necessary to take a boat trip. Waters here are not polluted, and visibility is usually good, unless there are heavy winds and choppy seas.

La Guancha is a sprawling compound of publicly funded beachfront, located 3 miles (4.8km) south of Ponce's cathedral. It has a large parking lot, a labyrinth of boardwalks, and a saltwater estuary with moorings for hundreds of yachts and pleasure craft. A tower, which anyone can climb free of charge, affords high-altitude vistas of the active beach scene. La Guancha is a relatively wholesome version of Coney Island, with a strong Hispanic accent and vague hints of New England. On hot weekends, the place is mobbed with thousands of families who listen to recorded merengue and salsa. Lining the boardwalk are at least a dozen emporiums purveying beer, party-colored drinks, high-calorie snacks, and souvenirs. Weather permitting, this free beach is good for a few hours' diversion at any time of the year.

Although snorkeling is good off the beaches, the best snorkeling is reached by boat trip to the offshore island of **Caja de Muertos,** or **Coffin Island,** an uninhabited key that's covered with mangrove swamps and ringed with worthwhile beaches. A government ferry used to take beach buffs to the wild beaches here, but it was needed for passenger service between Fajardo and Vieques. Today, a private outfitter, **Island Adventures,** c/o Rafi Vega, La Guancha (© **787/ 842-8546**), will haul day-trippers there for a full-day beachgoers' outing ($35 per person with or without snorkeling equipment). Advance reservations (which you can make yourself or leave to the desk staff of whatever hotel you opt for in Ponce) are necessary, as most of this outfit's excursions don't leave unless there are a predetermined number of participants.

The city owns two **tennis complexes,** one at Poly Deportivos, with nine hard courts, and another at Rambla, with six courts. Both are open 5am to 9pm Sunday through Friday and 8am to noon on Saturday, and are lit for night play. You can play for free, but you must call to make a reservation. For information, including directions on how to get there, call the **Secretary of Sports** at © **787/ 840-4400.**

One of Puerto Rico's finest and newest courses is the **Costa Caribe Golf & Country Club** ⚑⚑ (© 787/812-2650), on the site of the recommended Ponce Hilton & Casino (see "Where to Stay," below). This 27-hole course charges from $60 to $85 for guests to play 18 holes. The beautifully landscaped holes, commanding views of the ocean and mountain, are laid out in landscaped former sugar-cane fields. No. 12 hole, one of the most dramatic, calls for a 188-yard carry over water from the back tees. Trade winds add to the challenge. The three nines can be played in 18-hole combinations, as conceived by golf architect Bruce Besse. The greens are undulating and moderate in speed, averaging 666 square yards. Golf carts are included in the greens fees, and both gas and electric carts are available.

You can also go to **Aguirre Golf Club,** Route 705, Aguirre (© 787/853-4052), 30 miles (48km) east of Ponce (take Hwy. 52). This 9-hole course is open from 7:30am to sunset Tuesday through Sunday with $20 greens fees ($15 on holidays). Another course, **Club Deportivo,** Route 102 Km 15.4, Barrio Jogudas, Cabo Rojo (© 787/254-3748), lies 30 miles (48km) west of Ponce. This course is an 18-holer, open daily from 7:30am to 6pm. Greens fees are $35 during the week and $40 on the weekend.

SHOPPING

If you feel a yen for shopping in Ponce, head for the **Fox-Delicias Mall,** at the intersection of calles Reina Isabel and Union, the city's most innovative shopping center. Among the many interesting stores is **Regalitos y Algo Más** (no phone), located on the upper level. It specializes in unusual gift items from all over Puerto Rico. Look especially for the Christmas tree ornaments, crafted from wood, metal, colored porcelain, or bread dough, and for the exotic dolls displayed by the owners. Purchases can be shipped anywhere in the world.

At the mall, the best outlet for souvenirs and artisans' work is **El Palacio del Coquí Inc.** (© 787/841-0216), whose name means "palace of the tree frog." This is the place to buy the grotesque masks (viewed as collectors' items) that are used at Carnaval time. Ask the owner to explain the significance of these masks.

Utopía, Calle Isabel 78 (© 787/848-8742), conveniently located in Plaza Las Delicias, has the most imaginative and interesting selection of gift items and handicrafts in Ponce. Prominently displayed are *vegigantes,* brightly painted carnival masks inspired by carnival rituals and crafted from papier-mâché. In Ponce, where many of these masks are made, they sell at bargain prices of between $5 and

$500, depending on their size. Other items include cigars, pottery, clothing, and jewelry; gifts imported from Indonesia, the Philippines, and Mexico; and rums from throughout the Caribbean. Julio and Carmen Aguilar are the helpful and enthusiastic owners, who hail from Ecuador and Puerto Rico, respectively.

In a small workshop outside Ponce, woodcarver Domingo Orta has been gaining international publicity for his *santos,* religious figurines that locals believe have the power to perform good deeds. San Antonio of Padua, for example, is said to have great matchmaking skills and is eagerly collected by unmarried girls. The works of Orta, hailed as the best in his field, are showcased at the **Mi Coquí Gallery** (© 787/841-0216) on Calle Marina, off Plaza Las Delicias.

WHERE TO STAY
EXPENSIVE

Ponce Hilton & Casino 🌟🌟 *Kids*   On an 80-acre (32ha) tract of land right on the beach at the western end of Avenida Santiago de los Caballeros, about a 10-minute drive from the center of Ponce, this is the most glamorous hotel in southern Puerto Rico. Designed like a miniature village, with turquoise-blue roofs, white walls, and lots of tropical plants, ornamental waterfalls, and gardens, it welcomes conventioneers and individual travelers alike. Each unit has tropically inspired furnishings, ceiling fans, and a terrace or balcony. All the rooms are medium-size to spacious, with adequate desk and storage space, tasteful fabrics, good upholstery, and fine linens. Each is equipped with a generous tiled bathroom with a tub/shower combo. The ground-floor rooms are the most expensive.

The food at one of the hotel's restaurants, **La Cava,** is the most sophisticated and refined on the south coast of Puerto Rico. For less expensive buffet dining, you can also patronize **La Terraza,** which serves the best lunch buffet in Ponce (see "Where to Dine," below).

Av. Caribe 1150 (P.O. Box 7419), Ponce, PR 00716. © 800/HILTONS or 787/259-7676. Fax 787/259-7674. www.hilton.com. 153 units. $205–$345 double; $450 suite. AE, DC, DISC, MC, V. Self-parking $4.50, valet parking $10. **Amenities:** 2 restaurants; 2 bars; lagoon-shaped pool ringed with gardens; 27-hole golf course; 2 tennis courts; fitness center; bike rentals; playground; children's program; business center; room service; babysitting; laundry service; dry cleaning; rooms for those w/limited mobility; casino; night club. *In room:* A/C, TV, minibar, coffeemaker, hair dryer, iron, safe.

MODERATE

Hotel Meliá *Value*   This city hotel with southern hospitality, which has no connection with the international hotel chain, attracts businesspeople. It is located a few steps from the Cathedral of Our Lady of Guadalupe and from the Parque de Bombas (the red-and-black firehouse). Although this old and somewhat tattered hotel was long ago outclassed by the more expensive Hilton, many people who can afford more upscale accommodations still prefer to stay here for the old-time atmosphere. The lobby floor and all stairs are covered with Spanish tiles of Moorish design. The desk clerks speak English. The small rooms are comfortably furnished and pleasant enough, and most have balconies facing either busy Calle Cristina or the old plaza. The shower-only bathrooms are tiny. Breakfast is served on a rooftop terrace with a good view of Ponce, and Mark's at the Meliá thrives under separate management (see "Where to Dine," below). *Note:* There's no pool here.

Calle Cristina 2, Ponce, PR 00731. © 800/448-8355 or 787/842-0260. Fax 787/841-3602. www.hotelmeliapr.com. 73 units (shower only). $95–$120 double; $130 suite. Rates include continental breakfast. AE, MC, V. Parking $3. **Amenities:** Restaurant; bar; room service; rooms for those w/limited mobility. *In room:* A/C, TV, dataport, hair dryer, iron, safe.

INEXPENSIVE
Hotel Bélgica   In the hands of a skilled decorator with a large bankroll, this Spanish colonial mansion from around 1911 could be transformed into a very chic bed-and-breakfast. Until then, however, you'll be faced with a combination of historic charm and modern junkiness, overseen by a brusque staff. You might find this cost-conscious spot wonderful or horrible, depending on your point of view and room assignment. The most appealing accommodations are nos. 8, 9, and 10; these rooms are spacious and have balconies that hang over Calle Villa, a few steps from Plaza Las Delicias. Each unit has a small tiled shower-only bathroom. This venue is for roughing it, backpacker-style. The hotel is devoid of the standard amenities, and no meals are served, but there are several cafes in the area.

Calle Villa 122 (at Calle Unión/Concordia), Ponce, PR 00733. © 787/844-3255. Fax 787/844-3255. www.hotelbelgica.com. 20 units (shower only). $75 double. MC, V. *In room:* A/C, TV, no phone.

WHERE TO DINE
EXPENSIVE
La Cava ✦✦ INTERNATIONAL   Designed like a hive of venerable rooms within a 19th-century coffee plantation, this is the most appealing and elaborate restaurant in Ponce. It has a well-trained staff, a sense of antique charm, well-prepared cuisine, and a champagne-and-cigar bar. Menu items change every 6 weeks but might

include duck foie gras with toasted brioche, Parma ham with mango, cold poached scallops with mustard sauce, fricassee of lobster and mushrooms in a pastry shell, and grilled lamb sausage with mustard sauce on a bed of couscous. Dessert could be a black-and-white soufflé or a trio of tropical sorbets.

In the Ponce Hilton, Av. Caribe 1150. © **787/259-7676.** Reservations recommended. Main courses $26–$30. AE, DC, DISC, MC, V. Mon–Sat 6:30–10:30pm.

Mark's at the Meliá 𝕬𝕬𝕬 INTERNATIONAL   Mark French (isn't that a great name for a chef?) elevates Puerto Rican dishes into haute cuisine at this eatery. You'd think he'd been entertaining the celebs in San Juan instead of cooking at what is somewhat of a Caribbean backwater. French was hailed as "Chef of the Caribbean 2000" in Fort Lauderdale. With his constantly changing menus and his insistence that everything be fresh, he's still a winner. You'll fall in love with this guy when you taste his tamarind barbecued lamb with yuca mojo. Go on to sample the lobster *pionono* with tomato-and-chive salad or the freshly made sausage with pumpkin, cilantro, and chicken. All over Puerto Rico you get fried green plantains, but here they come topped with sour cream and a dollop of caviar. The corn-crusted red snapper with yuca purée and tempura jumbo shrimp with Asian salad are incredible. The desserts are spectacular, notably the vanilla flan layered with rum spongecake and topped with a caramelized banana, as well as the award-winning bread-pudding soufflé with coconut vanilla sauce.

In the Hotel Meliá, Calle Cristina. © **787/284-6275.** Reservations recommended. Main courses $16–$30. AE, MC, V. Tues–Sat noon–3pm and 6–10:30pm.

MODERATE

El Ancla 𝕬𝕬 PUERTO RICAN/SEAFOOD   Motorists who wish to escape from the city drive 2 miles (3.2km) south of Ponce to El Ancla, which is especially known for its seafood. Lying in a commercial port area, it offers fresh and well-prepared Puerto Rican dishes and makes a good outing from Ponce.

A favorite here is red snapper stuffed with lobster and shrimp, served with either fried plantain or mashed potatoes. Other specialties are filet of salmon in caper sauce and a seafood medley of lobster, shrimp, octopus, and conch. Most of the dishes are reasonably priced, especially the chicken and conch. Lobster tops the price scale. The side orders, including crabmeat rice and yuca in garlic, are delectable.

Av. Hostos, Playa Ponce. © **787/840-2450.** Main courses $15–$36. AE, DC, DISC, MC, V. Sun–Thurs 11am–10pm; Fri–Sat 11am–11pm.

La Montserrate PUERTO RICAN/SEAFOOD   Beside the seafront, in a residential area about 4 miles (6.4km) west of the town center, this restaurant draws a loyal following from the surrounding neighborhood. A culinary institution in Ponce since it was established 20 years ago, it occupies a large, airy, modern building divided into two different dining areas. The first of these is slightly more formal than the other. Most visitors head for the less formal, large room in back, where windows on three sides encompass a view of some offshore islands. Specialties, concocted from the catch of the day, might include octopus salad, several different kinds of *asopao*, a whole red snapper in Creole sauce, or a selection of steaks and grills. Nothing is innovative, but the cuisine is typical of the south of Puerto Rico, and it's a family favorite. The fish dishes are better than the meat selections.

Sector Las Cucharas, Rte. 2. (C) **787/841-2740.** Main courses $17–$29. AE, MC, V. Daily 11am–10pm.

La Terraza (★) INTERNATIONAL   During the design phase of the Ponce Hilton, a team of architects devoted one of its biggest, sunniest, and most interesting interior spaces to this dramatic-looking restaurant, where two-story walls of windows sweep the eye out over the greenery of the hotel's garden. Lunchtimes focus on a well-stocked buffet that dominates rooms off to the side of the eating area. At nighttime, except for a sprawling soup-and-salad bar (access to which is included in the price of any main course), the buffet is eliminated in favor of a la carte dining that's choreographed by a carefully trained staff. Menu items change with the seasons but are likely to include grilled grouper with either lemon butter or *criollo* sauce; T-bone steaks with béarnaise, red-wine, or mushroom sauce; a succulent chateaubriand that's prepared for two diners at a time; and lobster that's available in several different ways.

In the Ponce Hilton, Av. Caribe 1150. (C) **787/259-7676.** Breakfast $5–$19; lunch buffet $22 ($24 on Sun); dinner main courses $24–$36. AE, DC, DISC, MC, V. Daily 6:30–11:30am, noon–3pm, and 6:30–10:30pm.

INEXPENSIVE

Café Tomas/Café Tompy (Value) PUERTO RICAN   The more visible and busier section of this establishment functions as a simple cafe for neighbors and local merchants. At plastic tables often flooded with sunlight from the big windows, you can order coffee, sandwiches, or cold beer, perhaps while relaxing after a walking tour of the city.

The family-run restaurant part of this establishment is more formal. The discreet entrance is adjacent to the cafe on Calle Isabel. Here, amid a decor reminiscent of a Spanish *tasca* (*tapas* bar), you can enjoy such simply prepared dishes as salted filet of beef, beefsteak with onions, four kinds of *asopao*, buttered eggs, octopus salads, and yuca croquettes.

Calle Isabel at Calle Mayor. 𝒞 787/840-1965. Breakfast $3.25–$5.25; main courses lunch and dinner $7–$18. AE, MC, V. Restaurant daily 11am–11pm; cafe daily 7am–midnight.

2 Mayagüez ⊛

98 miles (158km) W of San Juan; 15 miles (24km) S of Aguadilla

The largest city on the island's west coast, Mayagüez is a port whose elegance and charm reached its zenith during the mercantile and agricultural prosperity of the 19th century. Most of the town's stately buildings were destroyed in an earthquake in 1918, and today the town is noted more for its industry than its aesthetic appeal.

Although it's a commercial city, Mayagüez is a convenient stopover for those exploring the west coast. If you want a windsurfing beach, you can head north of Rincón, and if you want a more tranquil beach, you can drive south from Mayagüez along Route 102 to Boquerón.

Although the town itself dates from the mid–18th century, the area around it has figured in European history since the time of Christopher Columbus, who landed nearby in 1493. Today, in the gracious plaza at the town's center, a bronze statue of Columbus stands atop a metallic globe of the world.

Famed for the size and depth of its **harbor** (the second-largest on the island, after San Juan's harbor), Mayagüez was built to control the **Mona Passage,** a route essential to the Spanish Empire when Puerto Rico and the nearby Dominican Republic were vital trade and defensive jewels in the Spanish crown. Today this waterway is notorious for the destructiveness of its currents, the ferocity of its sharks, and the thousands of boat people who arrive illegally from either Haiti or the Dominican Republic, both on the island of Hispaniola.

Queen Isabel II of Spain recognized Mayagüez's status as a town in 1836. Her son, Alfonso XII, granted it a city charter in 1877. Permanently isolated from the major commercial developments of San Juan, Mayagüez, like Ponce, has always retained its own distinct identity.

Mayagüez

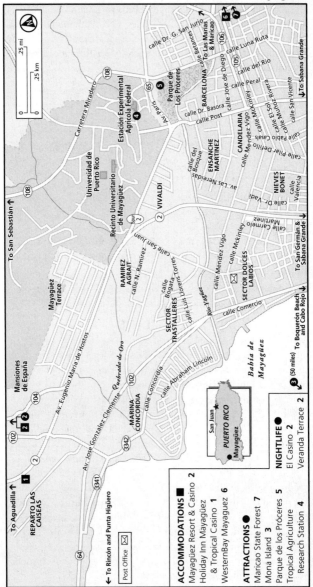

ACCOMMODATIONS ■
Mayagüez Resort & Casino 2
Holiday Inn Mayagüez
& Tropical Casino 1
WesternBay Mayaguez 6

ATTRACTIONS ●
Maricao State Forest 7
Mona Island 3
Parque de los Próceres 5
Tropical Agriculture
Research Station 4

NIGHTLIFE ●
El Casino 2
Veranda Terrace 2

Today the town's major industry is tuna packing. In fact, 60% of the tuna consumed in the United States is packed here. This is also an important departure point for deep-sea fishing and is the bustling port for exporting agricultural produce from the surrounding hillsides.

ESSENTIALS

GETTING THERE   **Cape Air** (© 800/352-0714; www.flycape air.com) flies from San Juan to Mayagüez twice daily (flying time: 40 min.). Round-trip passage is $180 per person.

If you're driving from San Juan, head either west on Route 2 (trip time: 2½ hr.) or south from San Juan on the scenic Route 52 (trip time: 3 hr.). Route 52 offers easier travel.

GETTING AROUND   **Taxis** meet arriving planes. If you take one, negotiate the fare with the driver first because cabs are unmetered here.

There are branches of **Avis** (© 787/832-0406), **Budget** (© 787/832-4570), and **Hertz** (© 787/832-3314) at the Mayagüez airport.

VISITOR INFORMATION   Mayagüez doesn't have a tourist-information office. If you're starting out in San Juan, inquire there before you set out (see "Visitor Information" on p. 52).

BEACHES & TROPICAL GARDENS

Along the western coastal bends of Route 2, north of Mayagüez, lie the best **surfing beaches** in the Caribbean. Surfers from as far away as New Zealand come to ride the waves. You can also check out panoramic **Punta Higüero** beach, nearby on Route 413, near Rincón. For more information, see the "Rincón" section on p. 172.

South of Mayagüez is **Boquerón beach** ⊛⊛, one of the island's best, with a wide strip of white sand and good snorkeling conditions.

The chief attraction in Mayagüez is the **Tropical Agriculture Research Station (Estación Experimental Agrícola Federal)** ⊛ (© 787/831-3435). It's located on Route 65, between Calle Post and Route 108, adjacent to the University of Puerto Rico at Mayagüez campus and across the street from the **Parque de los Próceres (Patriots' Park).** At the administration office, ask for a free map of the tropical gardens, which have one of the largest collections of tropical plant species intended for practical use, including cacao, fruit trees, spices, timbers, and ornamentals. The grounds are open Monday through Friday from 7am to 4pm, and there is no admission fee.

Mayagüez is the jumping-off point for visits to unique **Mona Island,** the "Galápagos of the Caribbean." See the box below for details.

Not far from Mayagüez is **Maricao.** You can reach Maricao from Mayagüez by heading directly east along Route 105, which will take you across mountain scenery and along fertile fields until you reach the village.

From Maricao, you can take Route 120 south to Km 13.8, or from Mayagüez you can take Route 105 east to the **Maricao State Forest** ⚘ picnic area, located 2,900 feet (884m) above sea level. The observation tower here provides a panoramic view across the green mountains up to the coastal plains. Trails are signposted here, and your goal might be the highest peak in the forest, Las Tetas de Cerro Gordo, at 2,625 feet (800m). A panoramic view unfolds from here, including a spotting of the offshore island of Mona. Nearly 50 species of birds live in this forest, including the Lesser Antillean pewee and the scaly *naped* pigeon. Nature watchers will be delighted to know that there are some 280 tree species in this reserve, 38 of which are found only here.

SHOPPING

This city wasn't a shopping mecca until the opening of the **Mayagüez Mall,** Av. Hostos 975 at Route 2 (✆ **787/265-3245**). Although geared more to local residents than visitors, this mall offers some 150 outlets, selling a little bit of everything—both practical merchandise such as clothing and island handicrafts.

WHERE TO STAY

Holiday Inn Mayagüez & Tropical Casino   This six-story hotel competes with the Mayagüez Resort & Casino (see below), which we like better. However, the Holiday Inn is well-maintained, contemporary, and comfortable. It has a marble-floored, high-ceilinged lobby, an outdoor pool with a waterside bar, and a big casino, but its lawn simply isn't as dramatically landscaped as the Mayagüez Resort's surrounding acreage. Bedrooms here are comfortably but functionally outfitted in motel style. Each unit includes a tiled bathroom with a tub/shower combo.

Rte. 2 no. 2701 (Km 149.9), Mayagüez, PR 00680-6328. ✆ **800/HOLIDAY** or 787/833-1100. Fax 787/833-1300. www.holiday-inn.com. 142 units. $113–$147 double; $197 suite. AE, DC, DISC, MC, V. **Amenities:** Restaurant; 2 bars; outdoor pool; gym; business center; limited room service; laundry service; rooms for those w/limited mobility; casino. *In room:* A/C, TV, dataport, coffeemaker, hair dryer, iron, safe.

Mona Island: The Galápagos of the Caribbean

Off Mayagüez, the unique island of **Mona** ★★★ is a destination for the hardy pilgrim who seeks the road less traveled. You'll find no hotels here, so a pup tent, backpack, and hiking boots will have to do. Snorkelers, spelunkers, biologists, and eco-tourists find much to fascinate them in Mona's wildlife, mangrove forests, coral reefs, and complex honeycomb, which is the largest marine-originated cave in the world. There are also miles of secluded white-sand beaches and palm trees.

Uninhabited today, Mona was for centuries the scene of considerable human activity, from the pre-Columbian Taíno Indians to guano miners to Columbus to the notorious pirate Captain Kidd, who used Mona as a temporary hideout.

Mona can be reached by organized tour from Mayagüez. Camping is available at $10 per night, but only from mid-April to late November. Everything needed, including water, must be brought in, and everything, including garbage, must be taken out. For more information, call the **Puerto Rico Department of Natural Resources** at ✆ 787/722-1726.

The only way to get to Mona Island is by private boat or through tour operator **Orca Too** (✆ 787/851-2185), which arranges day transport to the island. Tours cost $135 per person.

Mayagüez Resort & Casino ★   Except for the ritzy Horned Dorset Primavera (p. 174), this is the largest and best general hotel resort in western Puerto Rico, appealing equally to business travelers and vacationers. In 1995, local investors took over what was then a sagging Hilton and radically renovated it, to the tune of $5 million. The hotel benefits from its redesigned casino/country-club format, and 20 acres (8.1ha) of tropical gardens that include five species of palm trees and eight kinds of bougainvillea, for starters.

The hotel's well-designed bedrooms open onto views of the pool, and many units have private balconies. Units tend to be small, but they have good beds. The restored bathrooms are well-equipped with makeup mirrors, scales, and tub/shower combos.

The restaurant **El Castillo** ℞ is the best-managed large-scale dining room in western Puerto Rico, known for generous lunch buffets and a la carte dinners. Menu highlights include seafood stew served on a bed of linguine with marinara sauce, grilled salmon with mango-flavored Grand Marnier sauce, and steak and lobster.

The **Veranda Terrace** lounge, open daily until 1am, has a lush view of a manicured tropical garden and is a relaxing place for a rum-based cocktail. **El Casino** is the completely remodeled 24-hour casino, where you can try your luck at blackjack, dice, slot machines, roulette, and minibaccarat.

Rte. 104 Km .3 (P.O. Box 3781), Mayagüez, PR 00680. (C) **877/784-6835** or 787/832-3030. Fax 787/265-3020. www.mayaguezresort.com. 140 units. $185–$250 double; $325 suite. AE, DC, DISC, MC, V. Parking $4.50. **Amenities:** Restaurant; 3 bars; Olympic-size pool and children's pool; 3 tennis courts; small fitness room; Jacuzzi; steam room; playground; room service; massage; babysitting; laundry service; rooms for those w/limited mobility; casino. *In room:* A/C, TV, dataport, minibar, coffeemaker, iron, Wi-Fi.

WesternBay Mayaguez ℞   For years this was the old Parador El Sol, welcoming visitors to Puerto Rico's third city since 1970. In 2007 new owners took it over, adding 30 rooms and restoring the public lounges and private accommodations with better furnishings, offering more comfort. In time for the winter season in early 2008, all of these renovations are expected to be completed, which perhaps will make this hotel the most up-to-date in town. The six-floor restored hotel is central to the shopping district and to all major highways, lying 2 blocks from the landmark Plaza del Mercado in the heart of Mayagüez.

Calle Santiago Riera Palmer 9 Este, Mayagüez, PR 00680. (C) **787/834-0303.** Fax 787/265-7567. www.westernbaymayaguez.com. 81 units. $75–$95 double; $105 triple. Rates include continental breakfast. AE, MC, V. Free parking. **Amenities:** Restaurant; bar; pool; room for those w/limited mobility. *In room:* A/C, TV, hair dryer.

9

Western Puerto Rico

The scenery of western Puerto Rico varies from a terrain evoking the Arizona desert to a dense blanket of green typical of Germany's Black Forest. Some 8 centuries ago, the Taíno Indians inhabited this western part of Puerto Rico, using it as a site for recreation and worship. Stone monoliths, some decorated with petroglyphs, remain as evidence of that long-ago occupation. The interior has such attractions as the Taíno Indian Ceremonial Park, Río Camuy Cave Park, Arecibo Observatory, and the Karst Country. Along the west and south coasts, you'll find white sandy beaches, world-class surfing conditions, and numerous towns and attractions. There are modest hotels from which to choose, as well as a few noteworthy *paradores,* a chain of government-sponsored, privately operated country inns. But the waters of the Atlantic northwest coast tend to be rough—ideal for surfers but not always good for swimming.

There is a tremendous difference between a holiday on the east coast of Puerto Rico (see chapter 10) and one on the west coast. Nearly all visitors from San Juan head east to explore the El Yunque rainforest (see chapter 7). After that, and perhaps a lazy afternoon on Luquillo Beach, they head back to San Juan and its many resorts and attractions. Others who remain for a holiday in the east are likely to do so because they want to stay at one of the grand resorts such as El Conquistador (p. 190).

Western Puerto Rico is where the Puerto Ricans themselves go for holidays by the sea. The only pocket of posh here is the Horned Dorset Primavera Hotel at Rincón (see "Rincón," below). Rincón is also the beach area most preferred by windsurfers. Other than that, most locals and a few adventurous visitors seeking the offbeat and charming head for the southwestern sector of the island. This is the real Puerto Rico; it hasn't been taken over by high-rise resorts and posh restaurants.

Puerto Rico's west coast has been compared to the old U.S. Wild West. There is a certain truth to that. The cattle ranches on the rolling upland pastures south of the town of Lajas will evoke home for

Western Puerto Rico & the Southwest Coast

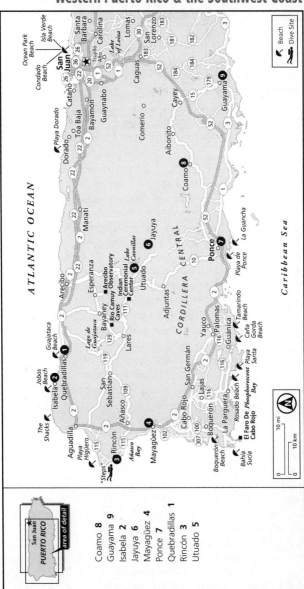

ATLANTIC OCEAN

Caribbean Sea

Ocean Park Beach
Isla Verde Beach
Condado Beach
San Juan
Santa Barbara
Carolina
Lomas
Santa Lorenzo
183
181
182
30
San Lorenzo
Trujillo Alto
Lake of Loíza
Caguas
184
179
Guayama ❾
Cataño
Guaynabo
Bayamón
Toa Baja
Playa Dorado
Dorado
Comerio
Cayey
15
Aibonito
52
Coamo ❽
1
Manati
Arecibo
Esperanza
Arecibo Observatory
Indian Ceremonial Center
Bayaney
Río Camuy Caves
Lago de Guajataca
Lares
Utuado
Jayuya ❻
Lake Caonillas
Adjuntas
CORDILLERA CENTRAL
Ponce ❼
La Guancha
Playa de Ponce
Guajataca Beach
Quebradillas ❶
Jobos Beach
Isabela ❷
San Sebastián
Añasco
Yauco
Palomas
Guánica
Tamarindo Beach
Caña Gorda Beach
The Shacks
Aguadilla
Playa Higüero
Rincón ❸
Añasco Bay
"Steps"
Mayagüez ❹
San Germán
Lajas
Cabo Rojo
Boquerón
La Parguera
Playa Rosado Beach
Playa Santa
Boquerón Beach
El Faro De Cabo Rojo
Phosphorescent Bay
Bahía Sucia

10 mi
10 km

area of detail

San Juan
PUERTO RICO

Coamo 8
Guayama 9
Isabela 2
Jayuya 6
Mayagüez 4
Ponce 7
Quebradillas 1
Rincón 3
Utuado 5

Beach
Dive Site

those who come from northwest Texas. Others have compared the peninsula of Cabo Rojo in Puerto Rico to Baja, California.

This western part of Puerto Rico also contains the greatest concentration of *paradores,* attracting those who'd like to venture into the cool mountainous interior of the west, a wonderful escape from pollution and traffic on a hot day.

1 Rincón

100 miles (161km) W of San Juan; 6 miles (9.7km) N of Mayagüez

North of Mayagüez, on the westernmost point of the island, lies the small fishing village of Rincón, in the foothills of La Cadena mountains. It's not a sightseeing destination unto itself, but surfers from as far away as New Zealand say the area's reef-lined beaches, off Route 2 between Mayagüez and Rincón, are the best in the Caribbean. Surfers are particularly attracted to **Playa Higüero** 🐠🐠🐠, the beach at Punta Higüero, on Route 413, which ranks among the finest surfing spots in the world. During winter, uninterrupted swells from the North Atlantic form perfect waves, averaging 5 to 6 feet (1.5–1.8m) in height, with ridable rollers sometimes reaching 15 to 25 feet (4.6–7.6m).

The best snorkeling is at a beach gringos have labeled **Steps.** The waters here are more tranquil than at the beaches attracting surfers. Steps lies right off Route 413, just north of the center of Rincón.

Endangered humpback whales winter here, attracting a growing number of whale-watchers from December to March. The lighthouse at El Faro Park is a great place to spot these mammoth mammals.

Many nonsurfers visit Rincón for only one reason: the Horned Dorset Primavera Hotel, not only one of the finest hotels in Puerto Rico, but one of the best in the entire Caribbean.

ESSENTIALS

GETTING THERE & GETTING AROUND   If you rent a car at the San Juan airport, it will take approximately 2½ hours to drive here via the busy northern Route 2, or 3 hours via the scenic mountain route (no. 52) through Ponce to the south. We recommend the southern route.

In addition, there are two flights daily from San Juan to Mayagüez on **Cape Air** (© **800/352-0714;** www.flycapeair.com). These flights take 40 minutes, and round-trip fare is $180. Taxis meet planes arriving from San Juan. Because these cabs do not have meters, always negotiate the fare in advance.

There are branches of **Avis** (© 787/832-0406), **Budget** (© 787/832-4570), and **Hertz** (© 787/832-3314) at the Mayagüez airport.

VISITOR INFORMATION There is no tourist-information office in Rincón. Inquire in San Juan before heading here (see "Visitor Information" under "Orientation" in chapter 3).

SURFING & OTHER OUTDOOR PURSUITS

Despite its claim as the windsurfing capital of the Caribbean, there are very definite dangers in the waters off Rincón. In November 1998, three surfers (two from San Juan, one from the U.S. mainland) drowned in unrelated incidents offshore at María's Beach. These deaths are often cited as evidence of the dangerous surf that has misled some very experienced surfers. Local watersports experts urge anyone who's considering surfing at Rincón to ask a well-informed local for advice. When the surf is up and undertows and riptides are particularly strong, losing a surfboard while far offshore seems to be one of the first steps to eventually losing your life.

Windsurfing is best from November to April. The best beaches for surfing lie from Borinquén Point south to Rincón. There are many surfing outfitters along this strip, the best of which is **West Coast Surf Shop,** 2 E. Muñoz Rivera at Rincón (© 787/823-3935), open Monday through Saturday from 9am to 6pm and Sunday 10am to 5pm. A local surfing star, Darren Muschett, is the resident instructor here. Rates for lessons vary, but the outlet rents both long and short boards, charging $35 for 24 hours.

The windsurfers who hang out here like **Sandy Beach** because it does not have the stones and rocks found on some of the other beaches in the area. Also, from December to February it gets almost constant winds every day. Windsurfers wait on the terrace of Tamboo Tavern (see p. 178) for the right wind conditions before hitting the beach.

Oceans Unlimited, Highway 115 Km 12.2, Rincón (© 787/823-2340), is a dive charter operation servicing the entire west coast of Puerto Rico. It offers scuba diving and snorkeling charters to Desecho Island and Mona Island in a 48-foot (15m) vessel. All-inclusive camping and diving charters to Mona Island are offered, along with dive instruction, whale-watching, winter sunset cruises, and fishing charters.

Another good scuba outfitter is **Taíno Divers,** 164 Black Eagle Marina at Rincón (© 787/823-6429), which offers local boat charters along with scuba and snorkeling trips. Other activities include kite-boarding, whale-watching expeditions, and sunset cruises. Fees are $109 for a two-tank dive, $725 for a half-day fishing-boat rental, and $55 for snorkeling.

The most visible and sought-after whale-watching panorama in Rincón is **Parque El Faro de Rincón (Rincón's Lighthouse Park),** which lies on El Faro Point peninsula at the extreme western tip of town. Within its fenced-in perimeter are pavilions that sell souvenirs and snack items, rows of binoculars offering 25¢ views, and a stately looking lighthouse built in 1921. The park is at its most popular from December to March for whale-watching, and in January and February for surfer gazing. The park is locked every evening between midnight and 7am. Otherwise, you're free to promenade with the locals any time you like.

The park's snack bar is called **Restaurant El Faro,** Barrio Puntas, Rte. 413 Km 3.3 (no phone). Platters of American and Puerto Rican food, including *mofongos,* steaks, and burgers, cost from $13 to $19. When is it open? The owner told us, "I open whenever I want to. If I don't want to, I stay home."

Punta Borinquén Golf Club, Route 107 (© **787/890-2987**), 2 miles (3.2km) north of Aquadilla's center, across the highway from the city's airport, was originally built by the U.S. government as part of Ramey Air Force Base. Today, it is a public 18-hole golf course, open daily from 6:30am to 6:30pm. Greens fees are $20 per round; a golf cart that can carry two passengers rents for $30 for 18 holes. A set of clubs can be rented for $15. The clubhouse has a bar and a simple restaurant.

WHERE TO STAY
VERY EXPENSIVE
Horned Dorset Primavera Hotel 🌟🌟🌟 This is the most sophisticated hotel in Puerto Rico, and it's one of the most exclusive and elegant small properties anywhere in the Caribbean. Set on 8 acres (3.2ha), it was built on the massive breakwaters and sea walls erected by a local railroad many years ago. Guests here enjoy a secluded, semiprivate beach; this narrow strip of golden sand is choice, if small.

The hacienda evokes an aristocratic Spanish villa, with wicker armchairs, hand-painted tiles, ceiling fans, seaside terraces, and cascades of flowers. This is really a restful place. Accommodations are in a series of suites that ramble uphill amid lush gardens. The decor is tasteful, with four-poster beds and brass-footed tubs in marble-sheathed bathrooms.

Rooms are spacious and luxurious, with Persian rugs over tile floors, queen-size sofa beds in sitting areas, and fine linen. Bathrooms are equally roomy and luxurious. Twenty-eight suites are set at the edge of the property, some with private pools; the Primavera suites are 1,400-square-foot (130-sq.-m), two-story town houses, each with two full bathrooms and a private terrace with plunge pool.

The hotel's restaurant, **Horned Dorset Primavera,** is one of the finest in Puerto Rico (see "Where to Dine," below).

Rte. 429 (P.O. Box 1132), Rincón, PR 00677. © **800/633-1857** or 787/823-4030. Fax 787/823-5580. www.horneddorset.com. 39 units (all suites). Winter $1,377–$1,865 suite for 2; off season $717–$1,023 suite for 2. Rates include MAP (breakfast and dinner). AE, MC, V. Children under 12 not accepted. **Amenities:** 2 restaurants; bar; 3 outdoor pools (1 infinity); fitness center; room service; massage; laundry service. *In room:* A/C, hair dryer, safe.

EXPENSIVE

Rincón of the Seas ✹✹   Although it hardly knocks Horned Dorset Primavera off the charts, this Art Deco resort with its custom-made furnishings is a glamorous oceanfront address set in a botanical garden. With balconies opening onto sea vistas, the resort features large bedrooms with modern amenities. Even the least expensive accommodations are first-rate, ranging from standard doubles to beach cabanas and suites. Casual elegance rules the day, with such extra touches as hand-painted murals and marble floors. Acclaimed chef Robert Ruitz has been hired to oversee the cuisine and he turns out a combination of fusion, mainly Mediterranean and Asian-inspired dishes. The hotel bar is unique with hand-painted murals, rich vegetation, and exotic birds. Digital effects "interpret" the island's rainforest, El Yunque.

Rte. 115 Km 12.2, Rincón, PR 00677. © **866/2-RINCON** or 787/823-7500. Fax 787/823-7501. www.rinconoftheseas.com. 112 units. Winter $235–$255 double, $285 beach cabaña, $495 suite; off season $190–$205 double, $235 cabaña, $410 suite. AE, MC, V. **Amenities:** 3 restaurants; 2 bars. *In room:* A/C, TV, dataport, coffeemaker, hair dryer, iron, safe.

MODERATE

Casa Isleña Inn ✹ *Finds*   "Island House" is created from a simple oceanfront former home right on the beach. Behind its gates, away from the water, is a private and tranquil world that offers a series of medium-size and comfortably furnished bedrooms decorated in bright Caribbean colors and designs. Each room has a neatly maintained shower-only bathroom. A natural tidal pool formed by a reef is an 8-minute stroll from the inn. At the tidal pool and from the inn's terraces guests can enjoy views of Aguadilla Bay and Mona Passage. In winter, while standing on the terraces, you can often watch the migration of humpback whales.

Rte. 413 Km 4, Barrio Puntas, Rincón, PR 00677. ℂ **888/289-7750** or 787/823-1525. Fax 787/823-1530. 9 units (shower only). $115–$185 double. Extra person $15. AE, MC, V. **Amenities:** Restaurant for breakfast and lunch; bar; outdoor pool; room for those w/limited mobility. *In room:* A/C, TV, no phone.

Lemontree Oceanfront Cottages ★ (Finds) Right on a good, sandy beach, these spacious apartments with kitchenettes are for those who don't want to limit themselves to hotel rooms and meals. With the sound of the surf just outside your private back porch, these well-furnished seaside units can provide a home away from home, with everything from ceiling fans to air-conditioning, from paperback libraries to custom woodworking details. The property is well-maintained. Families enjoy the three-bedroom, two-bathroom oceanfront suites called "Papaya"; the "Mango" and "Pineapple" accommodations are ideal for two people. Each unit contains a midsize shower-only bathroom. The least expensive units, "Banana" and "Coconut," are studio units for those who want a kitchen but don't require a living room. The cottages lie a 10-minute drive west of Rincón.

Rte. 429 (P.O. Box 200), Rincón, PR 00677. ℂ **888/418-8733** or 787/823-6452. Fax 787/823-5821. www.lemontreepr.com. 6 units (shower only). Winter $120–$150 double, $180 quad, $195 for 6; off season $105–$135 double, $155 quad, $180 for 6. AE, MC, V. **Amenities:** Nonsmoking rooms; rooms for those w/limited mobility. *In room:* A/C, TV, kitchenette, coffeemaker, Wi-Fi.

INEXPENSIVE

The Lazy Parrot Set within an unlikely inland neighborhood, far from any particular view of the sea, this place has a better-than-average restaurant and clean, well-organized bedrooms. Each unit is comfortable, even if not overly large, with light-grained and durable furnishings that might seem appropriate for the bedroom of a high-school senior in a suburb on the U.S. mainland. Bathrooms are simple, functional, and workable, each with a shower, but not at all plush. Lazy Parrot was built as a private home in the 1970s and then transformed into the inn you see today. The place is just as well-known for its restaurant as it is for its rooms. Meals are served in an open-sided aerie on the building's uppermost floor.

Rte. 413 Km 4.1, Barrio Puntas, Rincón, PR 00677. ℂ **800/294-1752** or 787/823-5654. Fax 787/823-0224. www.lazyparrot.com. 11 units. $110–$125 double. Rates include continental breakfast. AE, DC, MC, V. **Amenities:** Restaurant; bar; pool; room service; babysitting. *In room:* A/C, TV, fridge.

Parador Villa Antonio   Ilia and Hector Ruíz offer apartments by the sea in this privately owned and run *parador.* The beach outside could be nicer, but the local authorities don't keep it as clean as they ought to. Surfing and fishing can be enjoyed just outside your front door, and you can bring your catch right into your cottage and prepare a fresh seafood dinner in your own kitchenette (there's no restaurant). This is a popular destination with families from Puerto Rico, who crowd in on the weekends to occupy the motel-like rooms with balconies or terraces. Furnishings are well-used but offer reasonable comfort, and the shower-only bathrooms are small.

Rte. 115 Km 12.3 (P.O. Box 68), Rincón, PR 00677. © 787/823-2645. Fax 787/823-3380. www.villa-antonio.com. 61 units (shower only). $96–$128 studio (up to 2 people); $125–$144 2-bedroom apt (holds up to 4 people); $120 junior suite; $128 suite. AE, DISC, MC, V. **Amenities:** 2 outdoor pools; 2 tennis courts; playground; babysitting; laundry service; nonsmoking rooms; rooms for those w/limited mobility. *In room:* A/C, TV, coffeemaker, iron, safe, Wi-Fi.

Villa Cofresi   Set about a mile (1.6km) south of Rincón's center, this is a clean, family-run hotel with a view of the beach. Thanks to the three adult children of the Caro family, the place is better-managed than many of its competitors. Bedrooms are comfortable and airy, with well-chosen furniture that might remind you of something in southern Florida. Each unit has a white-tile floor and a small bathroom with a tub and shower. Most rooms have two double beds; some have two twin beds. The two units that tend to be reserved out long in advance are nos. 47 and 55, which have windows opening directly onto the sea.

The in-house restaurant, **La Ana de Cofresi,** is named after the ship that was captained by the region's most famous 18th-century pirate, Roberto Cofresi. Hand-painted murals highlight some of his adventures. Open Monday through Friday from 5 to 10pm and Saturday and Sunday from noon to 10pm, it charges $8 to $30 for well-prepared main courses that are likely to include fish consommé, four kinds of *mofongo,* breaded scampi served either with Creole sauce or garlic, and very good steaks, including a 12-ounce New York sirloin. All rooms are nonsmoking.

Rte. 115 Km 12, Rincón, PR 00677. © 787/823-2450. Fax 787/823-1770. www.villa cofresi.com. 80 units. Winter $135 double, $160 suite; off season $115 double, $140 suite. AE, DC, MC, V. **Amenities:** Outdoor pool; room service; rooms for those w/limited mobility. *In room:* A/C, TV, kitchenette, fridge, coffeemaker, hair dryer.

WHERE TO DINE
VERY EXPENSIVE
Horned Dorset Primavera ⚮⚮ FRENCH/CARIBBEAN   This is the finest restaurant in western Puerto Rico—so romantic that people sometimes come from San Juan just for an intimate dinner. A masonry staircase sweeps from the garden to the second floor, where soaring ceilings and an atmosphere similar to that in a private villa awaits you.

The menu, which changes virtually every night based on the inspiration of the chef, might include chilled parsnip soup, a fricassee of wahoo with wild mushrooms, grilled loin of beef with peppercorns, and medallions of lobster in an orange-flavored beurre-blanc sauce. The grilled breast of duckling with bay leaves and raspberry sauce is also delectable. Mahimahi is grilled and served with ginger-cream sauce on a bed of braised Chinese cabbage. It's delicious.

In the Horned Dorset Primavera Hotel, Rte. 429. ✆ **787/823-4030.** Reservations recommended. Fixed-price dinner $76 for 5 dishes, $110 for 8 dishes. AE, MC, V. Daily 7–9:30pm.

MODERATE
Tres Palmas Restaurant ⚮ NEW CREOLE   In Rincón visitors no longer have to depend on the two luxe properties (see "Where to Stay," above) for fine dining. The opening of Tres Palmas has improved the local dining scene considerably. The modern structure itself is unimpressive—but not the Caribbean dishes served with a certain flair. You can stop in before your reservation to enjoy a "sundowner" in the bar. Some of the freshest fish and shellfish along the western coastline is served here, but the kitchen also does meat dishes well, especially some of the best cuts of aged beef. The owners, Mr. and Mrs. José Ramirez, welcome you personally, tempting you with such dishes as conch or lobster salad for an appetizer, perhaps delectable crab claws. The signature main dish is coconut lobster, although you can also delight in grilled filet of various fish, including mahimahi, red snapper, or salmon. One of the best pasta dishes is shrimp fettuccine a la carbonara. For dessert, we'd recommend their caramel pecan cake or the *cazuela de calabaza* (pumpkin delight).

Rte. 413, Rincón. ✆ **787/823-6010.** Main courses $14–$18. MC. Daily noon–3pm and 6–10pm.

INEXPENSIVE
Tamboo Tavern AMERICAN   The allure of this place derives from the crowd of surfing enthusiasts who gather here for drinks

and fuel before braving the sometimes-treacherous waters at Sandy Beach. The staff pride themselves on knowing the latest surfing conditions. Burgers and sandwiches are the most frequently ordered items, and rum-and-Cokes and piña coladas are enduringly popular, too.

Sandy Beach. © **787/823-8550.** Reservations not accepted. Main courses $5–$25 dinner. MC, V. Bar daily noon–2am; restaurant daily noon–9:30pm.

2 *Paradores* of Western Puerto Rico

One program that has helped the Puerto Rico Tourism Company successfully promote the commonwealth as "The Complete Island"— the *paradores puertorriqueños*—will help make your travels even more enjoyable.

The *paradores puertorriqueños* (p. 40 for more details about these government-sponsored inns; p. 41 for a map) are a chain of privately owned and operated country inns under the auspices and supervision of the Commonwealth Development Company. These hostelries are easily identified by the Taíno grass hut that appears in the signs and logos of each one. The Puerto Rico Tourism Company started the program in 1973, modeling it after Spain's *parador* system, although many of the *paradores* here are mere shanties compared to some of the deluxe Spanish hostelries. Each *parador* is situated in a historic or particularly beautiful spot. They vary in size, but most share the virtues of affordability, hospitable staffs, and high standards of cleanliness. Most but not all of their rooms are air-conditioned, and each room has a bathroom.

For more information about *paradores,* contact the **Puerto Rico Tourism Co.,** P.O. Box 9023960, Old San Juan Station, San Juan, PR 00902 (© **787/721-2400;** www.gotoparadores.com).

Tips *Mesones Gastronómicos*

For authentic island cuisine, you can rely on the *mesones gastronómicos* **(gastronomic inns).** This established dining network, sanctioned by the Puerto Rico Tourism Company, highlights restaurants recognized for excellence in preparing and serving Puerto Rican specialties, especially fresh fish, at modest prices. Regrettably, there are no maps listing these myriad restaurants, but their signs are easy to spot as you drive around the island.

JAYUYA

The village of Jayuya, southwest of San Juan and north of Ponce, lies in the middle of the Cordillera Central, a mountain massif. From San Juan, travel west along Highway 22, going past the town of Barceloneta until you come to the junction of Route 140; head south to the town of Florida, passing through some of the most dramatic scenery in Puerto Rico. Continue along Route 140 until you come to the junction of Route 141, signposted southwest into Jayuya.

Jayuya is a small town that still retains strong Taíno cultural influences, particularly in the language. At the Jayuya Indian Festival in mid-November, you'll see crafts markets, parades, and displays of Taíno dances. The festival honors the patron saint of the town, Nuestra Señora la Monserrate.

Here you'll also find the Parador Hacienda Gripiñas (see below), a former coffee plantation, where you can glimpse the good old days in Puerto Rico. In 1950 Jayuya received worldwide attention when *independentistas* proclaimed the "Republic of Puerto Rico" and held the town under siege until the National Guard was called in.

WHERE TO STAY & DINE

Parador Hacienda Gripiñas 🎏   A former coffee plantation about 2½ hours from San Juan, Parador Hacienda Gripiñas is reached via a long, narrow, and curvy road. This home-turned-inn is a delightful blend of old-world hacienda and modern conveniences. The plantation ambience is created with ceiling fans, splendid gardens, porch hammocks, and more than 20 acres (8.1ha) of coffee bushes. You'll taste the homegrown product when you order the inn's aromatic brew.

The modest rooms vary in size, and all are kept very tidy. Each unit has a small, tiled shower-only bathroom. For meals, we suggest the restaurant's Puerto Rican dishes rather than the international cuisine. You can swim in the two chilly mountain pools, soak up the sun, or enjoy the nearby sights, such as the Taíno Indian Ceremonial Park at Utuado. Boating and plenty of fishing are just 30 minutes away, at Lake Caonillas. The *parador* is also near the Río Camuy Caves. All rooms are nonsmoking.

Rte. 527 Km 2.5 (P.O. Box 387), Jayuya, PR 00664. ✆ **787/828-1717.** Fax 787/828-1719. 20 units (shower only). $125 double. Rates include 2 meals a day. AE, MC, V. From Jayuya, head east via Rte. 144; at the junction with Rte. 527, go south 1½ miles (2.4km). **Amenities:** Restaurant; 2 outdoor pools; room service. *In room:* A/C, TV, safe.

UTUADO

Another good base in the Cordillera Central massif is the little mountain town of Utuado, which lies northwest of Jayuya (see above). This is the heartland of karst, an irregular limestone terrain with sinkholes, underground streams, and caverns. This unique landscape was created over several millennia by heavy rainfall. Utuado is a stronghold of *jíbaro* ("hillbilly") culture, reflecting the mountain life of the island as few other settlements do.

Petroglyphs left over from the Taíno civilization have been found in the area. One depicts an Indian woman with frog legs and an elaborate headdress. From Utuado, you can continue west for 20 miles (32km) on Route 111 to Km 12.3, to reach the Taíno Indian Ceremonial Center (see "Life After Death for the Taíno Indians," below).

WHERE TO STAY & DINE

Casa Grande Mountain Retreat   This *parador,* situated on 107 lush and steeply inclined acres (43ha) of a former coffee plantation in the Caonillas Barrios district, about 1½ hours from San Juan, originated in the 19th century as a hacienda. Thanks to Steve Weingarten, a retired lawyer from New York City, the isolated compound functions today as a simple, eco-sensitive hotel. The cement-sided core of the original hacienda is on view in the lobby and in the likable eatery, Casa Grande Cafe, which serves an array of well-prepared international and Puerto Rican Creole-style dishes. Nonguests can eat here daily from 7:30am to 9:30pm.

Accommodations lie within five wood-sided cottages (four units to a cottage, some of them duplex) scattered throughout the surrounding acreage. Each unit has deliberately simple, spartan-looking decor with exposed wood, airy verandas, a balcony, a hammock, a view of the mountains, and a small bathroom with shower. None have TV, phone, or air-conditioning—as such, they're popular with urbanites who want to get back to nature, and some come here to brush up on yoga and meditation skills. A nature trail is carved out of the surrounding forest. Under separate management, a riding stable offers horseback riding a short distance away.

P.O. Box 1499, Utuado, PR 00641. (C) **888/343-2272** or 787/894-3900. Fax 787/ 894-3900. www.hotelcasagrande.com. 20 units. $80–$95 double. AE, DISC, MC, V. From Arecibo, take Rte. 10 south to Utuado, then head east on Rte. 111 to Rte. 140; head north on Rte. 140 to Rte. 612 for ¼ mile (.4km). **Amenities:** Restaurant; bar; outdoor pool; laundry service; nonsmoking rooms. *In room:* Ceiling fan, safe, no phone.

Life After Death for the Taíno Indians

The Taíno Indians who lived in Puerto Rico before Europeans came here were ruled by *caciques* (chiefs), who controlled their own villages and several others nearby. The Taínos believed in life after death, which led them to take extreme care in burying their dead. Personal belongings of the deceased were placed in the tomb with the newly dead, and bodies were carefully arranged in a squatting position. Near Ponce, visitors can see the oldest Indian burial ground uncovered in the Antilles, Tibes Indian Ceremonial Center (p. 155).

Still standing near Utuado, a small mountain town, **Parque Ceremonial Indígena-Caguaña (Indian Ceremonial Park at Caguaña),** Route 111 Km 12.3 (℘ **787/894-7325**), was built by the Taínos for recreation and worship some 800 years ago. Stone monoliths, some etched with petroglyphs, rim several of the 10 *bateyes* (playing fields) used for a ceremonial game that some historians believe was a forerunner to soccer. The monoliths and petroglyphs, as well as the *dujos* (ceremonial chairs), are existing examples of the Taínos' skill in carving wood and stone.

Archaeologists have dated this site to approximately 2 centuries before Europe's discovery of the New World. It is believed that the Taíno chief Guarionex gathered his subjects on this site to celebrate rituals and practice sports. Set on a 13-acre (5.3ha) field surrounded by trees, some 14 vertical monoliths with colorful petroglyphs are arranged around a central sacrificial stone monument. The ball complex also includes a museum, which is open daily from 8:30am to 4:30pm; admission is $2, free for children under 12.

There is also a gallery called Herencia Indígena, where you can purchase Taíno relics at reasonable prices, including the sought-after Cemis (Taíno idols) and figures of the famous little frog, the *coquí*. The Taínos are long gone, and much that was here is gone, too. This site is of special interest to those with academic pursuits, but of only passing interest to the lay visitor.

QUEBRADILLAS

Quebradillas is one of the sleepy municipalities of northwest Puerto Rico. With its flamboyantly painted houses, narrow streets, and spiritualist herb shops, it is like a town of long ago. Quebradillas lies 70 miles (113km) west of San Juan, only about a 15-mile (24km) trip from the city of Arecibo along Route 2.

The Atlantic waters along the northwest coast of Puerto Rico tend to be rough, with the rugged coastline seemingly plunging right into the ocean. Both snorkelers and scuba divers are drawn to a protected beach area known as **The Shacks,** close to the town of Isabela, northwest of Quebradillas. The reefs and coral caverns here are some of the most dramatic in Puerto Rico. Surfers also flock to Isabela's Jobos Beach. Neither beach, however, is ideal for swimming.

Also northwest of Quebradillas lies beautiful **Guajataca Beach,** with its white sands, raging surf, and turbulent, deep waters. This is a fine beach for sunning and collecting shells, but it's a *playa peligrosa* (dangerous beach) unless you're a skilled swimmer. You can also visit **Lago de Guajataca,** another beautiful spot, by heading south for 7 miles (11km) on Route 113. This man-made lake is a lovely place for hiking, and it's the site of two *paradores* (see below). The staff at these government-sponsored inns will give you advice about jaunts in the **Guajataca Forest Reserve** to the immediate west.

WHERE TO STAY & DINE

Hotel El Guajataca *Kids*   You'll find this place on a rolling hillside reaching down to a surf-beaten beach along the north coast. Stay here for the stunning natural setting, and don't expect too much because the hotel itself is somewhat seedy. Each room is rather standard and has its own entrance and private balcony opening onto the turbulent Atlantic. Bathrooms are slightly battered but functional, each with a tub.

Served in a glassed-in dining room where all the windows face the sea, the cuisine isn't much more memorable than the accommodations, with little care going into the preparation of the often-canned ingredients. A local musical group plays for dining and dancing on Friday and Saturday evenings. There are two swimming pools (one for adults, another for children), plus a playground for children.

Rte. 2 Km 103.8 (P.O. Box 1558), Quebradillas, PR 00678. *©* **800/964-3065** or 787/895-3070. Fax 787/895-3589. www.hotelelguajataca.com. 38 units. $107–$118 double. AE, MC, V. From Quebradillas, continue northwest on Rte. 2 for 1 mile (1.6km); the *parador* is signposted. **Amenities:** Restaurant; bar; 2 outdoor pools; room service; laundry service; dry cleaning; coin-op laundry. *In room:* A/C, TV, safe.

Parador Vistamar   In the Guajataca area, this *parador*, one of the largest in Puerto Rico, sits like a sentinel surveying the scene from high atop a mountain overlooking greenery and a seascape. There are gardens and intricate paths carved into the side of the mountain, where you can stroll while enjoying the fragrance of the tropical flowers. Or you might choose to search for the calcified fossils that abound on the carved mountainside. For a unique experience, visitors can try their hand at freshwater fishing just down the hill from the hotel (bring your own gear). Flocks of rare tropical birds are frequently seen in the nearby mangroves.

Bedrooms are comfortably furnished in a rather bland motel style. Bathrooms with either shower or tub are functional, but without much decorative zest. There's a dining room with an ocean view where you can have a typical Puerto Rican dinner or choose from the international menu.

A short drive from the hotel will bring you to the Punta Borinquén Golf Course. Tennis courts are just down the hill from the inn itself. Sightseeing trips to the nearby Arecibo Observatory (p. 139)—the largest radar/radio telescope in the world—and to Monte Calvario (a replica of Mount Calvary) are available. Another popular visit is to the plaza in the town of Quebradillas. All rooms are nonsmoking.

Rte. 113 N no. 6205, Quebradillas, PR 00678. (℃) **888/391-0606** or 787/895-2065. Fax 787/895-2294. www.paradorvistamar.com. 55 units, each with either shower or tub. $80–$120 double. Up to 2 children under 12 stay free in parent's room. AE, DISC, MC, V. At Quebradillas, head northwest on Rte. 2, then go left at the junction with Rte. 113 and continue for a mile (1.6km). **Amenities:** Restaurant; bar; 2 outdoor pools; room service; rooms for those w/limited mobility. *In room:* A/C, TV.

ISABELA

On the northwestern coast, a 1½-hour drive west of San Juan, the town of Isabela captures the flavor of the west, although it's far less known by visitors than Rincón and Mayagüez. Its pastel-colored, whitewashed houses border the sea, known for its surfing and swimming beaches.

Tragedy has struck repeatedly in the area because of the geographical location of Isabela, which has made it the victim of both tidal waves and earthquakes since it was first settled. The locals don't survive on tourism, but on such industries as shoemaking and textiles. In spite of manufacturing, many small farms still dot the area.

Isabela enjoys a reputation for horse breeding. This activity is centered around Arenales, south of the town, where a number of horse stables are located.

The area abounds in good beaches, including Jobos Beach, directly west of Isabela on Route 466. The beach is set against a backdrop of cliffs, the most dramatic of which is El Pozo de Jacinto. Nearby at a beach called "The Shacks," both snorkelers and scuba divers enjoy swimming among the reefs, teeming with rainbow-hued fish and the coral caverns.

WHERE TO STAY & DINE

Villas del Mar Hau 🔗 *(Kids)*   Opening onto a long private beach, this family-friendly *parador* complex is peppered with West Indian–style cottages in vivid Caribbean pastels with Victorian wood trim. The location is midway between the west coast cities of Arecibo in the east and Aguadilla in the west, right outside the smaller town of Isabela. Under the shelter of Causuarina pine trees, most guests spend their days lying on Playa Montones. The huge tidal "wading" pool is ideal for children. The place is unpretentious but not completely back-to-nature, as the beachfront cottages are well-furnished and equipped, each with a balcony and with capacities for two to six guests. Some have ceiling fans, others have air-conditioning, and all units are equipped with small, tiled, shower-only bathrooms. Since 1960 the Hau family has run this little beach inn. The on-site restaurant is well-known in the area for its creative menu featuring fresh fish, shellfish, and meats.

Rte. 466 Km 8.3, Playa Montones, Isabela, PR 00662. ℱ **787/872-2045.** Fax 787/830-4988. 39 units (shower only). $100–$150 for 2; $140–$175 for 4; $190–$250 for 6. AE, MC, V. From the center of Isabella, take Rte. 466 toward Aguadilla. **Amenities:** Restaurant; bar; barbecue area; outdoor pool with snack bar; tennis courts; beach toy rentals; photocopy and fax; convenience store; babysitting. *In room:* A/C, TV (in most rooms), kitchenette, coffeemaker.

COAMO

Legend has it that the hot springs in this town, located inland on the south coast about a 2-hour drive from San Juan, were the Fountain of Youth sought by Ponce de León. It is believed that the Taíno peoples, during pre-Columbian times, held rituals and pilgrimages here as they sought health and well-being. Between 1847 and 1958, the site was a center for rest and relaxation for Puerto Ricans and others, some on their honeymoons, others in search of the curative powers of the geothermal springs, which lie about a 5-minute walk from **Parador Baños de Coamo.** Nonguests can come here to use the baths, but the experience is hardly special today. The baths are in poor condition.

WHERE TO STAY & DINE

Parador Baños de Coamo   The spa at Baños de Coamo features this *parador,* offering hospitality in traditional Puerto Rican style. The Baños has welcomed many notable visitors over the years, including Franklin D. Roosevelt, Frank Lloyd Wright, Alexander Graham Bell, and Thomas Edison, who came here to swim in the on-site hot springs. Since those days and since those long-departed visitors, spas have become state-of-the-art in many places, including San Juan and some nearby resorts. Such is not the case here; maintenance is poor, and the bathrooms show signs of aging. (Locals sometimes purchase a day pass and use the pool, which leads to noise, confusion, and overcrowding on weekends.)

The buildings range from a lattice-adorned two-story motel unit with wooden verandas to a Spanish colonial pink stucco building, which houses the restaurant. The bedrooms draw a mixed reaction from visitors, so ask to see your prospective room before deciding to stay here. Many of the often-dark rooms are not well-maintained, and the bathrooms seem more appropriate for a campsite. Mildew is also evident. The cuisine here is both Creole and international, and the coffee Baños-style is a special treat.

P.O. Box 540, Coamo, PR 00769. © **787/825-2186.** Fax 787/825-4739. www.banosde coamo.com. 48 units. $80–$85 double. AE, DISC, MC, V. From Rte. 1, turn onto Rte. 153 at Santa Isabel; then turn left onto Rte. 546 and drive west 1 mile (1.6km). **Amenities:** Restaurant; bar; 2 outdoor pools; room for those w/limited mobility. *In room:* A/C, TV.

10

Eastern Puerto Rico

The northeast corner of the island, only about 45 minutes from San Juan, contains the island's major attractions, El Yunque rainforest and Luquillo Beach (see chapter 7), as well as a variety of landscapes, ranging from miles of forest to palm groves and beachside settlements. Here you will find one of the best resorts on the island, El Conquistador Resort.

This is also the site of Fajardo, a preeminent sailor's haven, where you can catch ferries to the islands of Vieques and Culebra.

1 Las Croabas

35 miles (56km) E of San Juan

Las Croabas, near Fajardo, is the site of the El Conquistador Resort. El Conquistador was the leader in luxury resorts in the Caribbean from the 1960s through the late 1970s. Celebrities Elaine May, Jack Gilford, Celeste Holm (with her husband and two poodles), Elaine Stritch (and her dog), Amy Vanderbilt, Jack Palance, Burt Bacharach, Angie Dickinson, Omar Sharif, Marc Connelly, Maureen O'Sullivan, and Xavier Cugat attended its grand inaugural festivities. Its circular casino, in black and stainless steel, appeared in the James Bond movie *Goldfinger.* The original hotel closed in 1980, but it was reborn in 1993 as the distinctive $250-million El Conquistador we have today.

GETTING THERE

El Conquistador staff members greet all guests at the San Juan airport and transport them to the resort. Guests at the resort can take a taxi or a hotel courtesy car, or they can drive a rental car to Luquillo Beach. The cost of a taxi from the San Juan airport averages around $60.

If you're driving from San Juan, head east on Route 3 toward Fajardo. At the intersection, cut northeast on Route 195 and continue to the intersection with Route 987, at which point you turn north.

Las Cabezas de San Juan Nature Reserve

Las Cabezas de San Juan Nature Reserve is better known as El Faro, or "The Lighthouse." Located in the northeastern corner of the island, it is one of the most beautiful and important areas in Puerto Rico. Here you'll find seven ecological systems and a restored 19th-century Spanish colonial lighthouse. From the lighthouse observation deck, majestic views extend to islands as far off as St. Thomas in the U.S. Virgin Islands.

Surrounded on three sides by the Atlantic Ocean, the 316-acre (128ha) site encompasses forestland, mangroves, lagoons, beaches, cliffs, offshore cays, and coral reefs. Boardwalk trails wind through the fascinating topography. Ospreys, sea turtles, and an occasional manatee are seen from the wind-swept promontories and rocky beach.

The nature reserve is open Wednesday through Sunday. Reservations are required; for reservations during the week, call ⓒ **787/722-5882,** and for reservations on weekends, ⓒ **787/860-2560** (weekend reservations must be made on the day of your visit). Admission is $7 for adults, $4 for seniors and children under 12. Guided 2½-hour English and Spanish tours are conducted at 9:30, 10, and 10:30am, and 2pm (English-only tour at 2pm).

OUTDOOR ACTIVITIES

In addition to the lovely beach and the many recreational facilities that are part of the El Conquistador (p. 190), there are other notable places to play in the vicinity. Don't forget that not far from Las Croabas is **Luquillo Beach,** one of the island's best stretches of sand (see chapter 7).

WATERSPORTS   For a cruise, your best bet in Las Croabas is **Erin Go Bragh Charters** (ⓒ 787/860-4401; www.egbc.net). The 50-foot (15m) ketch is operated by Capt. Bill Henry, who is licensed to carry six passengers. The boat is available for day charters and sunset and evening cruises, and it has equipment for watersports, including windsurfers, masks, and fins. A full-day tour costs $85 per person, including a barbecue lunch.

For scuba divers, the best deal is offered by the PADI outfit **La Casa del Mar,** at the Puerto del Rey marina, the lowest level of the El Conquistador (*(C)* **787/863-1000,** ext. 7917). You can go for ocean dives on the outfitter's boats, a one-tank dive costing $69 or a two-tank dive for $99; tanks and weight belt are an additional $25. A PADI snorkel program, at $50 per person, is also available.

In Fajardo, the Caribbean's largest and most modern marina, **Puerto del Rey** (*(C)* **787/860-1000**), has facilities for 70 boats, including docking and fueling for yachts up to 200 feet (61m) and haul-out and repair for yachts up to 90 feet (27m). The marina has boat rentals, yacht charters, and watersports, plus shops and a restaurant.

Some of the best snorkeling in Puerto Rico is in and around Fajardo. Its beach, **Playa Seven Seas,** is not as hotsy-totsy as Luquillo Beach, but is an attractive and sheltered strip of sand. The beach lies on the southwestern shoreline of Las Cabezas peninsula and is crowded on weekends. For even better snorkeling, walk along this beach for about half a mile (.8km) to another beach, called **Playa Escondido ("Hidden Beach").** Coral reefs in clear waters lie

---

Top Caribbean Spa: The Golden Door

Perched atop a stunning 300-foot (91m) bluff overlooking the Caribbean Sea and the Atlantic Ocean, the **Golden Door** 𝑅𝑅, in Las Casitas Village complex at the El Conquistador Hotel (𝒞 **787/863-1000**), is the most sophisticated, well-managed, and comprehensive spa in the Caribbean, and it is one of the finest in the world. One of only three branches of a spa founded in Escondido, California, and today administered by the group, it's devoted to the relaxation and healing of body, soul, and mind. Spa rituals are taken seriously; New Age mysticism is gracefully dispensed within a postmodern setting that's a cross between a Swiss clinic, a state-of-the-art health club, and a Buddhist monastery. Spa treatments begin at $160 for 80 minutes. You can exercise here for a fee of $25 per day. The spa is open daily from 6:30am to 8:30pm. American Express, MasterCard, and Visa are accepted.

---

right off this beach. We'll let you in on a secret: East from Las Cabezas is a marine wildlife refuge known as **La Cordillera,** or "The Spine." Off the mainland of the island, these are the most gin-clear and tranquil waters we have found to date in Puerto Rico. They are teeming with wildlife, including several species of fish such as grouper, but also lobster, moray eels, and sea turtles. On these islets you might even see a rare crested iguana. **Las Tortugas Adventures** (𝒞 **787/809-0253**) offers kayaking/snorkeling day trips there for $65 per person.

TENNIS   The seven Har-Tru courts at the **El Conquistador** 𝑅𝑅 are among the best tennis courts in Puerto Rico, rivaling those at Palmas del Mar. The staff at the pro shop is extremely helpful to beginning players. Courts are the least crowded during the hottest part of the day, around the lunch hour. If you're a single traveler to the resort and in search of a player, the pro shop will try to match you up with a player of equal skill.

WHERE TO STAY

El Conquistador Resort & Golden Door Spa 𝑅𝑅𝑅 *Kids*   One of the most impressive resorts in the Caribbean, with a flash and glitter that remains supremely tasteful, El Conquistador has an incredible array of facilities. Rebuilt in 1993 at a cost of $250 million, it encompasses 500 acres (202ha) of forested hills sloping to the sea. Accommodations are divided into five separate sections that share the common themes of Mediterranean architecture and lush landscaping. A replica of an Andalusian hamlet, Las Casitas Village seems straight out of the south of Spain; each of the plush, pricey units here has a full kitchen. A short walk downhill takes you to Las Olas Village, a cluster of tastefully modern accommodations. At sea level, adjacent to an armada of pleasure craft bobbing at anchor, is La Marina Village, whose balconies seem to hang directly over the water. All the far-flung elements of the resort are connected by serpentine, landscaped walkways and by a railroad-style funicular that makes frequent trips up and down the hillside. The accommodations are outfitted with comfortable and stylish furniture, soft tropical colors, and robes.

The resort has an array of restaurants and lounges; you could live here for a month and sample something new and different every day. One of the most comprehensive spas in the world, the Golden Door, maintains a branch in this resort. The hotel is sole owner of a "fantasy island" (Palomino Island), with caverns, nature trails, horseback riding, and watersports such as scuba diving, windsurfing, and snorkeling. About half a mile (.8km) offshore, the island is connected by free ferries to the main hotel at frequent intervals. Camp Coquí on Palomino Island is for children ages 3 to 12.

Av. Conquistador 1000, Las Croabas, Fajardo, PR 00738. (✆ **800/468-5228** or 787/863-1000. Fax 787/863-6500. www.elconresort.com. 918 units. Winter $364–$1,098 double, from $1,700 casita with kitchen for 1–6; off season $317–$640 double, $640–$1,379 casita with kitchen for 1–6. MAP (breakfast and dinner) $96 extra per adult per day, $45 extra per guest 17 and under. Children 16 and under stay free in parent's room. AE, DC, DISC, MC, V. Parking $10 per day, valet parking $20. **Amenities:** 9 restaurants; 7 bars; 7 pools; golf course; 7 Har-Tru tennis courts; health club; spa; watersports equipment rental and dive shop; children's programs; tour desk; business center; room service; massage; laundry service; dry cleaning; rooms for those w/limited mobility; casino; nightclub. *In room:* A/C, TV, minibar, fridge, coffeemaker, hair dryer, iron, safe, Wi-Fi.

WHERE TO DINE
EXPENSIVE

Blossoms ✹✹ CHINESE/JAPANESE   Blossoms boasts some of the freshest seafood in eastern Puerto Rico. Sizzling delights are prepared on *teppanyaki* tables, and there's a zesty selection of Hunan and Szechuan specialties. On the *teppanyaki* menu, you can choose dishes ranging from chicken to shrimp, from filet mignon to lobster. Sushi bar selections range from eel and squid to salmon roe and giant clams.

In the El Conquistador Resort. ℂ **787/863-1000.** Reservations recommended. Main courses $20–$45. AE, DC, DISC, MC, V. Daily 6–9:30pm.

Otello's ☞ NORTHERN ITALIAN   Here you can dine by candlelight in the old-world tradition, with a choice of indoor or outdoor seating. You might begin with one of the soups, perhaps pasta *fagioli,* or select one of the zesty Italian appetizers, such as excellently prepared clams Posillipo. Pastas can be ordered as a half-portion appetizer or as a main dish, and they include the likes of homemade gnocchi and fettuccine with shrimp. The chef is known for his superb veal dishes. A selection of poultry and vegetarian food is offered, as are shrimp and fish dishes.

In the El Conquistador Resort. ℂ **787/863-1000.** Reservations required in winter, recommended off season. Main courses $26–$42. AE, DC, DISC, MC, V. Daily 6–9:30pm.

Striphouse ☞ STEAKHOUSE   Of all the restaurants in El Conquistador Resort, this is the most American. If Ike were to miraculously return, he'd feel comfortable with this 1950s menu. The severely dignified baroque room was inspired by an aristocratic monastery in Spain. The massive gates are among the most spectacular pieces of wrought iron in Puerto Rico. The service is impeccable, the steaks tender, and the seafood fresh.

Special care is taken with the beef dishes, even though the meat is imported frozen. You can begin with the lobster bisque or Caesar salad, then move on to the thick cut of veal chop or the perfectly prepared rack of lamb. Prime rib of beef is a feature, as are the succulent steaks; try the New York strip or the porterhouse.

In the El Conquistador Resort. ℂ **787/863-1000.** Reservations required. Main courses $28–$41. AE, DISC, MC, V. Daily 6–10:30pm.

2 Palmas del Mar

46 miles (74km) SE of San Juan

An hour east of San Juan, the residential resort community of Palmas del Mar lies near Humacao. Here you'll find one of the most action-packed sports programs in the Caribbean, offering golf, tennis, scuba diving, sailing, deep-sea fishing, and horseback riding. Palmas del Mar's location is one of its greatest assets. The pleasing Caribbean trade winds steadily blow across this section of the island, stabilizing the weather and making Palmas del Mar ideal for many outdoor sports.

The resort is no longer what it was in its heyday in the early 1990s. Today it is a real-estate conglomerate that promotes vacation properties to investors, although outsiders can stay here as well. Many of the occupants are residents of San Juan who come here on weekends. Tourists are welcome, but most first-time visitors will find better accommodations up the coast, at the Westin Rio Mar (p. 147) or the El Conquistador (p. 190).

GETTING THERE

Humacao Regional Airport is 3 miles (4.8km) from the northern boundary of Palmas del Mar. It accommodates private planes; no regularly scheduled airline currently serves the Humacao airport. **Palmas del Mar Transportation** will arrange minivan or bus transport from Humacao to the San Juan airport for $80 from 8am to 5pm, with a minimum of four people ($20 for each extra person); for $90 from 7pm to 8am, with a minimum of five people ($20 for each extra person). For reservations, call ✆ **787/285-4323.** Call if you want to be met at the airport.

If you're driving from San Juan, take Highway 52 south to Caguas, then take Highway 30 east to Humacao. Follow the signs from there to Palmas del Mar.

BEACHES & OUTDOOR ACTIVITIES

BEACHES   Palmas del Mar Resort has 3 exceptional miles (4.6km) of white-sand beaches (all open to the public). Nonguests pay a $1 charge for parking and 25¢ for a changing room and a locker. The waters here are calm year-round, and there's a watersports center and marina (see "Scuba Diving & Snorkeling," below).

FISHING   Some of the best year-round fishing in the Caribbean is found in the waters just off Palmas del Mar. **Capt. Bill Burleson,** based in Humacao (✆ **787/850-7442**), operates charters on his customized, 46-foot (14m) sport-fisherman, *Karolette,* which is electronically equipped for successful fishing. Burleson prefers to take fishing groups to Grappler Banks, 18 nautical miles away, which lies in the migratory paths of wahoo, tuna, and marlin. A maximum of six people are taken out, costing $680 for 4½ hours, or $840 for 6 hours. Burleson also offers snorkeling expeditions to Vieques at $650 per person for up to 5 hours. He can also take you to other snorkeling locations as well.

GOLF   Few other real-estate developments in the Caribbean devote as much attention and publicity to their golf facilities as the

Palmas del Mar Country Club ★★ (© 787/285-2256). Today, both the older course, the Gary Player–designed Palm course, and the newer course, the Reese Jones–designed Flamboyant course, have pars of 72 and layouts of around 2,267 yards (2,073m) each. Crack golfers consider holes 11 to 15 of the Palm course among the toughest five successive holes in the Caribbean. The pro shop that services both courses is open daily from 6:30am to 6pm. The Flamboyant course and the Palm Course cost $100 for 18 holes; after 1pm, $75.

HIKING   Palmas del Mar's land is an attraction in its own right. Here you'll find more than 6 miles (9.7km) of Caribbean ocean frontage—3.5 miles (5.6km) of sandy beach amid rocky cliffs and promontories. Large tracts of the 2,700-acre (1,093ha) property have harbored sugar and coconut plantations over the years, and a wet tropical forest preserve with giant ferns, orchids, and hanging vines covers about 70 acres (28ha) near the resort's geographic center.

SCUBA DIVING & SNORKELING   Some of the best dives in Puerto Rico are right off the eastern coast. Two dozen dive sites south of Fajardo are within a 5-mile (8km) radius offshore.

Set adjacent to a collection of boutiques, bars, and restaurants at the edge of Palmas del Mar's harbor, **Palmas Dive Center** ★, Anchors Village, 110 Harbor Dr. (© **800/739-3483**), owns a 44-foot-long (13m) dive boat with a 16-foot (4.9m) beam to make it stable in rough seas. Pennsylvania-born Bill Winnie, a 5-year veteran of other dive operations in and around Palmas del Mar, offers $150 full-day "Discover Scuba" resort courses that are geared to beginners. They include classroom testing, presentation of a video on water safety, a practice session in a swimming pool, and a one-tank afternoon dive in the open sea. Also available are both morning and afternoon sessions of two-tank dives for experienced and certified divers only, priced at $99 each. Half-day snorkeling trips, priced at $65 per participant and departing for both morning and afternoon sessions, go whenever there's demand to the fauna-rich reefs that encircle Monkey Island, an offshore uninhabited cay.

TENNIS   The **Tennis Center at Palmas del Mar** ★★ (© 787/285-0717), the largest in Puerto Rico, features 13 hard courts and 5 clay courts, open to resort guests and nonguests. Fees are $25 per hour during the day and $33 per hour at night. Within the resort's tennis compound is a **fitness center,** which has the best-equipped gym in the region; it's open daily from 6am to 9pm. The center is $7 for guests and nonguests of the resort; members use the center at no charge.

WHERE TO STAY

Four Points by Sheraton Palmas del Mar Resort ☆ (Kids)   This long-dormant property came alive again in 2006, with Sheraton as the "helmer." Completely restored and imbued with a post-millennium update, the resort offers bedrooms that are spacious and handsomely furnished. The junior suites are especially comfortable and inviting. A plethora of on-site activities may keep you from ever leaving the premises: championship golf courses, a country club, a casino and pool bar, along with an "infinity pool," are just some of the offerings.

Furnishings are tasteful and exceedingly comfortable, typical of Sheraton's deluxe hotels. Available extras include private balconies, luxury bathrooms, and work desks. The hotel also offers business services for commercial travelers, plus a special pool for kids. The hotel restaurant offers a varied international menu (some dine here every night), and you'll also find a wine and cigar bar.

170 Calderon Dr., Humacao, PR 00791. ℂ 787/850-6000. Fax 787/850-6001. www. starwoodhotels.com. 107 units. Winter $288 double, $320 suite; off season $234 double, $258 suite. Children 11 and under stay free in parent's room. AE, MC, V. Self-parking $12, valet parking $15. **Amenities:** Restaurant; 2 bars; outdoor pool; kids' pool; golf courses; tennis courts; fitness center; scuba diving; business services; room service; laundry service; dry cleaning; nonsmoking rooms; rooms for those w/limited mobility; casino. *In room:* A/C, TV, fridge, beverage maker, hair dryer, iron, safe.

WHERE TO DINE

Thanks to the kitchens that are built into virtually every unit in Palmas del Mar, many guests prepare at least some of their meals "at home." This is made relatively feasible thanks to the on-site general store at the Palmanova Plaza, which sells everything from fresh lettuce and sundries to liquor and cigarettes.

Blue Hawaiian CHINESE   This is the best Chinese restaurant in the region. It combines Polynesian themes (similar to a toned-down Trader Vic's) with an Americanized version of Chinese food that's flavorful and well-suited to Puerto Rico's hot, steamy climate. Menu items include lobster with garlic-flavored cheese sauce, blackened salmon or steaks reminiscent of styles in New Orleans, and a superb house version of honey chicken. You'll find the place within the dignified courtyard of the resort's shopping center, with tables for

---

Finds **Where the Locals Go for Soul Food**

To escape the confines of the resort for the evening, drive over to a local dive, **Trulio's Sea Food** (*©* **787/850-1840**), just off Route 3 on Calle Isidro Andreux Andreu in the hamlet of Punta Santiago. This is strictly no-frills. Though very low in cost, the food is top-notch and even memorable, especially the fried plantain filled with sea conch. The shrimp in garlic sauce will have you asking for more, and you can also order perfectly baked lobster in garlic sauce. Also try the grilled whole red snapper in garlic and onions. You get the point now: Garlic is king here. Puerto Ricans rave about the chef's dessert specialty, which is poundcake soaked in sweet milk. It tastes better than it sounds and is like soul food to the locals because it's just like Mom used to make.

---

alfresco dining. Your host is Tommy Lo, former chef aboard the now-defunct ocean liner SS *United States.*

In the Palmanova Shopping Center. *©* **787/852-0897.** Reservations recommended. Main courses $14–$45. AE, MC, V. Daily noon–10:30pm.

Chez Daniel *©* FRENCH   It's French, and it's the favorite of the folks who tie up their yachts at the adjacent pier. Normandy-born Daniel Vasse, the owner, along with his French-Catalonian wife, Lucette, maintain a dining room that is the most appealing in Palmas del Mar. Chez Daniel shows a faithful allegiance to the tenets of classical French cuisine, placing emphasis on such dishes as bouillabaisse, onion soup, and snails as well as lobster and chicken dishes. Among recent culinary delights sampled here were *osso buco* simmered in white wine and a cassoulet in the style of Toulouse in southwestern France (white beans with pork products). For dessert, consider a soufflé au Cointreau.

Marina de Palmas del Mar. *©* **787/850-3838.** Reservations required. Main courses $27–$40 dinner, $8.50–$13 lunch, $42 Sun brunch (includes 1st drink). AE, DISC, MC, V. Wed–Sun noon–3pm; Wed–Mon 6:30–10pm. Closed June.

3 *Paradores* of Eastern Puerto Rico

Most of the government-certified inns called *paradores* are found in western Puerto Rico (see "*Paradores* of Western Puerto Rico," in chapter 9), though there are two along the eastern coast that are ideal for escapists.

The Fajardo Inn 🟊 *(Finds)*   A good base for those visiting El Yunque, this inn is ideal for those who are seeking a location in the east and don't want to pay the prices charged at the El Conquistador (p. 190). Lying on a hilltop overlooking the port of Fajardo, this *parador* evokes a Mediterranean villa with its balustrades and grand staircases. The midsize bedrooms, most of which open onto good views, are spotless, and each has a small shower-only bathroom. The inn and its pool are handsomely landscaped. A few steps from the inn is an older building, The Scenic Inn, which offers access to all of Fajardo Inn's facilities at lower rates—$73 per night for a double—for those who don't mind a room without phone or view. The Fajardo Inn's restaurant specializes in Creole and continental cuisine, especially fresh fish, with indoor and outdoor dining.

Parcela Beltrán 52, Fajardo, PR 00740. © **787/860-6000.** Fax 787/860-5063. www.fajardoinn.com. 105 units (shower only). $100–$150 double; $132–$300 suite. AE, DISC, MC, V. A 15-min. walk east of the center of Fajardo. **Amenities:** 2 restaurants; 2 bars; pool; snorkeling and diving arranged; room service; 1 room for those w/limited mobility. *In room:* A/C, TV, hair dryer, iron.

Hotel Parador Palmas de Lucía 🟊 *(Finds)*   In the southern corner of Puerto Rico, where accommodations are scarce, this government-affiliated *parador* is a knockout discovery. It lies at the eastern end of Ruta Panorámica, a network of scenic, winding roads along which you can take in some of the finest views in the Caribbean before coming to rest at Palmas de Lucía, just steps from the pleasant sands of Playa Lucía. This is one of the newest hotels in eastern Puerto Rico, filling a vast gap in accommodations in this remote part of the island. The Lopez family are your hosts, and their complex combines colonial styling with tropical decoration. Each midsize bedroom is well-furnished and has a pool-view balcony and an efficiently organized, tiled shower-only bathroom. Rates rise dramatically over the weekend when this *parador* is heavily booked because of all the visitors exploring eastern Puerto Rico at that time.

Palmas de Lucía, routes 901 and 9911, Camino Nuevo, Yabucoa, PR 00767. © **787/893-4423.** Fax 787/893-0291. www.palmasdelucia.com. 34 units (shower only). Mon–Thurs $88 double; Fri–Sun $319 double. AE, MC, V. From Humacao, take Rte. 53 south to Yabucoa, to the end of the highway, where you connect with Rte. 901 to Maunabo. After a 2-min. drive, turn left at the signposted Carretera 9911, which leads to Playa Lucía. **Amenities:** Restaurant; bar; pool; gym; basketball court. *In room:* A/C, TV, fridge, coffeemaker.

Index

See also Accommodations index below.

ACCOMMODATIONS

FROMMER'S® COMPLETE TRAVEL GUIDES

FROMMER'S® DAY BY DAY GUIDES

PAULINE FROMMER'S GUIDES! SEE MORE. SPEND LESS.

FROMMER'S® PORTABLE GUIDES

FROMMER'S® CRUISE GUIDES

Alaska Cruises & Ports of Call

Cruises & Ports of Call

European Cruises & Ports of Call

FROMMER'S® NATIONAL PARK GUIDES

Algonquin Provincial Park
Banff & Jasper
Grand Canyon

National Parks of the American West
Rocky Mountain
Yellowstone & Grand Teton

Yosemite and Sequoia & Kings
 Canyon
Zion & Bryce Canyon

FROMMER'S® MEMORABLE WALKS

London
New York

Paris
Rome

San Francisco

FROMMER'S® WITH KIDS GUIDES

Chicago
Hawaii
Las Vegas
London

National Parks
New York City
San Francisco

Toronto
Walt Disney World® & Orlando
Washington, D.C.

SUZY GERSHMAN'S BORN TO SHOP GUIDES

France
Hong Kong, Shanghai & Beijing
Italy

London
New York

Paris
San Francisco

FROMMER'S® IRREVERENT GUIDES

Amsterdam
Boston
Chicago
Las Vegas

London
Los Angeles
Manhattan
Paris

Rome
San Francisco
Walt Disney World®
Washington, D.C.

FROMMER'S® BEST-LOVED DRIVING TOURS

Austria
Britain
California
France

Germany
Ireland
Italy
New England

Northern Italy
Scotland
Spain
Tuscany & Umbria

THE UNOFFICIAL GUIDES®

Adventure Travel in Alaska
Beyond Disney
California with Kids
Central Italy
Chicago
Cruises
Disneyland®
England
Florida
Florida with Kids

Hawaii
Ireland
Las Vegas
London
Maui
Mexico's Best Beach Resorts
Mini Mickey
New Orleans
New York City

Paris
San Francisco
South Florida including Miami &
 the Keys
Walt Disney World®
Walt Disney World® for
 Grown-ups
Walt Disney World® with Kids
Washington, D.C.

SPECIAL-INTEREST TITLES

Athens Past & Present
Best Places to Raise Your Family
Cities Ranked & Rated
500 Places to Take Your Kids Before They Grow Up
Frommer's Best Day Trips from London
Frommer's Best RV & Tent Campgrounds
 in the U.S.A.

Frommer's Exploring America by RV
Frommer's NYC Free & Dirt Cheap
Frommer's Road Atlas Europe
Frommer's Road Atlas Ireland
Great Escapes From NYC Without Wheels
Retirement Places Rated

FROMMER'S® PHRASEFINDER DICTIONARY GUIDES

French

Italian

Spanish

THE NEW TRAVELOCITY GUARANTEE

EVERYTHING YOU BOOK WILL BE RIGHT, OR WE'LL WORK WITH OUR TRAVEL PARTNERS TO MAKE IT RIGHT, RIGHT AWAY.

*To drive home the point,
we're going to use the word "right" in every single sentence.*

Let's get right to it. Right to the meat! Only Travelocity guarantees everything about your booking will be right, or we'll work with our travel partners to make it right, right away. Right on!

Here's a picture taken smack dab right in the middle of Antigua, where the guarantee also covers you.

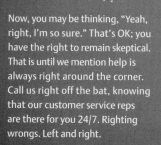

The guarantee covers all but one of the items pictured to the right.

Now, you may be thinking, "Yeah, right, I'm so sure." That's OK; you have the right to remain skeptical. That is until we mention help is always right around the corner. Call us right off the bat, knowing that our customer service reps are there for you 24/7. Righting wrongs. Left and right.

For example, what if the ocean view you booked actually looks out at a downright ugly parking lot? You'd be right to call – we're there for you. And no one in their right mind would be pleased to learn the rental car place has closed and left them stranded. Call Travelocity and we'll help get you back on the right track.

Now if you're guessing there are some things we can't control, like the weather, well you're right. But we can help you with most things – to get all the details in righting,* visit **travelocity.com/guarantee**.

*Sorry, spelling things right is one of the few things not covered under the guarantee.

I'd give my right arm for a guarantee like this, although I'm glad I don't have to.

** travelocity·
You'll never roam alone.™

IF YOU BOOK IT, IT SHOULD BE THERE.

Only Travelocity guarantees it will be, or we'll work with our travel partners to make it right, right away. So if you're missing a balcony or anything else you booked, just call us 24/7 1-888-TRAVELOCITY

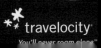

travelocity
You'll never roam alone

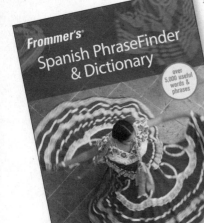